M000313801

HIGHWAYS TO THE END OF THE WORLD

EDWARD SIMPSON

Highways to the End of the World

Roads, Roadmen and Power in South Asia

HURST & COMPANY, LONDON

First published in the United Kingdom in 2022 by
C. Hurst & Co. (Publishers) Ltd,
New Wing, Somerset House, Strand, London, WC2R 1LA

Copyright © Edward Simpson, 2022

All rights reserved.

Printed in the United Kingdom by Bell and Bain Ltd, Glasgow

Distributed in the United States, Canada and Latin
America by Oxford University Press, 198 Madison Avenue,
New York, NY 10016, United States of America.

The right of Edward Simpson to be identified as the author of
this publication is asserted by him in accordance with the
Copyright, Designs and Patents Act, 1988.

A Cataloguing-in-Publication data record for this book
is available from the British Library.

ISBN: 9781787383975

www.hurstpublishers.com

CONTENTS

CONTENTS

ABBREVIATIONS

ABVP	Akhil Bharatiya Vidyarthi Parishad (All-India Student Council)
ADB	Asian Development Bank
AHN	Asian Highway Network
ASEAN	Association of Southeast Asian Nations
BJP	Bharatiya Janata Party
BOT	build-operate-transfer
CMGSY	Chief Minister's Gram Sadak Yojana
COALREAP	Coal Resource Exploration and Assessment Program
CPEC	China–Pakistan Economic Corridor
CRF	Central Road Fund
CRRI	Central Road Research Institute
DFID	Department for International Development
ECAFE	Economic Commissions for Asia and the Far East
ESCAP	Economic and Social Commission for Asia and the Pacific
GTSNY	Gramin Tola Sampark Nischay Yojana
IRC	Indian Roads Congress
KKH	Karakoram Highway

MGNREGS	Mahatma Gandhi National Rural Employment Guarantee Scheme
MMGSY	Mukhya Mantri Gram Sampark Yojana
MNP	Minimum Needs Programme
MPRDC	Madhya Pradesh Road Development Corporation
MSRDC	Maharashtra State Road Development Corporation
NDA	National Democratic Alliance
NHAI	National Highway Authority of India
NHDP	National Highways Development Project
NRR	National Rural Road Development Committee
NRRDA	National Rural Roads Development Agency
PMGSY	Pradhan Mantri Gram Sadak Yojana
PPP	public–private partnership
PWD	Public Works Department
RSS	Rashtriya Swayamsevak Sangh
UPA	United Progressive Alliance

INTRODUCTION
SIGNPOSTS

The question that gives direction and substance to this book is as follows: Why are so many roads being built in South Asia in an era of human-induced climate change?

Anthropological training encouraged me to understand the logic of social processes from the perspective of those engaged in them—in this case, roadmen building roads. What do they think they are doing? Over the course of the research, I have learned to see road building through the eyes of others as part of the development imperative, a right, a vision of the good life, a form of political communication—rather than simply the science of materials, carriageway design and project management methodologies.

The research gradually led me away from materials and processes to explore more broadly the 'culture' of roads and the ideologies they represent, intersect and do battle with. There are therefore no diggers or blueprints for bitumen spray nozzles in the text; instead, there are beliefs, loyalties, claims and, most importantly, the outline and analysis of underlying assumptions. This is a study of roads in the realm of ideas, discourse and rhetoric. The material shows how roads are intertwined with conceptions of national identity and ambition, internecine rivalry, public spectacle and other demonstrations of power and efficiency, progress and history.

In a critical global register, roads are relatively crude forms of infrastructure that emerged as part of a particular way of organising economic and social life. They are enlarged and paved versions of pathways that have been around for thousands of years and took a modern form in the twentieth century with mass road transport (cars, trucks and the like).[1] It is less well known that modern roads are highly marketed, promoted and sold to people like many other commodities. Numerous industries and financial regimes have strong vested interests in building roads and encouraging increasing levels of traffic. Through these efforts, roads are also associated with the future, engaging aspirations and motivating people to action. In this regard, they are particularly enchanted forms of infrastructure that contribute to the 'dromocratic' nature of many societies: mobility as the ruling principle of contemporary political life.[2] Roads are a hard, and generally dirty, element of the accelerating pace of modernity in which time and space are compressed by technology.[3]

An early Damascus moment during this research was the straightforward realisation that governments and many international organisations had departments to build roads and other departments to reduce carbon emissions. The aims of both were clearly at odds in the cold light of day, but in practice, the contradictory efforts were seldom given a second thought. On the ground, the relationship between the works of road builders and the long-term climate question received even less attention. Why?

In the ten years or so since I started the research, there has been increased public recognition that building roads now will perpetuate carbon-intensive living for many years into the future. This is described as 'path dependency', 'locking in' South Asian countries to the types of production and consumption that many international climate change negotiations have attempted to discourage. Some now see that road building in South Asia (as indeed elsewhere) will undermine efforts to reduce carbon emissions; targets will be missed, and the world will continue to warm at rates too fast for our long-term comfort. For many roadmen, however, climate change, and the need to reduce emissions, is only distantly related to their work. The disconnect is honest, slippery and profound all at the same time.

It is honest because road building itself does not come with tremendous carbon costs. Roads can be (and are) readily marketed as 'green' and 'sustainable', and the emissions of construction can be counted, reduced and neutralised by an official certification scheme. The problem then, for the roadman, is not so much the road but rather the internal combustion that takes place on the road once the speeches have been made and the inaugural ribbons cut. Meanwhile, the disconnect is slippery because this widespread reasoning has moral and logical limits, pushing responsibility into the future and on to others—but also because intractable questions of historical responsibility for emissions and global inequity are barely submerged in the defiant actions of roadmen. Lastly, it is profound because of the global humanitarian questions, but also because the disconnect takes us to the heart of the operation of contested knowledge, power, truth and how the world actually works. This book is written in these spaces of difficult knowledge, what I have chosen to call 'the politics of thought'.

The roadmen also know that roads bring with them increased levels of traffic and wealth built on resource consumption, a burn-stuff-to-prosper model. Build a road and the overall number of vehicles generally increases, as do levels of mobility and the general use of oil-based products. Indeed, roadmen are often proud that their labours yield such fruits and benefits. Yet, despite this dangerous promise of future growth, road building has been largely immune to climate scrutiny. Unlike coal-fired power stations, roads are almost invisible when the hunt is on for ways to reduce carbon emissions. It is as if roads are hidden in plain sight, camouflaged by familiarity and common sense against policy redress, sanction or outrage.

This book is about the historical and cultural processes that give roads such stealthy qualities. It is about the co-existence of contradictory forms of knowledge and uncertainty, the mechanisms through which revolutionary ideas become mass and routine, and the inequalities of the global climate moment. My contention is that road building has been naturalised by the twentieth century to the point of having become an unremarkable and common-sense activity against the backdrop of strategic underdevelopment in the colonial period and the excessive and frantic attention given to development in the post-colonial era.

On an interpersonal level, roadmen were not used to being questioned about what they were doing: 'Lunatic anthropologists!'

some said. On another level entirely, road building is so entrenched in general thought as a legitimate objective that it has expanded into personal and collective understandings of the self, rights and the future to the extent that there is little space to ask dissenting questions. Road building has become such a big idea that it is difficult to see round or through.

The madness of anthropologists notwithstanding (more on that later), roads do fundamentally organise many aspects of everyday life that are given energy and agency by fossil fuels: work, leisure, shopping, education, healthcare and kinship. Entire forests are seldom cut for roads, and, as I have already suggested, roads do not smoke like power stations or leave dramatic holes in landscapes like extractive industries (although material for building roads comes from somewhere). Instead, roads facilitate the removal of timber that may lead to wholesale deforestation, allow coal to be trucked to the power station to go up in smoke, and encourage the to-ing and fro-ing of people and spoils from minefields and elsewhere. Roads therefore transport ways of life that were refined in many parts of the world in the twentieth century. Roads carry with them a self-reproducing system that demands expansion and growth for success, which has contributed, in no small measure, to the unfolding climate disaster.

This book is also about the moral bind of one part of the world wanting to have lots more roads and the reasons for this want, while voices in other locations see such action as putting at risk the planetary public good. The greater part of the analysis is given over to tracing how roads became such a big idea and magnificent obsession in South Asia, an area where I have had long research engagement. Similar books could be written about somewhere else, a point to which I return in the postscript. A sharp focus on roads necessarily excludes other infrastructures and political and historical processes. I encourage you to see such myopia as a constructive method to read the past and sociology of the present. The history of South Asia told through the story of road development or the biography of Gandhi narrated through his use of the word 'road', for example, vividly illustrates the penetration, accretion and sedimentation of the 'road idea' on the Subcontinent.

I have used historical materials from the twentieth century to trace how road building gained moral and institutional momentum as the practice became central to nationalist and developmental projects in India and Pakistan. To follow the changing use of roads in the language of national political leaders is to chart by proxy the arrival and conquest of the motor road in popular, political and national consciousness. To study the changing ways roads are positioned and described in the policies of government is to reveal the ideological underpinnings of how a state believes, or wants, the world to work. These beginnings become the foundation for the grandiose fixations of later charismatic politicians, notably Nawaz Sharif in Pakistan and Nitin Gadkari in India. These flamboyant and controversial politician-roadmen are shown to have redefined 'road talk' as forms of utopian and hyperbolic promise built on the premise of a never-ending future.

In my view, it is not enough for anthropologists simply to understand and outline the worldview of others and to then rest content on their laurels. There should also be comparison, challenge and contest—climate change offers the resource for these things in the text. The book is fundamentally structured by time spent and interviews with roadmen, and this material is the most influential factor in the direction I have taken. However, what roadmen had to say about their work was astonishingly repetitive across the project. The most concentrated version: new roads bring development, reduce journey time and improve market access. In time, the repetition, although sometimes anaesthetising, became the focus of my analytical curiosity. Was there really so little to say? Was it that simple? Was it true? Why had the road meme gone global?

I harbour doubt about the wisdom of the new road mantras: new roads are a *particular* kind of development, *increase* overall numbers of journeys and promote a form of market that operates *without* carbon costing. I often wondered why I held these objections so trenchantly. I often felt hypocritical, as I use roads and used to enjoy road trips before I thought hard about where petroleum came from and where it went after propelling me through the countryside. There is, therefore, a deliberate self-reflexive edge in the text, playing genuinely and with ambivalence at the limits of authorial authority.

Roadmen often caused me to doubt myself and my convictions. I sometimes ran out of road quite quickly when trying to work out why my point of view was discordant with theirs. I hope they—or the combination of them and me—might challenge you too. This book is not about me, although I feature prominently in parts of it, because I think my own uncertainties and silences are occasionally illustrative of broader processes and recurrent patterns in thought politics.

Much road debate is framed in terms of left and right or in a cynical scepticism about corporate motivation versus trust in the market as a force for general good. These default positions emerged repeatedly and usually created adversarial impasses. It might well be the case that the politics of the left and right was the greatest popular distraction to have emerged with capitalism. During the research, it most definitely was the case that political polarity cultivated prescriptive and inflexible positions in debate. These positions were often pre-formed without the need for evidence, because both problem and solution were already known and given by political frames, dispositions and attendant theories of cause and effect.

To mix it up a bit, the research project on which this book is based organised roundtable discussions to bring different views into a common space. These feature in the text. A second form of ethnographic material takes us on to the road, and later to fume-filled toll booths in the heart of India, the health complaints of overworked government officials in Pakistan, and the piecemeal logic of one of the world's largest rural road-building schemes in India. However, we also developed another methodology, to 'read' roads as forms of governance and knowledge, to counter the astonishingly repetitious stories we heard about both the positive and negative effects of roads (for a phenomenon so far-reaching, subversive or deviant forms of commentary are an extreme minority sport).

The text is ordered around road trips as method and mode of analysis. The major journey is along India's State Highway 31 (SH31), which both begins and finishes the book. The first leg allows roads to speak for themselves and facilitates our reading of signs, scripts and things we see and hear in the landscape. We learn how regional history can help us understand roads in the present as a form of commodity. Archives reveal how roads became embedded in the institutions, political plans and imaginations of nations and people. The road is shown to have a biography and style, explicable through the work of Indian roadmen and their experiments with materials, standards and fonts.

We later traverse three of the Subcontinent's famous road infrastructures to understand the interwoven terrains of geopolitics and propaganda. These major routes have taken on mythological status, due to their historical depth, engineering bravado or contested claims on territory. At this stage, we take the road at face value, as an intervention in a difficult and enduring landscape, and read from that the exercise of political will and the extension of sovereign ambition. We build on these earlier trips through territory and history when we later travel through the coal borderlands of Gujarat in India and Sindh in Pakistan to analyse how roads unfold symbols and signs to make patriotic citizens, whose spectacular and nationalistic experiences are affirmed by the joys and associations of the road itself.

Lastly, we arrive at the show-not-tell conclusion, returning us to the SH31 in Madhya Pradesh. This is an intense reading of the road, now looking at the territory, semiotics, history and political economy. Research undertaken on and along the road is used to argue with the roadmen about what roads do and why, exploring the politics of evidence and trails of money. The picture that emerges challenges established geopolitical narratives of the region, finding both basic humanitarian concern and freewheeling international capital along the highways and byways of the Subcontinent. In learning how to read roads holistically, through intense interdisciplinary scrutiny and intimacy, we shift our focus to the things that were seldom said in interactions with roadmen but that turn out to be fundamental to roundly answering the central question: Why are so many roads being built in South Asia in an era of human-induced climate change?

***

This book uses the form of the road as a way of telling a story, carving a route through landscapes, lives and the politics of thought of road building. We explore the most visible infrastructural geography of South Asia, its key institutions and the standard narratives among roadmen. We also narrate the twentieth- and twenty-first-century history of roads in the region through the speeches and actions of politicians, including Mahatma Gandhi and Jawaharlal Nehru, tracing the consolidation of the road idea and the later liberalisation of the sector. Our road trips in Gujarat and Sindh teach us about comparative national identity projects in India and Pakistan, as do the political strategies of the Subcontinent's greatest contemporary road builders: Pakistan's Nawaz Sharif and India's Nitin Gadkari.

While most of the chapters will be familiar in style and approach to readers of argumentative and interpretive scholarship, the SH31 road trip that bookends the narrative is experimental in nature, methodology and approach; as such, it requires some additional explanation. As elaborated in Chapter 2, I actively use Jim Phelan's idea that roads give shape to lines of thought, Michael Fairless's characterisation of the road as a microcosm of larger processes, and Frank Morley's technique of stripping the road of all common sense.

The first leg takes us south along the SH31 in Madhya Pradesh. The stories of life and influence we encounter serve as an introduction to how to read roads, as forms of governance and technology but also as a means of linking themes and events—both literally and metaphorically. The story rings with ideas of development, 'opening up' and smoothing out the bumps of the world. Following Morley's style, I untangle events in the surrounding countryside as both linked to the road and given a narrative form by the journey. The SH31 is shown to be connected to other roads and regions, sometimes over a great distance, in this case through a historic opium economy that looked to the west coast of India and to Sindh. Life along the road also speaks of the intrigues of modern religious nationalism in India, which becomes a recurrent theme focused on the older competing regionalist idea of Central India.

Between this initial road trip and the second leg on the same road, the text emboldens the reader with knowledge of the history and common claims made for road building—the truth on the ground. When we return to SH31, the road now demands that we look beyond the grub of the hard shoulder and the visible material infrastructure of the road itself.

This final stretch takes us into ideas eloquently expressed by the philosopher and sociologist Bruno Latour: globalisation has outgrown the earth, particularly in relation to the consumption of fossil fuels.[4] He writes: 'If the [modernisation] project has become impossible, it's because there is no Earth capable of containing its ideal of progress, emancipation, and development ... the planet is *much too narrow and limited* for the globe of globalisation.'[5] Again: '[F]rom the post-war period on, thanks to oil, nations have been entering the reign of an Economy that believes it can do without material limits!'[6] In Latour's words, global elites, having realised the world is limited, have decided to go offshore, unmooring themselves from a world in common. Once I understood that the unmoored world was not a rhetorical figment of overheating Gallic intellect, I had to learn to navigate all over again on the SH31. Simply, I learned that what I could see and what roadmen told me to see was not all there was.

As we near the end of our journey, SH31's toll booth emerges as the extractive portal between the moored and unmoored, the gateway between this world and the one beyond the mooring. Following the money takes us to a tax haven island, as we hop into the offshore realms Latour evokes in relation to the shrinking resources and promises of endless growth. The ideas proselytised by many roadmen now begin to appear as the words of the foot soldiers of capital, rather than the purveyors of pro-poor development. Local and national economies appear to sustain roads—not always the other way around, as roadmen often claimed.

The road is part of the economy of the elite, the poor paying to service people who have been made invisible to them. In the spirit of the market, all benefit. In the spirit of market criticism, the benefit is extremely unevenly distributed; the carbon costs remain uncounted, and if they are accounted for, they are tallied as India's emissions rather than those of the Americans who profit from the road. At the hard edge of global debt, circulation and predation, the road runs through an unequal world in which scale, friction and speed take us along invisible routes, away from the visible and beaten track on to a path towards climate crisis.

1

ON THE ROAD
STATE HIGHWAY 31

SH31 is in the state of Madhya Pradesh in Central India. The road runs north–south, or Jaora–Ratlam–Lebad. This journey starts where many people end their own: in a shrine famous for healing.

The grandson of the last king of Jaora presides over the Hill of Hussain. He is eighty-two years old and proud to have no damaging vices. His ancestors ruled Jaora and during the colonial period were well known as pro-British Muslims with a fondness for beagles and polo. They established a shrine on the Hill of Hussain in the mid-1880s, following visions of the tombs of Muhammad's companions and mysterious lights in nearby forests.[1] They constructed memorials to the companions of the Prophet amid the graves of their own dead.

The shrine brought together Islamic notions of grace, power and martyrdom with local ideas of kingship. The combination had wide appeal and, although the royal palaces no longer contain sacred or secular power, the shrines now attract tens of thousands of visitors every year. Pilgrims come in search of cures for trouble, affliction and disease. According to our host, the king's grandson, there is no segregation, no bias—'we have more Hindu visitors than Muslims'. There is no entry fee, but donations are expected. Stiff competition to control the shrine suggests there is a lot at stake in the coming and going of people who pass through.

The poetry written in praise of the nineteenth-century kings describes Jaora as the 'heart of India', potent words about geography, culture, blood and lifeforce pumping through a circulatory system to all parts of the country. We begin our journey here to signal that travel in the region has history, and that there are precedents for paying to transgress barriers. Pilgrims have long sought intercession from the shrine's occupants, reaching across the divide between the living and the dead.

Sweet-smelling incense smoke billows across the courtyard. In the near distance, the overcome writhe and speak in tongues. Our conversation moves from shrines, miracles and royalty to roads. In our host's view:

> The roads were in such a shoddy condition, and during the monsoon they were unpliable. The people were absolutely helpless, but now they have been converted into three-lane, four-lane and five-lane. Things have changed like a wonder! The surface was very stony and negligible, but then it has been converted into a surface like a tabletop and the comparison is so great that I cannot tell you! There have been many advantages as far as commerce is concerned and all services that can avail of locomotion are flourishing today … The way these roads have helped people … it's fantastic!

The stony and negligible surface of the old two-lane state highway was expanded to four lanes of tabletop between 2009 and 2011; the operation is called 'widening' or 'four-laning'. Over the last twenty years, I have seen this operation performed many times throughout Western India, as the road network has been upgraded at tremendous speed. Traffic is kept moving through the construction site as sections of both old and new carriageways are used as contraflows, an elongated slalom.

In villages and towns, 'widening' is most visible and violent, as generally the preference remains to expand existing roads rather than to bypass settlements. 'Widening' involves 'cutting' existing buildings. Typically, surveyors mark the buildings to be cut, and demolition crews then hack these buildings back to the surveyor's mark. Often sections of the building remain standing and are put back to use.

The shopkeepers who crowd the roadside as it leaves Jaora take pride in the attractive displays of goods they make visible to passing traffic. The roadside location is the value of their businesses. They also remember commotion, protest and anger when their shops were purchased through compulsory orders and they were relocated to make way for the widened road, and some years before that for drainage and surface improvements. The jostling and competition for new commercial space went on for many years, leaving scars on people and buildings.

Shopkeepers are often well organised and connected with political groups and guilds and are hence well placed to protest and lobby. Consequently, road widening in urban areas is legally, politically and socially difficult and complex and requires a certain degree of force. As one international engineering consultant put it, unconcerned by cliché: 'if you want an omelette, then you have to break eggs'.

Petty bourgeois influence notwithstanding, after a protracted battle, the new 'four-laner' was 'cut' through Jaora. Strips of town were demolished and fences erected to prevent daily life from spilling back on to the new road. Drivers, travellers and pilgrims sip tea at the side of the road on a narrow-fenced access lane. The new commercial spaces are squashed between the new road and older properties. Everything has been compressed into the verge to open up the four lanes of tarmac for strangers to move uninterrupted through the town. Trucks from every part of the country creak and wallow over the 'speed breakers' (also known as 'suspension breakers' and 'sleeping policemen') before noisily accelerating from a crawl to a lumber, leaving fumes as wake. Passing through Jaora are the products of a growing industrial economy: local produce to the long-distance trade in everything from plastic ducks to motorbikes and wind turbines. Here India is on the move, as goods of all sorts are carted around the country.

Heading south, we pass grubby shacks of the road service economy: mechanics, tyre re-treaders, puncture repairs and petrol pumps. Years ago, the traveller would have passed out through city gates—

physical and symbolic markers of the urban edge of royal power. In post-colonial India, the fortifications and kings have long crumbled. Today, departure is marked by gantries erected by roadmen. In the past, there was a premium on entry to the markets and security of Jaora; now there is, in effect, a tax on leaving. Sovereignty has shifted from Princely States to private roads connecting urban India. The gantry spans four lanes and with a shouty font proclaims:

WESTERN M.P INFRASTRUCTURE AND TOLL ROADS PVT. LTD WELCOMES YOU.

At the side of the road, patties of cow dung mixed with straw dry in the sun to be used for cooking fuel. In the verge stands a white 'kilometre stone' with a green cap. The green is Indian Standard Shade 221 and denotes a state-level highway. These design standards were adopted in 1960, then revised in 1979 and 1981. The name of the 'destination junction', Lebad, is in 'standard font' 80-mm black lettering, while the distance, 125 km, is given in larger 130-mm lettering, denoting a place of importance: a 'terminal/starting station'. Adjacent to the kilometre stone is a metal pole painted in alternating thick bands of black and white (regulation stipulates three white, two black), displaying the sign for a numbered state highway, MP SH31, within a 'highway shield'.

Traffic moves on the left of the road, a legacy of Britain via the Commonwealth. The milestones display kilometres, a product of the metrification that took place in progressive and developmental India in the early days of Independence. Conducting research on roads, scratching every surface, has enlivened such commonplaces. Every piece of 'street furniture', every design and engineering convention, every colour, font and measurement has a story, a provenance. In the language of a senior British civil engineering consultant, national design codes are 'bibles'—usually without the additional volumes of commentary and interpretation. These books establish standard parameters for how roads are built and decorated and give national roads a distinctive character and feel.

Both the Central Road Research Institute (CRRI) and Indian Roads Congress (IRC), homes to the pioneers of the Indian road, have historically produced guidelines on the standards for all aspects of road, junction, drainage and signage design, including a manual for the design of the four-lane public–private partnership (PPP) highway we are travelling on.[2] Talking to the authors of the standards, it is quickly apparent that roads are social and historical products, made through debate, innovation, borrowing and compromise. Civil engineers proudly tell us how codes have been drawn up by commissions, working groups and overseas field trips and influenced by patterns of education and patronage among India's senior road builders.

The design of the shield on the SH31 sign is lifted straight out of US manuals, reflecting the influential role that country has played—rather silently—in late-colonial and post-colonial India. The shield reminds us that the Cold War was largely fought in India through the techniques of government and manufacture. While Nehru, who led India for seventeen years from 1947, socialist and protectionist in his approach, favoured the USSR as a partner for large state-led projects, it was often the US that won through at the level of detail on the ground. If we turn to look at the rear of the road sign, for example, we find what a potter would call the 'maker mark', intended not for casual users but for the expert who knows to look further than the visible public surfaces. The mark reveals that the sign was provided by a company called 3M (tagline: Science. Applied to Life).

3M is the Minnesota Mining and Manufacturing Company. In Delhi in November 2018, a sales representative of 3M told me that the products brought a new level of safety and quality to India's road signage. He was in the country to pursue national-level contracts through a trade show and was part of a delegation to lobby for new design protocols. Changes to safety and/or design standards are one of the greatest business opportunities in any country, and he was ultimately there to ensure that more of 3M's sticky and shiny products were required for every mile or kilometre of highway. The marketing materials he presented to me said: 'Wherever you go and however you get there, by air, water or land, from cargo ships to scooters, throughout the world of transport, you can find 3M.'

***

I first visited the heart of India in 2014 because I was interested in the engineering and social negotiation involved in road building, and the vexed question of what changes roads bring along with them. At the time, there was a massive and highly visible expansion of the road network. Roads were being widened and upgraded and new ones scraped through agricultural lands. Signs of investment and the machines of contractors littered the countryside, the tattered camps of the labourers bringing some humanity to landscapes of scarred and bulldozed red and brown earths. I was shown sites where half-constructed flyovers stopped in mid-air as they approached railway tracks, suggesting the traditional controversy in the country between road and rail had entered a new era. The atmosphere was wild, frenetic, as India was being networked with semi-privatised infrastructure. The scale of construction and the speed with which we were able to whip along the finished roads seemed disproportionate to the pace of everyday life in the countryside.

A few years into the research, in the cool and well-ordered offices of Madhya Pradesh Road Development Corporation (MPRDC; tagline: Connecting People Through Quality Infrastructure), the chief engineer explained how PPPs, or what he called 'PPP culture', had transformed the road network.[3] One of the very first public–private models for road building had been developed in the state in the 1990s. Over the next few years, Madhya Pradesh had gone from having the worst roads in the country to some of the best. There was marvel and astonishment in his tone as he recounted the story of growth and development.

The state had been notorious for spending money on roads that were never built, repeatedly. Levels of corruption had become something of a national joke. The chief engineer told us how PPPs were a 'social moment' or perhaps a 'social movement' (in retrospect we were not certain which) in the transformation of the fortunes of the state. There had been a bonanza in road building. MPRDC was established in 2004 on a model of 'corporatization, commercialization and outsourcing'.[4] Many of the employees from the state-run Public Works Department (PWD) simply moved offices to the MPRDC and carried on building roads in the state-owned private sector, which had nicer toilets, furniture and computers and a striking carport with ornamental shrubs leading to the entrance of the complex. I never got to speak to the CEO, but I did see him get out of a car to enter the building in a cloud of perfume and a brisk suit, his air that of a celebrity facing cameras on the red carpet.

The chief engineer kindly telephoned the divisional engineer, responsible for SH31, who was told to expect us the next day. He turned out to be friendly and hospitable and, over the next few years, repeatedly guided me and other researchers on the project along the SH31. On the first visit, I was garlanded with strings of colourful marigolds and given glasses of sweet tea as an honoured guest at the toll booths. We stopped to inspect new German road-building equipment decorated with Hindu swastikas, which hissed and whirred as groups of women bent double swept away the debris in its path with bundled grasses and twigs. I was given reams of paper, including the concession agreement and the revenue figures. As we saw him open doors, make data available and instruct those along the road to cooperate, it was quite clear that he was a man with power.

***

Back on the road, leaving Jaora and driving past the welcome signs, brilliant straggles of bougainvillea spew from the central reservation. The surrounding landscape is flat and tilled. Field views are frequent through vegetation and buildings along the road as the town gives way to a sprawl of truck stops. The rumbles and whines of moving goods fill our senses. Drivers tell us they prefer this highway over other long-distance routes; it has comforts and facilities that attract them. In this sense, they suggest, the road is a commodity and has been made more attractive than other routes.

Many of the *dhabas* (roadside eating houses) cater for drivers from particular parts of India, a localised appeal with a distinct blend of spice and the trust of familiarity on the road far from home. Himachal Una Kangado, Harayana Jammu, Pahadi, HP 12 Amb, Punjabi and Patel—names with regional and culinary connotations. Like many places catering for peripatetic truck drivers, some of these *dhabas* serve sex and opium along with food. Local political influence has allowed a concentrated zone to develop where truckers can eat and get laid and stoned in spaces at the side of the road with little interruption to their journey. The road itself has become a destination on their journeys. Built by the British to secure the supply of opium, the road now uses opium to secure a stream of toll revenue.

Unlike the soporific opium of Eastern India, the local Malwa variety has stimulant properties and is well suited for long drives on busy highways at night. Along the SH31, there are rumours of trafficking—opium hidden in secret compartments on trucks, opium in folds of the polluting shrouds of those whose lives were not saved on the Hill of Hussain, opium squeezed into cuts in the skin of camels.

The Malwa Plateau is opium country: a land shaped and given orientation by the trade and addicted to the revenue. The poppy has been grown here since the sixteenth century, probably earlier. Emperor Akbar's chroniclers and early Portuguese tourists noted the crop, suggesting trade was oriented to the Arabian Sea and predated the British.[5] Much of the early British colonial intervention in Malwa came with opium taxation and methods of controlling the trade, including, significantly, toll gates, as well as a distinct levy on the drug for the provision of infrastructure. When this trade was given a boost by colonial conditions in the early nineteenth century, pre-existing networks facilitated the shipment of the drug to the west coast, particularly through the ports of Bombay, Daman and Karachi. Some say the foundations of Bombay were built on the profits of Malwa opium.[6]

The colonial government had first developed a monopoly in Bengal opium, shipping it to China ostensibly to finance Britain's insatiable thirst for Chinese tea.[7] The British did not exercise the same tight territorial power over Central or Western India as they did in Bengal until the third Anglo-Maratha war ended in 1818.[8] The government then attempted to prohibit the export of opium through Bombay to protect their Bengal interests, which pushed the trade further north through the Portuguese territory of Daman and across the Thar Desert to Sindh: a 'new drug frontier', which then also brought Sindh into Britain's 'imperial orbit'.[9] In an important sense, controlling the trade in Malwa opium influenced the annexation of Sindh, seemingly far away in modern Pakistan, and the broader territorial vision of British power as it radiated into the provinces from Bombay.[10]

At the start of the nineteenth century, British authorities had entreated the Portuguese to intervene to disrupt the export of opium through Sindh. Britain's occupation of Portuguese India between 1805 and 1810 slowed the trade; however, it never ceased and, by 1819, now with British control of the region consolidated, the East India Company changed tack. Seeking to run the 'smugglers' out of business, and to further their own monopoly in Bengal opium, they began buying Malwa opium crop on the open market and selling it via the same Bengal merchants.[11]

This cunning strategy did not work. In 1823, the policy shifted to one in which defined quantities of opium would be bought at specified prices from the rulers of those opium-producing states under 'indirect rule' in Central India and Rajasthan, and sold through the British-controlled ports of Bombay and Calcutta.[12] As a consequence, the British East India Company entered into treaties with Jaora and other opium-producing states to this effect.[13]

As the trade in opium intensified in the first half of the nineteenth century, taxation became increasingly important for building and maintaining the routes that carried poppy products from Malwa to the coast. The Princely States of Ratlam and Sailana, both adjacent to SH31, constructed 'opium bungalows' and 'watching houses' to control and tax the drug as it moved through their territories.[14] Slightly further south, at Mhow, a major British military cantonment was established. Funds from the customs duties levied in the area went to the construction of a metalled road to link the military to the lucrative opium fields to the north. Work began on the route in the 1850s and, by 1870, if not earlier, a military road, complete with bridges, bungalows, wells and camping grounds, was in place along the route of what was to become the SH31.[15]

Critics of the colonial government asked good questions about the morality of cultivating poppies and promoting addiction as a way of making money. In 1894, the Indian Opium Commission examined production in Malwa, noting with concern the emergence of a speculative and high-risk futures market on the pricing of the crop.[16] Called on for evidence, the minister for Jaora, Yar Muhammad Khan, said that more than half the population was addicted.[17] At the time, Jaora produced 150,000 kg of opium, three-quarters of which went through Bombay.[18] The neighbouring town of Ratlam, our next major destination on the SH31, produced 2,200 chests for export each year, with a couple of hundred extra reserved for local consumption. Such was the scale of the trade that the Diwan of Ratlam, Cursetji Rustamji Thanewalla, warned prohibition would result in a loss of a quarter of state revenue.[19]

As we pass the truck stops on the way out of Jaora on the modern SH31 and marvel at the role of opium in making the region, we are passing along the modern iteration of a colonial military route constructed for the purpose of controlling a westwards-oriented opium trade. The military must also have had a presence to keep an eye on the affairs of the Princely States in the aftermath of the Maratha wars. At the time, the combined strategies of broad territorial domination aimed at controlling the long-distance trade routes and the militarisation of local routes, alongside mutually beneficial agreements with local rulers, appear to have succeeded, because by the 1850s, 60 per cent of Indian opium revenue came from Malwa.[20] Karl Marx estimated that around a sixth of the revenue of British India was derived from opium.[21] If we take these two gross and simplified figures at face value, then in the second half of the nineteenth century, 10 per cent of the revenue of the colonial activity in India came from Malwa opium. There was a lot at stake in the heart of India!

***

As we continue south of Jaora, we meet women who live nomadic lives with drivers, travelling with a truck or convoy of trucks before stepping down to join others. Some freight companies employ women as salaried workers to keep their fleets' drivers company. On the ground, we found realities harder. Clustered around Jaora are settlements where women sit on plastic chairs at the roadside to indicate that sex is available. One of these places is headed by a talkative man with one hand, the other lost in a car accident. He describes the sex trade as 'traditional work', the inheritance of the eldest daughter.

In the nineteenth century, the colonial military garrisons that attempted to control the opium trade encouraged the emergence of groups of hereditary communities of sex workers, many of whom have settled along SH31. California-based ethnographic filmmakers Orange Kite Productions have worked with the descendants of these communities for many years. Their patiently acquired road footage shows women getting in and out of trucks in the dusty beam of headlights. Their concern with social justice has brought them into contact with stories of trafficking, girls brought from Nepal after the earthquake of 2015, and apocryphal tales of missionaries and schools selling students into the sex trade. In their view, this region serves as a distribution centre for sex workers destined for Western and Northern India.

The settlement we visit is flyblown; a few men, beyond drunk, litter the shadow. Our one-handed interlocutor turns to talk about education in the villages. The trade has attracted organisations that offer health education and support to the women and introduce them to alternative forms of livelihood: one's first period does not have to mark one's first client. The girls themselves are reluctant to talk. Narratives shift clumsily between agency and coercion, choice and expectation, vocation and need. Working from home, their routine cooking and cleaning is punctuated by two- or three-minute encounters for which they charge Rs 200.

The Banchhara community was traditionally associated with rituals and practices of dance and entertainment, but with time they have become synonymous with sex work. They suffer routine discrimination in educational, vocational and other opportunities, stigma traceable to their inclusion as a 'Criminal Tribe' within the colonial regime's Criminal Tribes Act of 1871.[22] Moreover, popular discourse in Jaora and Ratlam links the community to both thieving and the traffic in opium.

This history of abjection is compounded by pressing economic necessities, blurring the lines between customary practice and commercial sex work, or simply eking out a living in the spaces at the side of the road. The girls told us that the widening of SH31 was not designed around them and had resulted in fewer truck drivers stopping at their settlements; in contrast to the *dhabas* to the south of

21

Jaora, there are no safe stopping places. Increasingly, their customer base has shifted from passing trucker trade to local men who visit by motorbike from nearby towns. It is almost as if the road builders bypassed them to direct passing traffic to the formal truck stops.

Twenty or so kilometres out of Jaora, the road bends to the right, passing the National Livelihood Resource Institute and the School of Rural Management, and here the truck stops suddenly disappear. We enter a new administrative region where planning rules have been differently enforced. The road alignment straightens to Mesawa before turning back to the left to head almost due south to Namli, where the highway skirts to the west of the village while the railway runs east.

As the countryside zips by, fields of bright flowers line sections of the road. These new market gardens and other forms of agriculture have been made possible by the road, which allows perishable goods to be transported to Indore and Bhopal. New forms of business and wealth have flowed into some pockets of the countryside. Farmers speak of the road as having brought wealth and opportunity. In other locations, often not that far away from the flourishing market gardens, the road has fragmented landholdings and access to land. The difference between these two conditions reminds us that there is nothing 'automatic' about what a road does to a region's wealth or mobility and that generalisation is difficult.

Road and rail cross just to the south of Namli. A massive pharmaceutical complex welcomes us to the outskirts of Ratlam. The SH31 skirts the factory before turning sharply east to start the cumbersome bypass of the town. Rivers and the extra-suburban sprawl of the town obstructed the work of the road builders. The route was compromised, and the carriageway enters and exits a bridge over the railway with dangerous curves. A small price to pay, the engineers reckoned, to avoid the extra costs, logistical and legislative difficulties involved in building a bridge that was not perpendicular to the tracks. Ratlam Junction is celebrated in Hindi songs about lovers on the station platform in the cool of the night, and it is also popularly known as the centre of the Indian rail network, with 192 different train services halting in the station.

The bypass skirts Ratlam as an arc of a circle, the sharp point of the compass rotating from the centre of the town. At a third of the way around, the road turns to the south-east. Ratlam is the main town along the route, popularly famous for puffed wheat snacks, gold and saris. It has a history of rioting, including multiple and often violent skirmishes involving Hindus and Bohras (a Shia Muslim community originally from coastal Western India known in the region for trade and their association with Hussain Hill in Jaora), as well as confrontations between student groups and the police, and communist-led strikes.[23] As a result, curfews and bans on public meetings were imposed, especially during the 1960s and 1970s.[24] Alongside these social tensions, Ratlam and its surroundings have suffered intermittently from famines and droughts, often disproportionately affecting tribal communities.[25]

This charged atmosphere may have contributed to the early success in Ratlam of the Rashtriya Swayamsevak Sangh (RSS), the grassroots Hindu nationalist organisation established in Nagpur in the 1920s. Many of the first village-level cells of the organisation were in the Central Provinces in which Ratlam was an important hub.[26] Indeed, by the 1980s, the town was seen as significant enough in Hindu revivalist circles for the Shankaracharya (head priest) of an important Hindu monastery in Kanchi, South India, to consider the Shankaracharya of Ratlam as a possible successor.[27]

Today, as in much of India, there are tensions between the RSS and Christian missionary groups, both of which compete for the devotion of tribal communities. Nationalist youth movements are active, coalescing around the high rates of unemployment and aspirations that are unmatched by opportunities. With the presence of organised Hindu nationalism comes a politicised awareness of minority religious groups, notably Christians and Muslims, and readymade structures of animosity and blame, which feed strongly into discourse about smuggling, mafias and anti-nationalism.

***

SH31 heads south-east out of Ratlam. Adjacent to the road is a joss factory called Shree Ram Products (tagline: Good Morning Retail $—underlined with a swirling black graphical highway). To the left is a private school, Himalaya International, a pyramid of glass representing a mountain peak at the entrance. To either side stretch substantial wings of brightly coloured architecture. The grounds are green, manicured and heavily irrigated. The school is dependent on the road, as Ratlam has spread like a slick along its flanks. The school 'story' is a fantastic assemblage of ideas:

> A mountain is composed of tiny grains of earth. The ocean is made up of tiny drops of water. Even so, life is but an endless series of little details, actions, speeches, and thoughts. And the consequences whether good or bad of even the least of them are far-reaching. The Himalayas represent the awe-inspiring power, beauty, and grandeur of Nature. Welcome to the Himalaya International—Where Earth Meets Sky!

SH31 is now surrounded by the unmistakable signs of land speculation, with fallow fields marked with chalk and stone to indicate building plots, future housing societies and more roads. The highway wiggles around Dharad and Bilpank. To the right are large reservoirs providing irrigation water. Impulsively, we leave the highway and turn towards the water. Our speed drops from 100 km per hour to 10 km per hour as we jolt and bump into rural India. The road round the reservoir leads into the hinterlands. The air is fresh, birds feast and play on the water. Poppies have been planted just away from the road; not very many of them, but they are not guarded, not even fenced.

The opium story did not end when the British left India. The railway between Ratlam and Bombay continued as a major and infamous smuggling route.[28] Before Independence, in the 1930s, the government opened two opium refineries for medical and commercial use. Today, the plant at Neemuch, to the north, houses the world's largest opium tank, resembling a swimming pool. Freedom, and the sudden importance of the international regulatory frameworks developed by the League of Nations, brought a sea-change in domestic policy. In 1949, the All-India Opium Conference adopted a resolution to curb opium use.

As opium became harder to procure, interest in heroin increased, and the value attributed to the by-products of poppies grew.[29] Consequently, soils of the region became increasingly attractive, and the state attempted to control the trade through a system of licences. The opium cultivators thus became a special category of agriculturalist, given relief when crops failed and the subject of sanction and penalty when production was high. The bureaucratisation of opium inevitably produced loopholes and new opportunities.[30] Rather than dying out, opium continued to be part of everyday life, and the new expectations of the command economy were incorporated into local life: marriages and loans negotiated on the basis of licensed opium lands as the fundamental asset of the region.[31] Efforts made to encourage farmers to grow other crops also failed because of the price difference between opium and other agricultural produce.[32]

Throughout the 1970s, there was concern about illicitly produced opium and products that leaked from state-run supply chains. There were well-known opium trafficking circuits linking Ratlam and Indore to Gujarat, with attempts by customs officials to curb the trade failing due to 'intimidation'.[33] The mid-1970s saw the arrest of smugglers operating on buses between Mandsaur and Pune via Jaora.[34] In the 1980s, Rajasthan enforced a prohibition on 'poppy husk' or 'poppy straw', the 'waste' parts of the poppy used for tea, which created new markets for the Malwa product. Those who were caught were indicative of far wider networks, because in the 1980s the US government, then led by Ronald Reagan, offered to 'make good' the losses of farmers in Malwa if they did away with opium production. They did not.

The question of how to control 'husk' arose again in the mid-1990s when the police and media 'discovered' cartels operating out of Ratlam and Neemuch to sell the product in Punjab and Rajasthan. In 1999, there were claims that officials from the Central Bureau of Narcotics (tagline: Make Health Your 'New High' in Life, Not Drugs—did they really need the last two words?) pocketed Rs 50 crore for providing fake opium licences.[35] Local politicians supported the increase in opium cultivation as a matter of expediency, the trade bringing prosperity to agricultural communities.[36] The claims of collusion between politicians and those controlling the black market went as high up as an unnamed former chief minister of Madhya Pradesh.[37]

Throughout the 1990s, there was a great deal of attention to drug addiction and HIV in India. Much discussed, too, were the links between heroin production and organised crime, including arms trading.[38] The state was seen to be losing control of the economy. With this region producing three-quarters of the country's opium, an aura of moral panic surrounded trains leaving Ratlam for Mumbai carrying young, unemployed drug mules with the refined product hidden about them, with the sting in the tail being that half of those arrested for trafficking were women and children.[39] In response, the state police established a 'narcotics control branch' to disrupt the trade.[40]

A few days earlier, we had stopped to talk with some nomads on the road. They offered us tea and opium, just there at the side of the road with the traffic passing. Of Malwa, it is said that the people have depth and sobriety; their land is flush with food and water. So, too, opium: it is on the highways and in the hedgerows; it is part and parcel of this land and society. The road is the way to move the product to where it is scarce, and where people will pay more. The stickiness and odour of opium make it difficult to move discreetly. The refined product is light and has less odour; morphine weighs a tenth of the raw material, while further refinement of morphine into heroin produces a drug that weighs a fifth of its precursor. Given these ratios, it is unsurprising that there is money in refinement. Who knows how much of this stuff is moving up and down the SH31, in false fuel tanks, in tyres and in the bloodstreams of the long-distance drivers?

The United Nations Office on Drugs and Crime (UNODC) seemed proud to have intercepted 102 kg of heroin, 51 kg of opium and 5.1 kg of morphine in 2002–3 in and around Ratlam, Neemuch and Mandsaur.[41] Data from the Central Bureau of Narcotics from the Office of the District Opium Officer, Jaora-I Division, list around 2,000 named licensed cultivators. If it is fair to assume that some might grow a little on the side, then the actual seized quantities of narcotic seem small. Indeed, there are police along the road, but not very many. No one ever said so, but was it simply a coincidence that SH31 was one of the first toll roads in Madhya Pradesh? The incentives for movement were unlikely to be diminished by the imposition of a toll, as the rulers of Princely Jaora and the British had found out two centuries earlier.

We bounce back on to the SH31 and accelerate to highway speed. Towards the end of the book, we will return here on a second road trip that takes us still further south from Ratlam to the junction village of Lebad. Together, these journeys take us a modest 125 km through a vast country. The book in the middle of these road trips is concerned with what I have chosen to call 'the politics of thought' about roads, people and institutions.

2

READING ROADS
THE POLITICS OF THOUGHT

Mumbai, 2019. I was attempting to explain what I had been working on for the last few years to an Indian sociologist. My research was about roads and what road builders, or 'roadmen' as they often describe themselves, thought of roads and of their work more broadly. The project combined the critical geography of South Asia with an enduring interest in how abstract ideas are made into concrete realities. Along the way, I had also developed a methodology to 'read' roads as routes, histories and modes of political economy.[1]

This methodology explored roads in a holistic sense, looking at the connections between roads and people, history and geography. This involved exploring how roads are interwoven with regional economies, such as in Central India, where the opium economy has given the road a distinctive orientation. More broadly, I had adopted an informal approach to geography: the focus was on South Asia, but the research crossed boundaries and brought together ideas and people from across the globe that are often deliberately separated.[2] The research, like the text of this book, moved almost seamlessly between India, Pakistan, Europe and North America. I was following flows of knowledge and power among road builders, as well as being led by the shape and force of roads themselves.

Over time, I had learned to associate roads with 'belief', ways of life and conviction. 'In essence,' I said to the sociologist, 'the project is about the politics of knowledge or thought—not tarmac or machinery. I struggle to convey my premise because roads usually evoke other things.' I recalled how one friendly reader of the initial research note had said: 'An unusual project. One does not usually associate roads with anything as refined as thought.' That reader was correct, insofar as the analysis and understanding went. Go further, however, beyond the commonplace assumptions, and roads 'open up' fundamental questions about the world, how we relate to one another and the future we are building.

The sociologist to whom I was describing my project was sympathetic, though she was senior and keen that I remember that. The second drink of the evening settled and, sensing an audience, I went on to recall how I had been deeply influenced by previous experiences in Gujarat, where I had seen how new roads brought comfort and hope to the beleaguered following an earthquake in 2001. The destruction had been terrible and left around 13,000 dead. As things were reassembled, four lanes of road ringed the provincial capital, Bhuj, as part of an 'infrastructural upgrade'.

In the evenings, friends would play cricket on the warm tarmac as the sun gave way to the chilly air of dusk. At weekends, the same friends would picnic on the road in the months before traffic was welcome—a blanket on the tarmac, dahl and chapatis on the blanket. The open space was a relief, away from the confines and choking construction dust of the old town. The road cut through virgin lands, 'jungle', they called it, as if disciplining nature for the trouble she had caused with the quaking earth. The unfinished edge of the road was more than a foot thick of layered tar and stone, a confident intervention over the shifting sands and scrubby acacia. As we played or ate, other people would come and go, looking in wonder, appreciation and disbelief.

I was interested in learning what people saw when they looked at roads. In Gujarat, the road was considered a marvel, taken by the people as evidence that the government was caring for them in the aftermath of disaster. After a heated debate in Oxford about the climate implications of road building, a minister for roads smiled and described the joy that lit people's faces when a road came to the village. 'You have to understand that,' he told me. I took his words to heart by trying to understand just that: the passion that many people feel for roads, as well as where this enthusiasm came from and what historical forces produce it.

I soon discovered that different aspects of roads are visible to different people; as I explained to the sociologist, engineers do not see the same things as chartered accountants. I paraphrased the narrative voiceover from a film that I had watched many times about the American steel industry to make my point:

> The modern highway, outgrowth of the motor age. ... Rolling along over the long straight stretches, often flanked by eye-filling scenery or rounding graceful curves, the traveller seldom thinks of the engineering skill and construction techniques utilised in the building of these ribbons of concrete and steel that make possible the miracle of modern transportation.[3]

Just as there are hidden technologies in roads, so too there are invisible ideas that lead to roads being built. To illustrate some of this thought, I reconstructed fragments from two contrasting interviews with road builders about the reasoning behind their work.

Brussels, 2015. The bistro table overlooks an elegant square, lit by the weak sun of a winter afternoon.

'We are asking road builders for their views on roads,' I say to the former commissioner. 'What effects do roads have? In your role in the European Commission, why did you build roads overseas?'

> First, it is important to realise that roads respond to the demand from people. Secondly, roads bring improved economic opportunities and enhanced social welfare. Thirdly, roads bring with them access to markets, jobs, health and education. Over my career, my concern was with roads, that is to say, road construction, finance and policy.

'What do you see when you look at a road?' I ask.

> I look at roads and I generally see difficulties, surface wear, faded road markings. Roads require maintenance. Politicians build roads and road networks much larger than they can afford to

maintain. They do not plan for maintenance. There are few votes in well-maintained roads; roads are noticed only when they are new or when roads have holes and fall into disrepair. The problem is that roads are managed as a bureaucracy rather than a business, and led by politics rather than research.

At the national level, the former commissioner continues, road expenditure is drawn from government budgets and thus competes with other public sectors for funds. 'The spending allocation for roads has little relationship to the underlying needs or economic importance of the asset—the political imperative wins out. The sector needs an overhaul: private players and a business ethos regulated by international standards.'

Delhi, 2016. Beneath office strip lights, yellowed computers and towers of neatly bound paper sit on the desk. I ask a senior civil engineer in the Indian government similar questions to those I had put to the former commissioner:

'Roads are a number one priority in this country,' the civil engineer responds:

> For decades, we had poor roads. The climate, monsoon, heat— we had potholes and unpassable roads. Roads bring development. Build a new road into a village and you open it up, new ideas, new opportunities. The girl gets education, the woman can get to hospital to give birth. The farmer can take his produce to market, the labourer can find work.

'What do you see when you look at a road?'

'I see promise. I see a government motivated to help the people.'

The sociologist liked these examples. Her interest in the project seemed to grow. 'What about corruption?' she asked excitedly. 'Roads are famous for corruption!' She reminded me of how, a few years ago, phone conversations between the political lobbyist Niira Radia and Indian government and business leaders had been leaked. In the transcript, the road ministry is described as a 'cash machine' (an ATM) for the minister in charge.[4]

I explained that while I had not been researching corruption directly, I had been trying to unravel the opaque structures of finance behind South Asia's roads. A series of high-profile leaks of offshore financial information had exposed the identities and interests of people moving money around the world, some of whom were linked to road building and infrastructural management. In London, financial advisors, brokers and agents were afraid of exposing themselves or their clients to media or tax investigations. The shutters came down on this world. Some screened my questions before agreeing to speak to me. Appointments were cancelled, and I received officious correspondence advising me of client confidentiality and insurance risks of various kinds. Three people kindly wrote with threats of legal action should I continue to ask questions.

'Oh, how interesting,' said the sociologist, clearly wearying of the conversation. To bring our interaction to a close, she said with conclusive flourish, 'After all is said and done, roads are necessary, *na?*'

***

That weighty political and moral questions on road building could be shut down by a reference to their apparent necessity is important. This moment resembled many comments by others who also blocked conversation by an appeal to the universal good of roads, a good so strong and obvious that it outweighed anything contestable. The sociologist, however, experienced as she was with the tendency of social science arguments to end openly, concluded her statement with a rhetorical '*na?*', both asserting the validity of her previous statement and leaving the path open for further debate.

Today, the marvel that I witnessed at the new roads in Gujarat is a distant memory from two decades ago. The jungle has gone now. The road brought leisure resorts and shopping centres as the town, Bhuj, expanded to meet the road, spreading like a slick of the oil that fuelled its growth.[5] Meanwhile, the leaked Radia Tapes remind us that road building is a notoriously venal business, and rumours of corruption still abound.

As the former commissioner suggested, to understand roads is to explore the primacy of the political imperative and the relegation of research and evidence-based decisions. In other words, politicians often deploy road building as a form of populist engagement, though the question remains as to why the promise of roads should command so much political power.

According to the civil engineer, national service and development are core preoccupations for many roadmen, and their actions and thoughts are informed by these senses of a greater good, progress and value.

The considered silence of London's financial advisors demonstrates how many of those involved in moving the money around had put years of effort and considerable resources into hiding and did not appreciate their identities being leaked. This points to other difficulties in understanding roads: some parts of the puzzle are highly visible, while others are invisible and only discoverable by chance or with educated guesses (which got better as the research progressed). Some road builders promote their work with billboards and even films and books. Some operate in the shadows, through subcontracts or third parties. Some discreetly place their logos on documents and road infrastructure where only other roadmen would know to look. Some deliberately hide all traces of themselves and use masks, fronts and 'secrecy jurisdictions' to remain unseen.

Consequently, there are roadmen whose work we can drive along, others whose work we can trace through paper, government offices and courts, and others still whose road building is only evident in elaborate internet trails and leaked papers. The Panama Papers put Nawaz Sharif, Pakistan's most notable road builder, straight into prison. Subsequent leaks of the Paradise and Pandora Papers by the International Consortium of Investigative Journalists also named others associated with roads in South Asia and elsewhere, who use the accommodating jurisdictions of tax havens—capitalism's outlaw foundations—to hide their loot.[6] Through ethnographic and archival research, this book attempts to explain how and why South Asia's roads usually fall beyond critical scrutiny. Along the journey, we examine the visible and invisible aspects of the road to reveal a broader political story.

***

In the autumn of 2017, Tommaso Sbriccoli spent six days walking along the verge of a 125-kilometre stretch of SH31 in Madhya Pradesh, Central India. Tommaso had previously spent time in the region conducting long-term research on nomadic communities and changing rural lives. Although he carried Italian coffee and pasta with him, Tommaso speaks Hindi, knows his way around and can handle himself in the country. Even so, SH31 turned out to be a tough gig; buffeted by traffic and dismayed by the filth of the roadside lodges, he observed hardness in the lives of those he encountered, pointing to an unforgiving land. Along the way, he asked people about the new highway and quickly noticed patterns in what they said.

'The first reply is that roads are good—they mean development, and this is good for everyone,' Tommaso said. 'But if I keep asking questions about possible problems, then people start to list a lot of them. After a while, you reach a point where you cannot tell how real the benefits are that are supposed to come with road building.' Once the positive impacts of the road had been enumerated, the conversation would usually shift to land. A village headman told Tommaso, 'The price of land has increased incredibly after the road was built. Many people in this village sold land on the road and bought cheaper land elsewhere.' If the conversation went further, said Tommaso, 'there was usually a mixed bag of lesser observations, repetitive along the entire length of SH31'.

The anthropologist's job, as I see it, is to get past the standard narrative or official account, in this case the idea that roads bring development. The recurrent statements that Tommaso encountered on SH31 are an example of how social science research methods can begin to do this. People develop simple and repetitive explanations for things, and in providing such answers, they also engage with what they perceive to be the expectations of those asking the questions. Stay longer, see more, learn more, and the standard narrative is revealed as a conceit that can become the object of analysis itself: the subject of this book.[7]

***

While anthropologists traditionally used to work alone, this book emerges from a team research project: 'Roads and the Politics of

Thought.' Researchers on the project spent time along the highways and byways, and in offices and toll booths, of South Asia, getting to know people and how they thought about and interacted with the roads in question. These roads became our 'fields', as anthropologists say, while the people who used, worked on and built the roads became our 'subjects', our task being to understand their beliefs about roads. We use the word 'belief' in an affirmative and positive sense, not as a cynical shorthand for something untrue or fanciful.

Most of the roadmen I talked to were educated in sciences and engineering and preferred to deal with what they saw as knowledge and evidence, rather than theories or beliefs. Their views are generally mainstream and reflect the global privileging of 'scientific' over interpretive or expressive frameworks. However, reading as a partial outsider, the so-called 'evidence' on roads is all highly contested and contestable, as we will see later. Rather than evidence informing meaning, it seemed to me that broader views of the world gave meaning to evidence: the interpretative practice determined how the 'data' would be read. In this way, 'evidence' is given power and legitimacy by communities of practitioners who share similar views on the world, perpetuated by education, ambition and recruitment practices.

The challenge taken up in this book is to explain how force and value come together in ideas about roads, and about roads and the world. How has 'necessity' been made? How has such necessity become common sense? To answer these questions, we conducted ethnographic fieldwork on and around particular roads in Pakistan, India, Sri Lanka, the Maldives and Réunion Island, some of which has found a way into this text.[8] The aim was to examine the organisation and culture of construction on the ground, in offices and within a broader array of national and international institutions, from provincial PWDs to global hedge funds and development banks. Overall, the project team learned how roads are built on paper and in law and language, how land is acquired, how routes are negotiated and determined, and what happens when they are bulldozed, graded and scraped into the earth.

Individually and collectively, we learned the language of road building, studying the manuals and procedural guidelines as well as how these were assembled. We traced how the logic and discourse of road building linked technocratic and moral ideas about roads to the environment, the economy, development and society in particular ways. The road builders' most common refrain—or standard narrative—is that roads generate wealth, reduce poverty and promote political stability, or at least security. This, broadly speaking, is also the position of the key institutions that promote, finance and construct roads in South Asia.

As part of the research, I enrolled in professional development courses for road and infrastructure managers and later became an instructor on one such course. As I gained more insight into the road world, I found I had the skills to take on consultancy work for road builders. Some of the contacts I developed through that work became 'key informants' outside our paid time. I hardened my nose as I presented research to seasoned roadmen and economists, audiences very different from the anthropology crowds I am used to. In earlier days, I attended the conferences of the International Road Federation and World Road Congress and other, smaller specialist and regional events on road finance, management, materials and technologies.

The project also engaged with colonial, engineering, online and newspaper archives. Various institutions have provided technical publications, manuals and discussion of materials and construction techniques, including the Institution of Civil Engineers in London (tagline: Shaping the World); the National Transport Research Centre in Islamabad (tagline: Transport Research for Better Connectivity & Prosperity); the CRRI in Delhi; and the IRC in Delhi. The tagline is an ethnographic artefact in this book and appears repeatedly as a representation of an organisation's intent, self-image and public ethos within broader national, international and cultural contexts.[9] Taglines vary surprisingly in aims and style; compare, as we go, those used by engineering firms in Pakistan with those in India. The words used in taglines often recall progress, surety and the future—three of the main professional concerns of those engaged in roadworks.

More generally, the internet provided the project with daily news alerts, social media material and endless homemade road movies, as well as the more specialist content of archive.org and the digital

Wayback Machine archive. I have also drawn extensively from a range of newspapers, but most systematically from *The Times of India* and Pakistan's *Dawn*. At various points, the project got stuck and I had to learn new research methods using company records and freedom of information laws.

In the following sections, I survey some of the literature on roads that has informed my project and outline how roads will be treated in this book.

The Road in Social Science Literature

Roads have been around for a long time and many great minds have had a great deal to say about them; I have elected not to provide a potholed history. Instead, I bring together four inspiring moments from the literature that are characterised by both intellectual exuberance and clarity to develop a framework of ideas about the road.

First is select critical commentary from the early 1970s by public intellectuals in the United States on the pitfalls of road building in light of the oil crisis and the implementation of the programme for inter-state highway construction. Here, the literature screams against the logic of road building and the progressive entanglement of American ways of life with oil and mobility. This body of work is the most concentrated and sophisticated set of statements against road mania, which, although echoed in later years in other parts of the world, reaches apotheosis during this period.

Second is an attempt by John Whitelegg, roadman gone rogue, in the United Kingdom in the 1990s to undermine the logic and authority of the road story by using its own terms of reference and data to show that roads did not do what was generally claimed for the economy, opportunity and geography.

Third, literature produced in the academic fields of social science and the humanities in the last few decades has explored the social effects of road building in various parts of the world. This work shows how roads and road building intersect with cultures and societies, how roads bring change, and how roads are associated with broader ideas of time, progress and development.

Fourth, those who study pathways are called 'hodologists'; in this instance, the hodologists are men who have spent much of their lives on roads and have thought hard about how roads and their journeys encouraged personal stories and regional histories to take particular road-like shapes.

Writing against the road in 1970s America

The early 1970s saw an outbreak of spirited engagement with roads and automobility, particularly in relation to urban form. These critiques enlivened themes also found in the earlier work of historian and sociologist of technology Lewis Mumford and the architect Victor Gruen. Mumford's *The Highway and the City* (1963) and *The Urban Prospect* (1968) took on the planning logic of the American Interstate Highway system. Gruen, now often accredited with the invention of the shopping mall, similarly envisioned the city as a place of residence and creativity rather than of transit and mobility, with the mall being the commercial focus of a broader human-centred urbanism. The mall was unfortunately the only element of this vision that took off, and it grew to be served by roads rather than Gruen's walkways.

Helen Leavitt's admonitory *Superhighway—Superhoax* (1970) was a sardonic critique of the inter-state highway system, written when her own home in Washington was threatened by road builders. *The New York Times* poignantly noted in review, 'Hell hath few furies like a lady confronted with a highway through her living room.'[10] Kenneth R. Schneider's *Autokind vs. Mankind* (1971) rages against the creation of America's 'automotive civilisation' and 'occupied society' inebriated by the 'mass autoism' of the highway boosters. The plaything of the rich became the necessity of the poor. 'Consider how the liberals warn us about the emergent tyrannies. Yet they fail to take note of the only species of tyranny presenting a clear and present danger: that of automobility.'[11]

The journalist Vance Packard's *A Nation of Strangers* (1972) picked up on his longer-term critique of planned obsolescence and the psychological manipulation of consumer society to argue that the mobility enabled by roads and cars was the root of social isolation and loneliness. In a similar vein, the architectural critic Martin Pawley described the automobile in his *The Private Future* (1973) as 'the shibboleth of privatisation', the symbol and the actuality of an individual's withdrawal from the community.

The 1973 oil crisis, sometimes known as the 'first oil shock', came about when OAPEC (the Organization of Arab Petroleum Exporting Countries) imposed an embargo on states supporting Israel during the Yom Kippur War. Oil prices rose and drew attention to patterns of dependence and environmental degradation. Against this backdrop, Ivan Illich's *Energy and Equity* (1974) described the work Americans put into their cars: 1,600 hours to travel 7,500 miles. The tone is mocking but the analysis is deft:

> He sits in it while it goes and while it stands idling. He parks it and searches for it. He earns the money to put down on it and to meet the monthly instalments. He works to pay for petrol, tolls, insurance, taxes, and tickets. He spends four of his sixteen waking hours on the road or gathering his resources for it.

In the 1970s, America led the way with automobile culture. Illich observed:

> In countries deprived of a transportation industry, people manage to do the same, walking wherever they want to go, and they allocate only 3 to 8 percent of their society's time budget to traffic instead of 28 percent. What distinguishes the traffic in rich countries from the traffic in poor countries is not more mileage per hour of lifetime for the majority, but more hours of compulsory consumption of high doses of energy, packaged and unequally distributed by the transportation industry.[12]

I grew up knowing about such books; their polemic arguments and tabloid-shouty covers from second-hand bookshops remained with me. I am thus reminded that published scepticism of roads has been around for as long as I have, and longer. I have unquestionably been influenced by these debates, but I take from them not simply the straightforward message that roads are part of capitalist expansion and vested interest, but rather that a more careful analysis of roads can shed light on other forms of knowledge, social life and political process. These books, for example, were themselves often a manifestation of the first major wave of post-Second World War environmental anxiety born of the oil crisis.

The arguments and sharp turns of phrase extracted above are strong and engaging and caught the imagination of rebels of the moment and those looking for alternatives. Like many such popular books, they sold well but were quickly remaindered. In the longer term, they changed little and did not absorb the ambition of North American petrolheads, contractors and concrete merchants.

One of Pawley's concluding questions, slightly repackaged, is however particularly hard to shake: Has road building made America more culturally and therefore politically right wing, as the values of individualism and social distinction have been naturalised through vehicles? My suspicion is that this is a left-wing question to begin with.[13] Politics is everywhere in road-thought, and whether you drive on the left or the right, so to speak, is particularly influential in how you frame and assess the arguments.

Whitelegg questions the road builders

I was about four years into my own project when I came across a book called *Critical Mass* (1997) by John Whitelegg. John had developed a critique of the ideas that kept roadmen in business, by using their own data, language and terms of reference to plot a different world from the one that suggested business-as-usual and more-of-the-same-please. I tracked him down, and he kindly agreed to a chat, the headline of which was his frustration at not having found a way to make people act on what he had to say.[14]

In the 1990s, John had attempted to explain why the British government continued to organise society and economy around the automobility of roads, especially when there was strong evidence (as interpreted by him) to suggest that costs outweighed benefits. He questioned the assumptions that roads create jobs and economic growth and provide equal and greater access to opportunities. He saw these ideas as wishful thinking and as part of a Faustian bargain, the sacrifice of everything to satisfy desire.

John argued that the car had been sold as a vehicle of freedom, which carried in its boot and paintwork the notions of progress, independence and growth. The advertising industry had connected cars with images of speed, power, open roads, breath-taking scenery and sex—images so powerful that the beholden could not see the flaws in the four-wheeled monsters they had been socialised to adore. Indeed, John made it sound like being in love. Love is often blind to other kinds of reason.

John saw that the attractiveness of the economic model, as well as the car itself, was so strong that transport planners had failed to reflect adequately on the consequences of their road building. Significantly, traffic forecasting and statistical modelling did not incorporate the feedback mechanism that linked new road construction to the generation of yet more traffic—so-called 'flow paradoxes'. Likewise, the evidence had also been ignored that showed how new transport infrastructure resulted in larger market areas being supplied from a smaller number of production and distribution points. In this sense, new roads had not created jobs, as is commonly argued, but had instead redistributed and centralised them—and, in some cases, actively contributed to their loss.

Across Britain, John saw that high levels of mobility and energy-intensive production had led to the decline of traditional communities. He pointed out that cars meant people spent less time on the street talking to one another, which led in particular to the isolation of children and the elderly. In the grander scheme, the car and the cult of individual mobility had contributed to the emptying out of the countryside. For many, this development was a blessing, a glad farewell to stifling relations, familiarity, close kin and repetitive rituals. For others, however, there is the sense of loss and fragmentation that comes with increasing anonymity, individualisation and secularisation. While this sharply one-way-or-the-other characterisation is simplistic, it serves to show that the past and the future ushered in and out by roads are far from value neutral.

John saw that competitive regional development within the UK, where local authorities kept piling up the concrete and tarmac to keep ahead of the neighbours in terms of jobs, supermarkets and growth rates, was the automobile equivalent of 'an arms race'.

John's solution was for a 'critical mass' of opinion, thus the title of his book, to rebel against the idea of automobile economic growth as the central principle on which to organise society.

In his project to articulate and question the unspoken assumptions underpinning the mass automobility of roads, John was successful to a great extent, though he would perhaps acknowledge that more work could have been done to clarify and simplify his arguments—not least because in the UK, the critical mass did not emerge. In short, little happened, and John was ostracised for challenging the creed of automobility.[15]

Reflecting on this literature, we find that those who shouted at the highwaymen in America in the 1970s saw their task as something akin to swerving across the carriageway and into a head-on collision. The wreckage of their arguments now reads as cars of the same period appear—oversized, wallowing, pointy and often beige or brown. In contrast, John Whitelegg attempted a different epistemological move. Instead of direct opposition, he took the arguments and premises of roadmen to draw alternative conclusions and then attempted to sell these to a reading public to generate a critical mass of non-roadmen who would take up the anti-road charge. Both approaches have limitations. The first closes dialogue; the second assumes, possibly quite incorrectly, that the emergent critical mass will understand the premises of the roadmen and then run with a heterodox interpretation in good faith.

The other lesson to take from this historical literature is that people tend to be more concerned with what is at stake when, like Helen Leavitt, they are faced with a highway through their living room. Then, roads magically shed their invisibility.

Anthropology of the road

Through repeated interactions with roadmen, it became obvious to me that anthropology was an esoteric, if not to say narrow-minded, form of knowledge. Many of my interlocuters did not grasp the point of it, not because they are simple-minded but because anthropology is a specialist discipline—it is not, as many anthropologists seem to think, common sense. Consequently, throughout, I have tried to maintain a high level of self-reflexivity and an ecumenical relationship to anthropological conventions, both to explain the discipline as I go along and to broaden the terms of debate and bring different forms of knowledge into conversation. In this section, I review what anthropologists have had to say about roads, but I also explain why they have said what they have.

First, however, a vignette to illustrate. We are in a small meeting room in a UK government department. My hosts are charged with spending money through consultancy firms to build roads overseas, with a particular interest in projects in parts of South Asia. I have been invited to talk about anthropological approaches to road building and how these understandings may enhance the work of civil and transport engineers. By this point, I have learned to see transport as a force that conveys messages to people about who they are, what the government wants for them, and how the future can be seen. These messages are subtle and engage with emotions, hopes and fears.

I suggest to my hosts that knowing that transport infrastructure can generate optimism, loyalty and political capital could enhance the quality of communication and engagement with what they call 'recipient' and 'beneficiary' populations. Road infrastructure engages with people's aspirations, who they want to be, how they imagine themselves in the future; roads summon the glossy lives of car adverts, ideas of freedom and power. I was on a roll. In the back of my mind, I was applying the work of the great theorists of power and ideology to everyday road planning. Suddenly, one of my hosts interrupted. 'Sorry,' he said, 'do you mean that we can put signs on the sides of buses?' My heart sank. My captivated audience was not spellbound but befuddled.

For anthropologists, objects and relationships carry meaning, symbolism and power. In this view, objects are not just material: they interact with the social world and become part of that world. Anthropologists can therefore study roads without considering the chemical composition of tarmac, engineering algorithms or land acquisition law, peculiar as this sounds for those who build roads. Roads are not simply technologies: they also establish the invisible rules and ideas that guide everyday life, and these are what anthropologists are generally interested in and write about (this is part of the madness of anthropology, which, when you are embedded and trained within this system of knowledge, seems perfectly reasonable and common-sensical).

This approach to roads can be understood in the broader anthropological context of looking beneath or beyond the sometimes dull surface of infrastructure to explore how it conveys meaning. Susan Leigh Star, one of the key voices in the field, acknowledges that infrastructure involving 'things such as plugs' can be 'mundane to the point of boredom', but that its anthropological interest lies in the way its meaning varies between groups.[16] Thus, technical issues of failure and repair 'surface invisible work' to deepen our understanding of the contemporary world in periods of both stability and crisis.[17] More recently, Brian Larkin highlights the diversity of frames through which infrastructure can be understood—technological, financial, biological—suggesting that anthropology has not settled on a coherent approach.[18] Other theorists of infrastructure place emphasis on 'agency' and 'rights'.[19]

Anthropology's focus on meaning extends to the specific study of roads, too. Back in the early 1990s, French anthropologist Marc Augé influentially theorised the motorway as one of the 'non-places' of the post-modern era, along with shopping malls and airports. Augé did not mean that nothing happened in these spaces; instead, he argued that the anonymous solitude of his 'non-places' offers the transitory and mobile occupant the sense of being part of some grand global scheme: a fugitive glimpse of a utopian city-world.

More conventionally, anthropologists describe roads as meaningful places.[20] Roads are seen to variously divide or shape communities, represent the state or different kinds of modernity, or bring an end to traditional ways.[21] Roads cut and connect space in particular ways that may build on existing divisions of ethnicity, class or language or may contribute to the generation of new social forms. Some scholars have studied life on roads and the changes brought about by the arrival of roads in places where there were previously none.[22] In such studies, roads emerge as sites of potent meaning and culture where emotions and affects such as hope and desire, fear and danger, nationalism and hatred are brought into sharp relief.[23]

Sociologists and geographers have seen roads as part of the continued appeal of the story of individual freedom and movement and the grand narratives of modernisation and progress—particularly in relation to the car and automobility.[24] Roads may bring civilisation to a rude country, producers closer to a market, a port closer to a city or an army closer to a site of potential conflict. They may be part of an attempt to establish a democratic utopia or they may deepen inequality. Many build roads for investment, seeing profits in tolls, kickbacks, land prices and allied construction opportunities. Some people believe that roads bring peace, some that roads bring trouble.[25] Yet others emphasise the geopolitical messages emanating from roads in which roads themselves speak, a genre quite distinct from a formal focus on international relations and the pronouncements of generals or ministers. This has been turned into a cottage industry by the China-led Belt and Road Initiative and the new 'resource extraction roads' currently being built in parts of Africa.[26]

Historians have shown how road building passes through technological phases and financial fashions and how roads have been part of ideological projects.[27] The Nazis in Germany, for example, sought to build a nation with motorways.[28] The European Union also attempted to unite the continent through 'infrastructural Europeanism' represented by a motorway network.[29] Roads pass between power and governmentality and become the sites through which history is made and remade, where notions of citizenship are forged, and where capitalism operates in the most extreme and enchanting forms. Roads cease to be anodyne or the neutral means to a destination and instead become artefacts of culture and politics, mediums of change and hope, and vehicles of state-building, liberation and oppression.[30] Roads become places of exuberant meaning and radical action.[31]

However, there is another side to thinking about roads: they are often also seen as public and awful domains, where strangers intermingle to create unknowable fleeting societies, a liminal space. The anthropologist Adeline Masquelier draws on individual stories to place roads in Niger in a 'complex economy of violence, power, and blood'. The road, she argues, is not an uncomplicated symbol of modernity but rather a 'hybrid space' in which diverse religious, economic and technological strands of history are condensed alongside the 'perils and possibilities of modern life'.[32] Roads are home to spiritual forces, bewitched vehicles and the curses of gods and ghosts. These deadly road spirits are commentaries on the perils and possibilities of modern life, sometimes bearing striking resemblances to the seductive creatures of Western advertisements.[33]

The idea of a hybrid space, rather than a 'non-place' or a simply 'meaningful place', rings true of the roads we journey along in this book. Across South Asia, the trickster stands at the crossroads, in the boardroom and in the government office. The trickster is a boundary-crosser and shapeshifter, lying his way into the knickers, wallets and lives of passers-by. The trickster disrupts the world, and thus reshapes it. Playful, mischievous, subversive and amoral, tricksters are trouble, but they are also cultural heroes.[34] During the course of the research, the trickster dumped bodies in suitcases, raped, murdered and robbed. Death, tragedy, misfortune and the tangled steel and plastic of crashed vehicles are never far away on the highways of South Asia.

Overall, then, the social science literature identifies the stated and unstated assumptions as well as the intended and unintended consequences of infrastructural plans.[35] The focus here is primarily on the ideas that put roads into place, rather than on geopolitical games or the ways roads change the lives of those who live near them. The aim is to identify the fundamental and often submerged ideas and motivations that bring roads into existence, the 'affective', 'liminal' and 'subversive' elements.

Significantly, under this approach, these positions are also forms of cultural and identity politics and therefore find their way directly into technocratic plans and the means of their implementation. Thus, latent and abstract ideas gradually become material realities and structures that bring together force and value.

The wonderful and terrible qualities of roads make them hard and unwieldy to handle. It takes brave and risk-taking figures to embrace roads as political projects, to stake their careers and reputations on roads and road building. Road building is not easy; it might be lucrative, but the high stakes involved attract resistance, especially when living rooms are threatened. It is these qualities, particularly when combined with deregulation and marketisation, that make this world hard-nosed. The roadman is an alchemist, someone who overcomes landscape, opposition and process, who is driven and has a destination in mind.

Hodologists and the road

My final grouping of literature relates to hodology, the study of pathways and routes; a way of thinking surprisingly more readily taken up by those interested in brains and mental illness than by social scientists. Hodology shows us how the road itself plays a role in these processes combining force and value.

Following a long jail sentence, the Irishman Jim Phelan tramped the roads of England during the 1930s and 1940s. He became a hodologist and phenomenologist of sorts, in that he studied the 'ways of the road' and the 'run of the road'. Together, these enquiries led him to suggest that the shape of the road and the process of journeying influenced the ways travellers learned to present themselves. Tramps developed stories to encourage the generosity of those who lived along the roads. Phelan's contention was that these were not simply stories but that they were given particular forms by the road itself. Roads encourage narrative storytelling; the journey became a mode of thought. Phelan called these stories 'lines of guff', not fact, not fiction, but formed by the movement of people along roads: '[T]he learning to live on the road and the development of a fiction-technique, come with little practice.'[36]

Earlier, I noted the striking homogeneity of the beliefs that road builders shared and how I have tried to understand these ideas within communities of practitioners as the products of similar education and training. Our road builders design, manage and promote roads rather than tramp along them, but in the end, the stories are very similar to Phelan's 'lines of guff', formed by repetitive interaction with particular forms of infrastructure. It must also be said that the lines and views of road builders are often self-justificatory and are frequently intended to solicit the generosity—or support or vote—of those who live along roads. I use Phelan's theory as a companion to the anthropological preoccupation with implicit meanings and value.

When roads are spared a good thought, at least in the literature and society that made me, it is by the wanderer, the eccentric or the renegade who has something powerful to say. It is Jim Phelan or Michael Fairless or Frank Morley who went beyond the commonplace and turned the road into part of us. Phelan, as we already know, thought there was something beyond words in the relationship between tramping and the road that generated stories. Michael Fairless, a female writer with a male pen name, settled in East Anglia and wrote *The Roadmender* in 1902, a fictional account of a roadman who found beauty in labour and who saw the road and its immediate surroundings as a concentration of the universe (in this case a Christian one). Arguably, the metaphor is extended too far; nonetheless, the idea of road as mirror orients my thought.

Frank Morley's *The Great North Road* (1961) traces the history of Britain (and much else) from the Romans through the A1, the road that runs between London and Edinburgh. Morley was a mathematician of international stature, and the influence of his discipline shows in his prose style and the problems he set himself. Morley's staccato text succeeds in stripping the A1 of all tempting and easy common sense, showing how it had first come about through the vanity and uncertainty of Caesar; how it had influenced, rather than been shaped by, the Industrial Revolution; and how it contributed to a distinct ethos in the East of Britain that was absent in the West. In short, he saw that the road had made the country and the country had made the road in very particular ways. Reading Morley makes it impossible to pass along the dull, tattered and occasionally louche modern A1 without marvelling at the profound, influential and revolting things that have happened along the way. His form of hodology opens the country to new questions and ways of seeing; the road becomes an actor in making history.

For many of those we have spoken to, roads reflect striving, discovery, domination, growth and profit. Consequently, it makes sense that the road is a root metaphor in many languages for psychological and developmental journeys, and that it is central to the imagination of modernity and progress. Conversely, the circulation of human blood (arteries, capillaries) has become the base metaphor for the operation, description and analysis of road networks and

49

traffic. Roads and human bodies have become intertwined: roads have become part of human consciousness, part of what nations and people aspire to become. Roads are both medium and message, as well as mirrors and forms of storytelling.

***

My premise is that roads have become integral to the way we think about the world yet are seldom spared a thought. The road has become philosophically, morally and practically intrinsic to much of human life, so central to the story of modernity that it is often consigned to the edges of historical discourse. Roads have become a form of common sense and road builders the engineers of this common sense. I noticed that some people are disposed to tease the solidity and surety of common sense; others find questioning the obvious to be embarrassing and silly. I have encountered both in the course of this research, but most roadmen that I met belong to the latter category; if they did not, perhaps they would not be roadmen. Surfacing roads with common sense is not a natural reflection of ubiquity or banality, as such appearances are permitted by the historicity of the road being stripped away during construction and promotion. The road is transformed into optimistic discourse, promises and possible consumption; the road is not usually an option, but inevitable and necessary. The road is not only implicated in a certain type of mobilisation by capital, automobility, but it is also an active (if partial) agent in the reproduction of that structure and is hence utterly embedded in thought and history.

As I noted, some anthropologists have focused on the visibility of failing infrastructure as a way of undoing this enchanted entanglement. If this strategy is pushed further, when else does infrastructure become visible? We have seen that roads take on frightful qualities when they threaten living rooms and backyards. Perhaps, too, roads might shed the cloak of invisibility when they imperil the future, threatening to further change the climate, rubbish hard-won emission targets, and sustain ways of life that are unsustainable for the planet. The problem, as Whitelegg and the shouty Americans found, is that liberal facts and logic, or even moral reasoning, are impotent weapons when faced with the primacy of 'the market' and the mainstream imperative of economic growth.

Road Cosmologies

In South Asia, mobility is advertised as everything from a solution to poor health and educational outcomes to a source of happiness, smiles and elevated status. In India, the government argues that it is 'well established that building reliable access to rural transportation is a major enabler for social and economic development'.[37] In Pakistan, the government holds that 'development of modern transportation infrastructure plays a pivotal role in economic development and attracting investments'.[38] These ideas have a long history. In 1945, T.R.S. Kynnersley, a seasoned road planner, claimed for India that '[b]etter roads' bring 'education, health, wealth and happiness to the countryside'.[39]

Of course, not all road builders have the same convictions about their project or the world. At the core of their beliefs, however, is a readily recognisable association of engineered infrastructures with a view of progress that will be achieved through growth and consumption. There are also debates about construction technologies and network theory; at the edges, there are heretical views.

Three men sit around a table in a university setting in 2013: the late John Urry, one of the world's leading sociologists of mobility and climate change; Clive Bell, an economist who had conducted the most visible research at the time on rural road building in India for the World Bank (tagline: End Extreme Poverty and Promote Shared Prosperity in a Sustainable Way); and Rob Petts, a seasoned roadman with decades of experience of building rural roads in Africa and Asia. The topic of their discussion: What do new roads do to older places? The simplicity of the question disguises the complexity of possible answers and the multiple levels at which evidence could be sought, with the conversation illustrating how the politics of thought operate in relation to roads. The three men also introduce the difficult idea that individual views on roads have little to do with roads or evidence, but more to do with a broader vision of how the world works or should work, that is, their own political cosmologies.

Petts, an engineering development consultant as well as a road builder, was one of the old-ish hands within the 'roads for development' scene and had been influential in British government-funded projects to build roads for economic growth and the delivery of basic services in Africa and Asia. His position was that improved rural transport drives both sustainable rural development and national growth. Improvements to rural transport play a direct role in food security and ensuring that there is zero hunger. Poor rural transport means that the poor stay poor and disconnected from cities, education and employment. Connecting people to places and opportunities is a positive thing. His experience had taught him how to link road building to other development priorities, including sustainable development goals, so that roads had great rhetorical uplift. Of course, in his view, and as he was a consultant as well as an engineer, additional money and commitment were always needed to build and maintain rural road networks and develop sustainable rural transport services.

In different ways, Clive Bell and John Urry were sceptical of Rob's views, Clive on the basis of micro-economic data that showed that roads had differential effects on villagers rather than wholesale and generic benefits. We will return to Clive's data later, particularly in Chapter 4. John, who had spent decades researching mobility and climate change, also questioned the data but brought a touch of methodological cynicism to the debate, suggesting mobility had become a commodity and international development had become a means through which to promote that commodity. John snorted when Rob said that roads brought prosperity. The idea that roads led to economic growth was, in his view, a form of ideology, a belief in the market, rather than a view informed by research. John's broad sociological research on automobility and related activities led him to see that roads were one element of production and consumption cycles tied to oil; road building was a method of locking people into dependent relations and certain forms of consumption and ways of life.

With hindsight, as the conversation intensified, roads were left by the wayside, and the debate was clearly underpinned by broader notions of politics. These included beliefs in how things are connected or should be connected, in what freedom meant, in what the good life might be, in what purpose the state serves, and in what the future might hold. Three men gently arguing. On the surface, the topic was roads; in practice, there was engineering, sociology, welfarism, holism, a belief in numbers, mistrust of numbers, and both fear and optimism for the future.

In among competing viewpoints, roads became part of individual political cosmologies—perhaps crudely characterised as neo-liberal, empirical and socialist—as debate about materials and routes disappeared. Evidence was off the table, replaced by conviction oriented around personal politics in the broadest sense, emerging from the deeply personal experience of growing up at a particular time, somewhere, and with influential people, such as parents, around you. In the subsequent years of research, experiencing the zeal, confidence and conviction with which roadmen hold on to ideas and see different worlds in scant and fragmented evidence, has only firmed the importance of the revelatory moment.

John represented views that I am familiar with from universities. Clive represented what was then a novel view for me: one based on numerical measurement of human activity. Rob held the views that best represent those I became immersed in through this project. In a general sense, the 'free market' and the value of 'competition' prevail. Underlying these headlines are supporting ideas relating to creation/destruction and time/evolution and the transforming institutional context in which they work. Even 'government servants' (the 'public sector') tend to bend their beliefs in progress towards the private sector and the motivations and efficiencies encouraged by a profit motive.[40] There is loyalty to the state and to its institutions and codes, but the market represents a form of liberty and freedom and the most effective mechanism for development; the market is a more efficient means of enriching people than controlled planning by the state. This is not to say that the state is only mistrusted and resented, because in many contexts (and increasingly so over the course of the research) the state remained a facilitator of private enterprise and a guarantor of failing projects and private equity (and a source of cash for consultants in the private sector).

We move now from sitting around a table in London to corporate South Asia. Among the main private road builders in India are Reliance (tagline: Better Roads for a Developing India); IRB (tagline: Highway to Growth); Jaiprakash (tagline: No Dream Too Big); Nagarjuna (tagline: 40 Years in Nation Building); GVK (tagline: We Power Development); and Lanco Infratech (tagline: Always inspiring). As a board member of one of these companies put it:

> Roads are foundational for a developed economy. Roads facilitate our connectivity. In the current phase of India, the need of the hour is for the growth in the economy. Growth comes with connectivity and trade. That is why we place so much of our efforts on our nation's infrastructure. This is particularly true for the roads in the country as they remain the most common mode of transport for the people and have been poor in the past.

In Pakistan, taglines have a different emphasis: Habib (tagline: Quality Construction is our Benchmark); KBK (tagline: Engineers and Contractors); Mumtaz (tagline: A Registered Civil Engineering Company of National Repute); and SKB (tagline: Reshaping Your World!). As a manager within one of these companies put it:

> Road construction is considered one of the most important projects for a country, particularly Pakistan where roads have been in poor condition and construction quality. We work to optimise the logistics for successful delivery of road construction projects. Roads have changed the way we think about the country. We are working for even greater connectivity and lower travel times so as to grow the economy still more. Roads are key to economic growth and development.

Within these institutional environments, roadmen use the language of economics and growth-led development to describe their work. Those who build big roads such as national highways and trade corridors use the following terms with great frequency—'increasing efficiencies', 'accelerating growth', 'facilitating integration', 'improving living standards' and 'unleashing trade'. For those who build lower-order roads—particularly village access roads—words such as 'opening up' and 'connectivity' feed most repetitively into their self-description. In this formulation, the road is a facilitating and transformational infrastructure, part of an economic system built on the promotion of enterprising individuals and on the ideas that quality goods and services are always elsewhere and that the future of economic growth is infinite.

In both India and Pakistan, the 'market' in roads has different shades of meaning. The 'market' is associated with powerful industrial and entrepreneurial families who have grown and prospered alongside the emergence of the post-colonial state and who run some of the firms listed above. In Pakistan, the military is also keen on road building. In the upper echelons of both countries, governments and private entities have long collaborated in national projects, relationships evident in older road projects as well as in new forms of partnership. The gradual deregulation of economies has further opened this zone to international collaboration, adding new actors and entrepreneurs to the mix.

From the perspective of state employees, the 'market' is also present in the work of development banks. Roadmen in those organisations do not see their roles in such light but more as facilitators and enablers, although they generally wear sharper suits than government engineers. Since the late 1990s, many states in India have formed 'Road Development Corporations' to broker relationships and manage road infrastructure tenders and concession agreements. Building, maintaining and managing roads are a number of big private players; there are some start-ups, including offshoots of established enterprises newly attracted to roads by the infrastructural finance boom of the first decade of the twentieth century; there are many thousands of engineering, haulage and materials contractors; and countless smaller businesses, sometimes no more than labour gangs with contracts to clean signs or cut back foliage.

The roadmen whose voices and ideas feature in this book, as at our roundtable, are for the most part middle-aged and from the well-officed middle of this constellation from national and international civil engineering and consultancy firms and governments. Around them, much as in their offices, there are also the voices of the

55

apprentices and retired masters. The influence from people at the very top of organisations and at the other end of long chains of subcontracts also features, but more as an illustration of how the road world works than as the main ethnographic subject matter. In offices and out inspecting roads in cars, the middling roadmen of the early twenty-first century see their work as introducing market rationality to the irrational and closed provinces. Instead of relying on the dysfunctional welfarism of the state to provide employment, primary healthcare and education, they see roads as introducing capacity, 'choice' even, for people to get by on their own, to 'get on their bikes', or at least on to buses or into their small cars, to head off to find work and opportunity. In this sense, roadmen see their work as pedagogical and as making new citizens: transforming lives by 'enabled mobility'.

Compared to the community of academics I spend some of my time among, many roadmen are mercurial, quick-witted and spritely—qualities I have learned to associate with the symbolic and actual violence inherent in what they do, the energy required to change the world and to negotiate with those who object to their proposals. Building roads is hard, no matter how much general goodwill or state support there might be; there is also usually resistance and anger along the way. New roads or widened old roads (the more common method across South Asia) involve bulldozing lives, houses, lands and communities.

Peacetime displacement and attacks on private property produce visceral ire no matter where you are in the world: a fight for what is most dear and fundamental to those who are to be moved comes face to face with those promoting abstract ideas of development and progress. In these encounters, roadmen find themselves as the agents of sacrifice. Some anger might find expression in tenacious letter-writing or media campaigns and/or courts; some is also directed at the bodies of those seen to be responsible. I spent a memorable couple of days with a South African consultant in Western India. When we checked into the hotel, he pretended to be a travelling salesman—anything to avoid becoming a magnet for the public anger bubbling on the widened road outside the hotel if he were seen to represent the power to usurp private property and disrupt long-held intimacies. On this occasion, his pretend identity protected him; on other occasions, he told me, road building had been 'bumpier'.

Research on road protest quickly gets into deep questions of rights and the relationship between life and landscape. I have casually thought that in the last two decades, road building in South Asia and China was probably the largest single cause of recent displacement of people anywhere on earth. Given such pressures, roadmen are often skilled negotiators, capable of dealing with opposition and conflict. Displacement is necessary; the displaced are sacrificial, sometimes to 'development', sometimes to the 'greater good' and sometimes to the 'nation'.

An Indonesian roadman who had worked for an international consultancy in Pakistan for many years recounted: 'You have to destroy to make. Things have to be undone before they can be put back together again.' In such an attitude, there is a hard edge, given, I think, by the conditions and terms of this work at the interface between governments and populated landscapes. The world of public objection, litigation, angry protest and easily made allegations of corruption or favouritism hardens skins. The attrition and disruption required to build a road also contribute to explaining the half-hearted ways in which participatory planning processes are generally treated by roadmen.

The Indonesian continued: 'You see, roads are about transformation, and we all know that change is sometimes difficult for people. If you see a bigger picture, and you only look at the bigger picture, then it is possible to go on with the work.' I would often ask roadmen if they thought about those they displaced. 'Of course I do, but there have to be limits,' said a British-born engineering consultant. He continued with a smile: '[T]he last thing I want is an anthropologist telling me about this and that cultural value and what to do when I am building a road!' A British government engineer: 'Listening to people's stories about their land and traditions is all very well, sometimes even interesting, but ultimately I am here or there to build the road. I am not here or there not to build the road! The decision has already been taken.' Such pragmatic lines harden with longer teeth and a few bruises.

Roadmen often describe their work teleologically: the explanation of roads in terms of the purpose they serve rather than of the causes and conditions from which they have arisen. This compass is understandable given that they also look to roads for personal motivation, career progression and professional satisfaction. However, underlying this functional attitude, we also encountered a deep belief in infrastructural evolution, an idea rather akin to the social evolutionism of the nineteenth century. Then, people in Europe looked to places like India for evidence of their origins or previous states. Europe was India's future; India was Europe's past. India contained European civilisation in its earliest known form; both were different phases along the same path of human development.[41]

Today, many different road builders converge on the idea of an 'infrastructure deficit' to describe conditions in South Asia.[42] From Delhi: 'We will build roads and become like Western countries'; or from London: '*They* need roads to catch up.' In this view, roads are a universal indicator and measure of national progress, an evolutionary yardstick. Roadmen sometimes quantify these relations in technical terms of road density and length of network, or as a ratio of roads to people, usually aware of the confusions brought by other variables. Some roadmen have modelled the relationship between national wealth and road building, that is, when a country's GDP exceeds a certain level, it will build roads because of the capacity of the population to demand mobility. Others promote the idea of 'leapfrogging', arguing that roads have proven to be such a headache in Western countries that others may skip an evolutionary stage given the right governmental interventions and move straight to either electric mobility or car-free lives. This generally has not gone down well with interlocutors in South Asia, where the idea of development as a linear model of evolutionary economics remains strong and the thirst for petro-mobility is being pushed ever harder by advertising agencies.

To explore the emergence and embeddedness of such thought, the following chapters trace how roads have been historically produced by states as mechanisms, metaphors and monuments of control and progress. In the twentieth century, roads became nationalist projects, visions of hope and freedom. In the twenty-first century, roads have been 'off-shored' as engineering spectaculars, and, as an 'asset class', roads now allow money to move as well as vehicles.[43] As part of understanding why the road emerged from history with such force, the analysis attempts to de-naturalise the road, to make it live and contentious. This has often been a difficult task, which encountered resistance and hostility to the idea that belief in roads is a product of history rather than a divine or natural truth—a circumstance on which I offer periodic reflection along the way.

3

STANDARD GEOGRAPHY
AN INFRASTRUCTURAL CONTINENT

When I was younger, I attempted to ride a bicycle from Bangkok to Europe. My plan was quickly frustrated by land borders between Thailand and Burma, which were closed to me. I learned then that South East Asia and South Asia were disconnected, a condition borne of imperial and post-colonial politics. I flew from Bangkok to Calcutta, crossed the Howrah Bridge, and started to pedal west through the paddy and brick-kiln smoke of the Bengal winter. The road was rough, potholed and, to my eyes, unfinished at the edges, as the tarmac crumbled into rutted strips of compacted mud. The traffic was wild and unkind, the air dusty and acrid.

When I reached Europe nearly a year later, in 1991, I decided to study social anthropology. I thought that the subject would help me 'understand' the varied life I had encountered in the spaces at the side of the road over many kilometres in India, Nepal and Pakistan. A quarter of a century later, I return to the subject to now understand how those roads and side spaces got there and why they took such forms. These are not just incidental shapes in the landscape but are given form by history, bureaucracy and diplomacy.

The anthropologist Kathleen Stewart makes a similar point about the spaces at the side of the road in Virginia, suggesting they can

61

be read as zones of creativity on the one hand and as a measure of cultural ideas about progress and legitimacy on the other.[1] I also see them as quite specific types of places formed on the one hand by the interaction of historical forces through the standardisation of materials and measurements and on the other by speeding traffic passing such spaces by. Pavement materials, hard shoulders, truck stops, slip roads, culverts—not incidental, but by design.

The research has allowed me to see how the road in South Asia took on such distinguished shapes. The single strip of tarmac with compacted mud emerged from decades of experimentation, trial and error. It was not an accident or an unfinished project. The design allowed India to move at different speeds, trucks and cars occupying the fast-moving centre ground and pedestrians, carts and bikes on the 'soft shoulders'. Throughout the twentieth century, the idea of a country moving at different speeds was vital for those with an interest in planning and building roads.

The only map I carried on my bike was a line drawing of West Asia torn from a guidebook. I navigated with a compass, and although I preferred smaller roads, I repeatedly found myself on the trunk routes on my map that gave the continent a skeleton. Even then, most of these major highways were tolerable for a cyclist, but I still preferred to be in the wilds away from trucks, toxic tea and that hardened type of humanity—the civility of indifference—that forms where people are always coming and going. Some of the main routes, however, seemed impossible to avoid; they drew the traveller back no matter how determined the escape. Sometimes, there were no other roads, but more commonly it was because these roads already occupied the easiest paths through difficult landscapes, the paths of least resistance, as people had discovered or worked out many centuries previously.

At the time, I knew little of road networks, engineering and inter-governmental agreements. I do though vividly recall rusting signposts pointing to cities many kilometres and a few countries away, road numbers that were out of kilter with national numbering systems, and the conspicuously engineered and built-up border crossings between India and Pakistan, Pakistan and Iran, and Iran and Turkey. I later learned that there was an inter-continental vision in the system that had flourished briefly in the 1950s and 1960s in the aftermath of the Second World War; however, the project was quickly taken over by prior geographies: the divisions between Europe and Asia, Iran and South Asia, and South and South East Asia. Utopian road visions designed in an era of reconstruction and reconciliation were unable to defeat older, partly colonial notions of national and regional identity. These roads could not undo the geographies they were intended to counter. They ended up, despite the best intentions of the diplo-engineers who put them there, being agents of older borders rather than the forces of geographical liberation and free movement. National will and international animosity were more powerful than the levelling magic of the road.

The offence that had been caused by the 1988 publication of Salman Rushdie's novel *The Satanic Verses* meant that I would need creativity in order to obtain a visa for Iran. I used three unanticipated months in Pakistan to cycle up the fantastical Karakoram Highway (KKH) to Gilgit and west over the Shandur Pass to Chitral and back down to the plains. Those long and grinding climbs introduced me to another form of infrastructural diplomacy—one country building roads in another. Such constructions are often part of international strategising rather than pure gifts, although at the time it meant very little to me that China had built a road in Pakistan.

Overall, these formative experiences on the road introduced me to some of the important geopolitical infrastructural currents in the region: South Asia stopped, figuratively speaking, somewhere to the east of Calcutta. Attempts to unify or transcend diverse territory with road infrastructure had a long and repetitive history, of which the Grand Trunk Road is the best example and the then fading UN network was at the time the latest iteration. The mass of the Himalayas had been breached most effectively by China with the KKH into Pakistan, and this had altered the power dynamic in the region.

In what follows, I explore these three prominent geographical-infrastructural formations (China–Pakistan, networked Asia, and South–South East Asia). The literature on these projects is dominated by scholars of international relations and security. In contrast to their theoretical approaches, my interest is in elements of the political, bureaucratic and media performances that have been used to promote these schemes and make them real. My emphasis here is not on the 'whole story'—see signposts and scholarship in the footnotes for that—but on the geographical claims of road building and on select cultural aspects of 'making' and 'selling' projects. Road infrastructure is populist, evoking grand relationships in the exciting idioms of 'connectivity' and 'networks'; however, there are often also more intimate and moral elements to the persuasive propaganda, which evoke friendship, emotion and sacrifice, as well as state strength, conquest and domination over new territories.

Infrastructural ambition is as old as the hills, or at least as old as the desire to cross them. South Asia is littered with ancient traces, signed by monuments, ruins and wells that speak of previous visions and configurations of power with geography. 'Roads' (or pathways) have played roles in the consolidation and maintenance of various empires and dynasties. Similarly, pilgrimage traditions ground sectarian, regional and national routes into the landscape. In the colonial period, railways took priority as the infrastructure of trade and communication. The motor road came at the turn of the twentieth century and only gradually brought populism and mass movement into the equation. The change might have been quicker if leaders of those times had not been occupied with the anti-colonial struggle and emerging institutions had been better supported.

At Independence, things altered swiftly with the formation of a developmental state that placed roads at the heart of the rhetoric and practice of building new nations. In post-colonial South Asia, the road became *the* means of modernisation; 'roads became everything', as a senior bureaucrat in Delhi pithily put it as he outlined the growth of road planning and institutions in India in the second half of the twentieth century.

Significant roads in South Asia are often described as 'geopolitics' (by bureaucrats and academics), as the nation-building and power plays of the post-Independence decades coincided with a new focus on roads and reorienting territory. Road infrastructures are readily seen as expressions of competition and one-upmanship between nations and coalitions of interests. Through this lens, the Subcontinent is a battleground for ideas and plots, made real through infrastructure and other diplomacy, of those types I first vividly encountered on a bicycle.

In South Asia, the stakes are high. Jingoistic tensions over land and borders define the ways countries get along and relate to one another. Infrastructure, or the strategic positioning of a lack of infrastructure, becomes a form of diplomatic and cultural manoeuvre, aimed at the control of territory, trade and perhaps ideology. When viewed like this, the 'geopolitical' landscape is dominated by China, which is making highly publicised infrastructural interventions in Pakistan, Sri Lanka and Iran.

China and Pakistan: CPEC and Karakoram

The China–Pakistan Economic Corridor (CPEC; taglines: too numerous to list) is a sub-project within China's broader Belt and Road Initiative that aims to create new transport and communication networks across the world. In Pakistan, China has pledged to invest tens of billions of dollars to build roads, ports, industrial parks and power projects. For some in Pakistan, there is pride in the China association, that of a nation modernised by the infrastructural generosity of a superpower with no love for India. For sceptics, investment is in part borrowing by Pakistan, paving the way to indebtedness and mass indenture. Some see CPEC as a way to internationalise the renminbi, or to move dirty forms of production to Pakistan, or to surround India with secular infrastructure with latent military potential.[2]

The dominant message of CPEC is carried by the road connecting China via the KKH in the north of Pakistan to the southern port city of Gwadar. China, the story goes, will have direct access to the Indian Ocean, bypassing the Malacca Straits and bringing the country closer to Africa, the Middle East and Europe. While the contrasting explanations for CPEC might each to a lesser or greater extent be true, they also resemble the headline claims of organisations and advertising agencies that have global contracts to promote Chinese infrastructure.

In conversation in Karachi, the then chairman of Gwadar port gave more mixed messages: he was buoyed by his position at the end of tens of billions of dollars of investment; frustrated by the security situation; and blustery and evasive when it came to quantifying the level of trade passing through the port. It is also the case that both academic literature and publicity materials often describe the road as complete. On the ground, however, armed troublemakers and difficult geography make the 2,000-km road trip from an incomplete port in Baluchistan to a remote part of western China seem quite improbable as a trade route in the current climate.

Agencies promoting Chinese infrastructure have done the hard work of creating narratives. The beauty of a readymade narrative is that it is easy for journalists and academics to reproduce. Even if the coverage is critical, the narrative is still publicised. CPEC has similarly funded books, reports and films to contribute to the 'realisation' (please read this word literally) of the project. An explicit form is a music video, 'The Belt and Road Is How'.[3] The production emerged from Fuxing Road Studios, friends of the Chinese Communist Party's International Department. In the film, well-nourished 'global' children sing and gleefully interact with animated and cut-out representations of fast-moving geographies and infrastructures:

Verse

The belt connects the land, the road moves on the sea

[a high-speed train slides down the left of the screen while a container ship waits in port to the right of the girl singing].

The promise that they hold, is joint prosperity

[another girl wanders in a landscape of global monuments, pyramids, Parthenon and Coliseum that seems to have been penetrated by a hotel in Dubai called the Burj Al Arab Jumeirah; in the centre is Merlion (the mermaid lion of Singapore) and St Basil's Cathedral in Moscow].

We're breaking barriers, we're making history

[two boys step over an impassable range of snow-covered mountains (you already know which ones)].

The world we're dreaming of starts with you and me

[the same boys walk through a serene and uncluttered cityscape].

Chorus

The future's coming now, the Belt and Road is how

[the screen explodes with impossibly happy colours].

We'll share the goodness now, the Belt and Road is how.

[The girls stand aside, to let the boys take over with this rousing verse]:

Products and goods are only a part, from apples to cranes (they're state of the art!)

We're paving new roads, building more ports, finding new options (with friends of all sorts!)

It's a culture exchange, we trade in our wealth, we connect with our hearts (it strengthens our health!)

With our lines and our cables, diplomacy tables (we'll share in a world of prosperity!)

Oh! The futures coming now.

Chorus [and more verses].

The propaganda of Chinese infrastructure litters the internet and has also been pushed in different ways into governments and universities through funding for conferences and trade conventions with representatives of think tanks and lobbyists as chief guests. Websites, technical publications, databases and new institutes have ensured that CPEC is in the media and on the political and academic agenda, and that everyone in Pakistan knows about it.

Propaganda presents CPEC as a modern echo of the mythical and romantic silk routes: '[W]e advance side by side on the Silk Road.'[4] This route, however, is future-looking, 'game-changing' and a new era for Pakistan. In fact, much of what is proposed has echoes of British and Russian attempts in the nineteenth century to control trade between the sea and Central Asia. As I will discuss in the following section, the emphasis on logistics and connectivity in Pakistan, now taken up with great skill by China, also has an older and America-inflected post-colonial history. There is an additional grittier twentieth-century history, itself 'geopolitical', that traces China's interest in building roads across Pakistan back to the 1950s. In many ways, the KKH through the high mountains of the north was the first draft and a response to efforts made by the United Nations to construct other roads in the region.

Following the formation of Pakistan, diplomatic relations with China were established in 1950.[5] Various boundary issues between the two countries were resolved in the early 1960s. Official military assistance began in 1966. A strategic alliance was agreed in 1972 and economic cooperation in 1979. The KKH or the China–Pakistan Friendship Highway opened to non-military traffic in 1986 and became a minor wonder of the world and a high-profile symbol of the relationship between the two countries.[6] The highway is among the highest in the world, and its precarious and audacious engineering created a connection, perhaps as much symbolic as practical, which has played into the equations between Pakistan–Afghanistan and Pakistan–India ever since. India tended to view the KKH as a 'militarily sinister move' against its interests.[7]

From the vantage point of Pakistan, the KKH runs from Islamabad through Hasan Abdal to Abbottabad, into the Karakoram mountains to Gilgit, over the Khunjerab Pass, and across the border to Kashgar in the Uighur Autonomous Region of China. Supposedly also tracing one of the routes of the legendary Silk Road, what was a military and strategic road became an artery and agent of profound social transformation for the northern regions.

The highway 'opened up' the region, enabling the movement of people and goods and dramatically reducing travel times. A Swiss documentary film by Gabriela Neuhaus and Angelo Scudeletti negatively describes the road as a 'one-way street to globalisation'.[8] The road has transformed Gilgit, once a remote administrative centre, into a hub for commerce, transport and communications. The ready availability of cement from the lowlands has had a particularly important effect and allowed a construction boom that has reconfigured the architectural fabric and physical appearance of the region.

An army colonel with the National Highway Authority in Pakistan spoke about the transformation he had seen:

When a road is built in an area, those people do not die of hunger. I was on KKH in 1973–4. Between Gilgit and Abbottabad, there were only four persons who could count Pakistani currency. One was a maulana who was also our contractor. I was there for the construction. Once a helicopter came and they [the local people] put grass for it to eat. In 1976, there was an earthquake and the Australians and others gave blankets and the locals sold these for five rupees. From Pattan to Challas there was no road, it was only a mule track. People used to go on horseback. Food was dropped from the helicopter. There was not a silk road as such. In 1992, I went back to Narran and found that people who used to supply us eggs had become big contractors. In 1992, I took my children with me and found that on the way were many workshops, and people were speaking Urdu and running hotels.

The narration of such history simply introduces some of the elementary and contested structures inherent in the politics of road thought. The filmmakers saw the road as having eroded the culture and traditions of the region, ensnaring the population in a bland culture of global consumerism. The colonel, in contrast, saw in positive terms how the road had taught people how to count, make money and speak the national language. Same evidence, different conclusions. Is it the evidence or the conclusion that comes first? Is it the facts of the matter or the preceding worldview that determines whether the social change brought about by a new road through the high mountains is evaluated in positive or negative terms? Is the glass half empty or half full? These questions echo through the rest of this book.

Between 1,000 and 5,000 workers were killed in landslides and falls during the construction of the KKH. Many deaths were marked with monuments and by a cemetery at Danyor near Gilgit. In 2011, retired People's Liberation Army soldiers visited the cemetery to pay homage to the dead. Two years later, at a ceremony involving officials from both countries, local politician Wazir Baig laid the foundation stone for a new cemetery. He said: 'We are proud of the eternal friendship between Pakistan and China … [the KKH] serves as a bridge between people of the two countries.' Abdur Rehman Bukhari, the Chinese Overseas Association secretary general in

Gilgit-Baltistan, said: 'These labourers and engineers laid down their lives for Pak-China Friendship. We value their sacrifice.' In Islamabad the following month, Li Keqiang, the premier of the State Council of the People's Republic of China, made a speech entitled 'Making New Progress in Growing China–Pakistan All-Weather Friendship'. He announced the launch of 'big projects' to enhance financial and investment cooperation, infrastructure development, connectivity, maritime, energy, agriculture and defence cooperation. He also mentioned the heartfelt and loving relations between the two countries. In China, he said, they referred to 'Iron Pak', a friend as strong as iron:

> And here is a story that has deeply moved the 1.3 billion Chinese people: Near the city of Gilgit, there is a Chinese cemetery where over 140 Chinese workers who lost their lives in the construction of the Pakistani section of the Karakorum Highway (KKH) are buried. For over 30 years, some Pakistanis volunteered to work as cemetery keepers. One of them passed away due to illness a few years ago, but his child immediately took over as the new keeper of the cemetery. Today, the young saplings in the cemetery have grown into towering trees. We are truly proud to have such a devoted and enduring friend in Pakistan.[9]

The KKH paved the way for CPEC: the sentimental ideas of sacrifice and friendship that were evoked, along with the rejuvenation of the cemetery, point to a political and emotional way of selling an idea—foreplay, so to speak. A cynic might have pointed out that proportionally, many more workers from Pakistan lost their lives, and that for the cemetery to require restoration, it must have been neglected.

The UN Asian Highway Network

The KKH was constructed at a time when other countries were taking a keen interest in roads in the region. The project emerged, in part, from a particular context and form of international competition. After Independence and the end of the Second World War, new global institutions (which largely excluded China) were created for 'reconstruction' and peace building. Many of these initiatives came following the Bretton Woods agreement of 1944 and the creation of the International Monetary Fund. In South Asia, such developments carried with them the spirit of American victory and later the counter-currents of the Cold War.

The physical and political geography of divided South Asia interacted with a broader desire to promote connectivity and road transport. India had very few motorable borders, the mountains and sparse populations to the north and east offering little incentive for infrastructural expansion at the time. Pakistan had a desert border with Persia/Iran, which offered, at least in theory, a connection to Turkey and Europe. For both India and Pakistan, port-led development became key instruments of development policy given the barriers to overland trade and the absence of friendly and hospitable borders. Pakistan, however, also shared a mountainous border with China, which, as we have seen, was to become influential in the region as the two countries started to develop connections in the 1950s and to first dream of a road connecting China to the Indian Ocean coast of Pakistan.

At the same time, in the late 1950s, attempts were made to create an Asian Highway Network (AHN), the ambition of which may surprise those currently in the thrall of Chinese infrastructural propaganda, because the project has been neglected and side-lined, and never had the advertising budget currently used by China. The idea of AHN dates back to 1955, when the Highway Sub-Committee of the influential Economic Commissions for Asia and the Far East (ECAFE) met in Manila.[10] The AHN was to promote roads as means of transport, to encourage trade, tourism and regional economic and social development. The project used existing roads, except in cases where 'missing routes' necessitated new ones.

In April 1959, the *UN Review* ran a special feature detailing the history of roads from caravan routes to modern highways.[11] This piece also outlined the proposed routes, which speak to the 'geopolitics' of the period while also reflecting 'problems' and difficult borderlands that have not since gone away, as the regional map was not radically redrawn by new post-colonial powers. Key roads and border crossings were planned between Turkey and Iran as a way of linking Europe and Asia. Towards South Asia, routes from Tehran went to Kabul via Meshed, Herat, Farah and Kandahar in Afghanistan and another to Pakistan through Qum, Nain, Kerman and Zahidan. Zahidan was to be connected to Quetta with connections to Lahore and Karachi. A route from Kabul traversed the Khyber Pass and then ran onward through Peshawar, Lahore, Delhi, Agra, Calcutta and Imphal to the Burmese border, with a link from Raniganj to Kathmandu. Another route travelled from Agra to Indore (with a connection to Bombay), on to Hyderabad and Bangalore (with a connecting road to Madras), and finally to Colombo via a ferry between Danushkodi and Talaimanar in Ceylon. Other routes went through Burma to Thailand, and from there to Laos, Malaya, Singapore and Cambodia.

Meetings in Delhi and Karachi in 1959 brought roadmen from across the region to discuss the network and timescale for the project. The Karachi meeting recommended five years for the construction of the highway from Turkey to Singapore.[12] In 1961, discussions in Kathmandu finalised the alignments of the network, including standards for roads and bridges. In the early 1960s, survey techniques and the design of network road markers and milestones were agreed.[13] Of the main route—13,300 km from Tehran to Saigon—only 550 km remained to be built in several sections in Burma, East Pakistan and Thailand.[14]

In these early days, there was a rhetoric of 'reviving and adapting the ancient caravan routes that carried silk and tea trade of earlier centuries to become a network for modern highway traffic spanning the continent'.[15] The project was also linked, throughout the 1960s, to the Mekong River Dam project, which was another ECAFE scheme supported by the United States. In 1967, U. Nyun, then executive secretary of ECAFE, lauded the efforts as 'the most striking achievements of multinational or regional co-operation'.[16] Those behind the project, given their early successes, had the confidence to begin to think about linking Asia to Africa and Europe with roads.[17] In this optimistic environment, progress was a certainty: 'In scarcely more than a decade, what had been to most people an impractical dream had been transformed into a reality. The objective of an all-weather through-route from east to west, with suitable connections to other countries not falling on that route, had been nearly achieved.'[18]

As the 1960s wore on, the project began to fade, and the oil crisis of the early 1970s raised the cost of road transport. Financial assistance was suspended in 1975. In the 1990s, the AHN was revived as the Asian Land Transport Infrastructure Development project. New fashions in planning looked to 'integrated transport networks', primarily road and rail. Much of the earlier work was redone as new international agreements and standards were determined. By the turn of this century, new sources of finance were available for upgrading the network to the latest design standards.[19] By 2007, perhaps because of the new availability of funding, the Asian Highway was again incorporated into the national road plans of India, Nepal and Pakistan. ESCAP, the Economic and Social Commission for Asia and the Pacific, then began work in 2008 on a study looking at how best to transform transport corridors into economic corridors.[20] A new era had arrived in transport planning that still dominates much of the thinking in South Asia: connectivity, given by multi-modal transport and industrial and logistics facilities.[21] 'Corridors' became the new thing, primarily, given the sensitivity of the borders in South Asia, as national development projects.

Look and Act East

India's contemporary involvement with the AHN is through the 'Look East' policy, later renamed by the first Narendra Modi government as 'Act East'. Initiated in 1991 by Narasimha Rao to cultivate economic and strategic relations with South East Asia, the policy entailed road and rail projects accompanied by other tracks of diplomacy to even out the lumpy geographical and cultural territories between India and Thailand. The idea of connecting Delhi to Bangkok was part of a strategic competition with China as well as a fundamental intervention in anglophone colonial geography, where South and South East Asia are distinct regions, with different cultural traditions, and, in this case, separated by the conceptually confusing territory of Myanmar.[22] Afghanistan arguably has a similar conceptual status on the western periphery of South Asia.

The immediate context for looking east was given by economic liberalisation, structural adjustment and the end of the Cold War. In the geopolitical landscape of Look East in those early days, India's pursuit of economic reform followed China, a process initiated by Deng Xiaoping in the 1970s. This 'opening up', following the death of Mao and the end of the Cultural Revolution, had accelerated foreign trade and new forms of relations between China and South East Asia. Before 'the market' triumphed in the logic of India–China relations, questions of territory dominated. The Sino-Indian War of 1962 was waged over disputed borders in the Himalayas, sparked by the Chinese construction in the 1950s of a road between Xinjiang and Western Tibet that passed through Indian territory. The conflict was rooted in older disputes over sovereignty, dating from the early nineteenth century: Britain's colonial incursions in Aksai Chin, Manipur and Assam, and, later in that century, 'the Great Game' between Britain and Imperial Russia. For many years after 1962, and perhaps still today, China was seen as supporting a destabilising insurgency in the north-east.

Following its inauguration in 1967, India's view of the Association of Southeast Asian Nations (ASEAN) had been that it represented neo-colonial interests. India famously remained non-aligned. Moving into the 1970s and beyond, the relationship was defined by key political moments. These included New Delhi's support for Vietnam against the Chinese-backed Khmer Rouge following its 1978 invasion of Kampuchea (Cambodia) and subsequent recognition of Heng Samrin's People's Republic of Kampuchea.[23] In this context, 'Look East' sought to heal old wounds and make new friends in South East Asia through trade, development and military and security cooperation. There also came a shift in policy towards Burma. Once a staunch supporter of the pro-democracy movement, India signed a border trade agreement with Myanmar in 1994. Prior to this, 'Look East' had a strong maritime emphasis. Cooperative relations with Yangon allowed the focus to shift to overland routes and the development of the idea of a 'trilateral' India–Myanmar–Thailand highway.

In the mid-1990s, alongside rail and pipelines, infrastructural diplomacy focused on the road from Imphal in India to Tamu in

Myanmar, already part of the now-faded glory of the AHN. The new project was to re-develop the neglected roads, once part of the United Nations vision for the region. By 2002, at a meeting in Yangon, plans were dramatically expanded to include 1,360 km of a four-lane road crossing Myanmar from Moreh in India to Tha Ton in Thailand. The Indian government announced cooperation with ASEAN to extend the route to Laos, Cambodia and Vietnam, although this bluster did not amount to an actual road.

The friction between Chinese road building and India's 'Acting East' is particularly marked in India's north-east. While the north-east is seen as India's gateway to South East Asia, it is also landlocked and difficult terrain with many small states with varied interests. Tension came to a head in 2006 when the Chinese ambassador to India described the Indian state of Arunachal Pradesh as part of China, specifically 'Southern Tibet'.[24] In 2008, India announced the '1044-km trans-Arunachal highway' and the 'frontier highway' as a means of extending government control and stability. The government of Manmohan Singh (2004–9) prioritised road building in the region for national integration. Some of those we spoke to who had been part of a task force commissioned to research the highway pointed out that there was no formal political role for state governments in India's north-east as part of this programme, unlike that of China's south-western Yunnan province, which has played a crucial role in promoting transnational cooperation.[25]

From the outset of the AHN in the 1960s, it was recognised that for the project to gain traction it had to have history, in that case reviving the ancient silk trade routes (just as the KKH propaganda was to do). Such a status gives a road gravity, and a ready place in the imagination of a population that has been through a national education system. In more recent times, governments and institutions have taken this idea much further. To build a road, especially one with national ambition, or one that shows governmental strength, determination and courage, or one that shows superiority over previous political regimes, one has to build a communicative and moral infrastructure that tells the electorate about your actions and achievements. Building a road in the imagination of an electorate is perhaps as important as constructing one through the troubled and difficult ground of the region itself.

In the case of the trilateral highway project from India to Thailand, the propaganda machine has been running for a few years, with light and bouncy advertorials in national newspapers promoting tourism and claiming the road is open.

For example:

> In no time you'll be dumping all those pricey flights to Thailand from India and planning a wondrous road trip! ... Bangkok, undeniably, is one of the most favoured foreign destinations for Indians to travel to and with this super highway in action now, footfall from India is expected to increase by leaps and bounds.[26]

Other similar articles particularly recommend the Bob Dylan café in Shillong and the Kaziranga National Park in Assam. From Delhi or Chennai or Karachi or Beijing, there would be no reason to doubt such reports were genuine and that the government had pacified the disruptive locals and opened a land border with Myanmar. These advertorials are often accompanied by detailed instructions for visa applications and other travel arrangements, which give them an air of authenticity.

The Indo-Myanmar and Indo-ASEAN friendship car rallies were launched amid much fanfare in 2011 and 2012. In 2015, the government first announced the road was open for tourism and trade. In 2019, the same government promised it would be open before the end of the year. Conditions on the road, and the reluctance of the government in Myanmar to have Indians roving unaccompanied through the semi-militarised countryside, particularly after the coup in the spring of 2021, mean that the feasibility of this most bodacious post-colonial road trip is still some way off, but efforts with roads and propaganda are gradually beginning to change realities.

***

When I first cycled through South Asia, I used a compass to navigate. Then I was repeatedly drawn back to roads that followed the paths of least resistance through difficult terrain, the arteries of the UN network and the KKH. In geographic and allegorical registers, these roads became the easiest story to tell, as well as to travel.

These infrastructures are highly visible forms of government as distribution systems and forms of communication interwoven with continental topography over many centuries. The geopolitics they stand for, such as the difficulties of regional cooperation, suspicious and slow border crossings, the power-play between India and China, and the legacies of colonial government and Partition, have become the central themes of regional history. These, if you like, are the 'just-so' stories of South Asian roads.

These examples of 'infrastructural persuasion' are selected from many other kinds of arguments and material that are used to make geopolitical forms a reality on the ground and in the minds of people; while they may be partial, they are also illustrative of general tendencies. The children singing about infrastructure to promote China's Belt and Road Initiative become an extreme instance of infrastructural propaganda, an attempt to make something real through innocence and promise. In many parts of the world, however, governments and contractors use private agencies to make inspirational films, images and press copy for their infrastructure. The internet is awash with such materials, as infrastructural and consumerist dreams are built in people's minds as much as they are on the ground.

The earlier United Nations vision was more discreet, but it was radical in aiming to network Asia—a post-continental vision of connectivity where 'dreams became realities'. This was a high-level bureaucratic attempt to create new geographies. The project must have appeared as an exciting and utopian vision of a new world order to roadmen at international conference venues. But the scheme always lacked traction on the ground, and especially in the difficult contexts of borderlands between actual neighbours. The Indian Act East propaganda is of yet another kind, crude and bold in vision, but perhaps effective because of these qualities in a domestic context.

Looking back on my experiences with these infrastructures, I now have more confidence as a geographical and cultural navigator. Two decades of research experience in India, a generous research grant and a team of people with varied skills and predispositions allowed me to ditch the compass. I became able to navigate without state-sanctioned maps and cardinal points. This geographical philistinism has resulted in something akin to looking at one of those pictures that appears to be one thing at a casual glance, but in which something altogether different emerges upon a more fixed stare. The readily seen picture is the Subcontinent drawn with the established geopolitical lines that I have discussed. We can see the KKH as the first draft of CPEC and China's greater design. CPEC, heralded by loud calls (and songs) for attention, appears as a new line drawn thickly on the older map. India's response, Act East, is ushered in with a whimper in comparison, but it is still highly visible, ambitiously reorienting India and South East Asia.

As our attention became a stare, the scrutiny permitted by ethnographic proximity revealed other detail—nothing as systematic or as coherent as the established standard narratives of regional infrastructure. Gradually, as our senses began to master the fragmented materials, another picture started to emerge. What the hidden picture revealed is the deep presence of other countries, particularly America, on the roads of the region. Significantly, this is exerted not through promotional videos or other forms of geopolitical grandstanding, but instead, as other sections of this book discuss, through the victory of the Cold War, funds for technical road research and institutions, and the quiet establishment of road standards and the terms of trade. Indeed, as our research progressed, American ideas and corporations began to appear frequently, to the extent that they now rather dominate our story—but that is the research talking, not the bluster of international relations or propaganda.

The point here is not that the propaganda issued by India or China does not reflect tarmac realities, or that propaganda is an attempt to make realities. We should not be surprised by such things. Rather, propaganda has made some roads visible, and these have become the just-so standard and authoritative narratives of road building in South Asia. To be interested in roads in South Asia, when I started this project, was to be interested in CPEC, Look East and so forth. Roadmen expected me to ask them questions about these schemes— these were the standard narratives of the region, the headlines and, I dare say, the kinds of projects about which governments and media already had stories prepared.

I had intended for the project to go beyond, or at least below, the standard and repetitive narratives of geopolitics, to what was happening on the ground. In the end, and despite this clear aim, the research revealed something previously unseen, unreported and unanticipated—geopolitics without propaganda. On the road, and with roadmen, ethnographic research showed the influence of corporate America along the highways and byways of the Subcontinent.

4

STANDARD NARRATIVE
RURAL ROADS IN INDIA

The Vision

At the time of Independence, V.V. Ramanadham the distinguished economist and later champion of public enterprise, noted: 'If it is true that the strength of an army lies in its legs, it is more true that the strength of our agriculture lies in our roads.' The time has now gone when agriculture was the supportive backbone of the Indian economy.[1] Today, there is a massive and highly publicised rural road-building project oriented around the twin ideas of reduced transport costs (i.e. more transport) and speculation in land as a way of putting money into rural areas. The Pradhan Mantri Gram Sadak Yojana (Prime Minister's Village Road-Building Scheme, or commonly PMGSY) is represented slickly through targets, numbers and futuristic and technical language: half a million miles targeted within the first decades of the twenty-first century.

Imagine that: half a million miles, the moon and back and more, threaded through rural India. Fieldwork with roadmen across the country impressed on me the jubilance and pride they take from this achievement. For many of them, the populist appeal of roads is one thing, but within their professional circles and institutions, it is the structure and implementation mechanisms of the programme that have had 'transformative' and 'game-changing' effects.

Throughout the 2010s, PMGSY was advertised as having a budget of $50 billion; this figure has subsequently increased. In what follows, the arguments supporting the investment of such a large sum are outlined, explored and debated. The knowledge politics surrounding this programme are taken as an example of how, under certain circumstances, the assumptions that drive road building run so deep that they fall beyond scrutiny.

According to the World Bank, for example, in rural India: 'Government expenditure on roads has been found to have the largest impact on poverty reduction (163 persons lifted out of poverty with INR1 million investment) as well as a significant impact on productivity growth. Road investments have seen improved agriculture productivity, increased off-farm employment opportunities, and higher wages.'

The World Bank's stated purpose is to reduce poverty; therefore, given the efficiency of the investment, roads have become a priority. Other listed benefits of road building include 'doubling of farmers' incomes; reduction in freight charges by more than 60 percent; increase in literacy rate by 8 percent; increase in land prices by 80 percent; about 12 percent higher prices for agricultural produce; and timely help during medical emergencies, particularly for pregnant women'.[2]

Yet the published evidence on the actual effects of roads is thin, such that if one came to it cold without the common sense provided by a century of living with cars and roads, it would be discounted as fanciful.

***

We held a roundtable in Delhi in 2016 to address the question: What do new roads do to older places in specific relation to the PMGSY programme? We invited bureaucrats, academics, journalists and activists to debate these questions, with contrasting views on the programme reflecting the shades of opinion in India. In this chapter, I interweave voices from the roundtable with the story of the development of PMGSY. From my perspective, the story shows how constellations of institutions and priorities have come together with political will and the drag of history to make it appear as if road building is the only possible course of action. In the rhetoric of those roading rural India, this is their moment, this is what the national struggle has been for, their work is the pinnacle of a country's striving: the bureaucratic capacity to build good roads, and lots of them. There are no alternatives.

Surveying the extensive grey and promotional literatures and social media and having spoken to villagers in eight states across India about the programme, I found that these narratives are surprisingly repetitive and constant across diverse field sites: increased farm income, improved access to medical and educational facilities, daily wage migration and improved marriage proposals. It would seem fair to say that the government's message has reached the people. Indeed, what 'the people' say is not so very different from the words of the World Bank cited above. How are we to explain this remarkable congruence, where the peasant and the bank and the many people in between speak with such similar words?

From Independence in 1947, rural road building has been at the heart of India's developmental state primarily through a pride in public works and employment creation programmes. Alongside this, the village was cultivated as a devolved location for development work, not an independent republic but a place of democracy and primary health and education services. In essence, the state took welfare to the village, rather than villagers to welfare. Then, in a gradual reversal of this fundamental idea, the state now sees roads as a way of taking people from villages and delivering them to market-driven services in urban areas.

Later, we will trace the development of roads through the five-year planning cycle, as India moved from a planned economy towards the market. For now, we jump in at the deep end to look in detail at the latest hybrid form of organisation: the state-led facilitation of the market through national rural road provision. The road, along with water and electricity, has become the vehicle of development, rather than the aim of development. I have explicitly pursued the arguments that politicians and roadmen make in support of this approach and this scheme, and here pick up their assertions considering academic research from contemporary India and 'classic' studies on these questions from Nepal and elsewhere.

***

A $50 billion budget is a strong and round number, although the ambition was less when the scheme was launched at the start of the century. The plan was then to 'connect' tens of thousands of 'habitations'—a term used to include sub-settlements within entities classified as 'villages'—to 'all-weather' or 'black topped and asphaltic roads'.[3] The Bharatiya Janata Party (BJP) government then led by Atal Bihari Vajpayee (1999–2004) placed great emphasis through the planning process on infrastructure as a means of development.

As PMGSY successfully expanded, it became a 'flagship' programme—and strongly associated with the BJP. However, the conditions of its inception suggest that it was formed out of expediency rather than as the bearer of a standard. Partha Mukhopadhyay, one of the founding members of the Infrastructure Development Finance Company (tagline: Enabling India), was closely associated with the Prime Minister's Office when the National Highways Development Project (NHDP) was launched. According to him, PMGSY and the National Rural Roads Development Agency (NRRDA) were formed in the shadows of the more newsworthy highways projects. The planned additional cess, or tax, on fuel for highway construction was to place the burden on the rural population, a burden without any obvious benefit to them.[4] Thus, in Mukhopadhyay's view, PMGSY, which would bring roads to rural areas, became the legitimising programme to allow for grand highway projects.

In October 1998, Vajpayee announced the north–south and east–west highway corridors as the first in a series of major project announcements. A few months later, he launched the NHDP and laid the foundation stone in January 1999.[5] PMGSY was announced almost a year later by the president on 29 October 1999, and the National Rural Road Development Committee (NRRDC) was created on 6 January 2000.[6] After a progress review in May 2000, the government approved a budget for Phase I, which subsumed the previously announced project within the brand of the 'Golden

Quadrilateral Project', a massive road scheme intended to connect the major cities of India with upgraded highways. The Central Road Fund Act 2000 was not passed until towards the end of the year; the cess in the act thus came into force after the announcement of the highway project, suggesting the financing mechanism was either an after-thought or had played second fiddle to high-profile political promises. B. Rajender, joint secretary of the Ministry of Agriculture, described the relation thus: 'National highways were like the big brother, and rural roads were like the poor cousin; they never got attention they were supposed to get.'

The NRRDC was first chaired by Nitin 'Mr Flyover' Gadkari, then the leader of the opposition in Maharashtra. The report he oversaw was an 'action plan to accomplish 100% rural road connectivity by black topped road of 10 year durability in a time-bound and cost-effective manner'.[7] The decision to construct rural roads might not have been the first priority for the government until it realised that rural people were being asked to finance highway development. However, looking back on those early days, Rajesh Bhushan and Jugal Mohapatra, both former directors of the NRRDA, attribute credit for PMGSY to the promotion and encouragement of Gadkari. His 'magnificent obsession' (on which much more later) with road building as a mode of political engagement saw PMGSY emerge alongside the Golden Quadrilateral, as a way not so much of financing the highways but of generating a national vote bank.

The World Bank also played an important role in the inception of the scheme. Initially the bank led the programme, drawing on experiences of rural road-building programmes in other parts of the world, where roads fed into 'inclusive development' and 'poverty reduction' agendas. When Gadkari was asked to chair the national committee, he appears to have wrestled the programme from the World Bank and pinned it to the central government. He perhaps saw the political potential of making the project a 'national asset' and knew that institutions in India also had experience of rural road building through community development programmes and later employment-generation initiatives. Since then, the World Bank and the Asian Development Bank (ADB; tagline: Prosperous, Reliant, Inclusive, Sustainable) have played major but less visible roles in supporting and financing PMGSY, with both providing large loans and technical and conceptual assistance.[8]

Within the government, the scheme was placed with the Ministry of Rural Development. The joint secretary of the ministry is the ex-officio director general of the NRRDA—the agency responsible for executing PMGSY. The NRRDA has strategic responsibilities for the programme, coordinating with state-level agencies and maintaining online portals.[9] The CRRI, National Informatics Centre and Centre for Development of Advanced Computing play roles in quality monitoring of roads and design, as do various engineering colleges and universities. At the state level, there are around 1,500 Project Implementation Units with oversight of construction on the ground, with perhaps as many as 50,000 eligible contractors.

***

> For me, PMGSY in my mind was this paradigm shift in the rural development policy … The big difference was that instead of doing this micro thing … now we're providing this far-reaching or over-arching intervention, if you will. But more than that, we're going to build a road. We're going to change the environment, the ecosystem that you function in, and then you go and make your decision … and see if you can optimise things.[10]

At the 2016 Delhi roundtable, these words of development economist Shilpa Aggarwal cut to the heart of the 'enabling and empowering' ideology behind PMGSY. This is often contrasted with the 'welfaring and securitising' ideology of the Mahatma Gandhi National Rural Employment Guarantee Scheme (MGNREGS), launched by the Congress-led United Progressive Alliance (UPA) coalition in 2005. Increasingly, PMGSY has been used to fly the flag of the BJP-led National Democratic Alliance (NDA) coalition, with a focus on constructing 'enabling' infrastructure that the BJP's Vajpayee had pioneered. This shorthand gloss for associating policy bundles with political parties cuts across opinion makers, scholars and bureaucrats. In interviews, it was striking that roadmen referred to PMGSY as 'our' government's programme. Some of this is political positioning, of course, but there is also a difference in approach to the state and how to change things.

Aggarwal talked about 'optimising individuals' who would be empowered to make their own decisions on whether to send their children to school, deliver their babies in hospital, or use fertiliser in their fields. In fact, for her, seeing the increase in fertiliser use provided a moment of clarity. Previous governments had tried to encourage fertiliser use in agriculture through subsidies, with moderate success and at considerable expense:

> And that fertiliser thing, it was just something that really changed the way I thought about development economics. Because fertiliser is something that there have been so many interventions trying to get farmers to use more … really trying to get fertiliser use up, and it really doesn't happen. And it's absolutely mind-blowing that you put in roads, and it's not that farmers are stupid, they know what makes sense for them, and earlier it didn't make sense for them and now it does, so they just start using.[11]

PMGSY's popularity inspired many states to launch their own rural development programmes—various forms of CMGSYs (Chief Minister's Gram SadakYojanas), for example in Bihar, Madhya Pradesh and Gujarat. As the potency and popularity of the scheme continued to rise, the Indian government became increasingly aggressive with its targets. In Bihar, a rival road-building scheme was announced as a newly elected chief minister created a new ministry. The secretary was told to deliver on the roads because the chief minister wanted to retain his position in the next elections and thought he would do so if he provided better roads to rural areas than the central government.

PMGSY was a national scheme providing 'all-weather roads' for 'habitations' with populations greater than 500. In Bihar, MMGSY (Mukhya Mantri Gram Sampark Yojana) was launched in 2013 aiming to connect the habitations with populations of 250–499 (i.e. those neglected by the central government scheme). Going a step further in the state, GTSNY (Gramin Tola Sampark Nischay Yojana) was to connect habitations with populations below 250. With these schemes already in place, the government of Bihar also borrowed heavily from the World Bank to finance further rural road building on the premise that '[t]he underdeveloped rural road network is constraining the growth of rural areas'.[12]

Other states also developed their own programmes to diffuse the spotlight that PMGSY shone on the central government. As the journalist Nitin Desai argued during our Delhi roundtable, the fact that roads are built on central government cesses 'shows up' the rhetoric of devolving power to the state governments to manage development on their own terms. The result, as he put it, is a 'macho central state':

> A macho central state, as I call it, is, 'We guys [central government] do the infrastructure, you guys [state governments] do all the soft stuff like taking care of people's health.' And that's practically what's happened in the past two years, as money invested in roads has come at a cost to some other things. And it's clearly come at a cost of the spending decrease in health.

Narendra Modi has crystallised this position in a hundred speeches in which he says with admirable simplicity: 'The government should give the people roads, water and electricity. Job done!' In his first three years as prime minister (2014–17), a great emphasis was placed on PMGSY. During the previous Congress-led UPA government, rural roads had been subsumed within the broader Bharat Nirman development agenda, which also included housing, electricity, water supply and telecommunications. The subsequent BJP-led NDA government under Modi was consequently more easily able to claim PMGSY as its own, since the scheme started with Vajpayee, a BJP prime minister. Road development was once again given a distinct policy branding, and the logo is now recognised across India. By 2015, the PMGSY publicity machine claimed to have connected 112,500 villages with 454,048 km of road, reaching a rate of construction of over 100 km per day in 2014–15. By 2017, PMGSY claimed 517,600 km of rural roads connecting over 135,700 habitations at a peak rate of 130 km per day, a figure that NRRDC chairman Gadkari was fond of repeating.

***

The numbers are huge and the results highly visible, with PMGSY signboards littering the countryside, billboards advertising the government's efficiency and care. Most of those we spoke to in Delhi believe PMGSY to be one of the best central policies in independent India. In 2012, the Planning Commission acknowledged the work behind the project, describing its features as a 'gold standard'. We have already seen the influence of broad government policy agendas, Gadkari's mastery of roads as politics, and attempts made to distinguish political parties and governments within the growth of the PMGSY project. Among the roadmen, however, there are other stories, of individual skill, responsibility and pride in the figures that built road institutions.

In Delhi, the past directors of the CRRI are held in high esteem; their achievements and milestones in highway and rural road engineering are memorialised on the walls and in the publications of the institution, their personalities and temperaments taken as models for action. From Dr E. Zipkes (dir. 1950–4), a Swiss engineer and the first director of the institute, the qualities and accomplishments of eleven former directors are expounded: Professor S.R. Mehra (dir. 1955–68), 'a man of vision'; Dr Bh. Subbaraju (dir. 1968–77), renowned for his 'engineering acumen'; Professor C.G. Swaminathan (dir. 1977–83), remembered for his meticulous research; Dr M.P. Dhir (dir. 1983–9), who joined CRRI as a Scientist 'B' (a mid-ranking technical position) and amassed a broad range of skills that saw him develop new bullock carts and airport runways; Professor D.V. Singh (dir. 1992–6), who created international connections with the world's advanced research institutes on roads; Professor A.K. Gupta (dir. 1996–7), who instituted research on new computer modelling in CRRI and intensified interactions with the World Bank; Professor P.K. Sikdar (dir. 1998–2004), who injected a rigorous research mindset among the scientists of the institute, and who prepared the base documents for PMGSY and the Golden Quadrilateral Project; Dr P.K. Nanda (dir. 2004–7), who also joined as a Scientist 'B' and worked his way up within the institute; Dr Vikram Kumar (dir. 2007–8), a man of 'dynamic leadership'; and Dr S. Gangopadhyay (dir. 2009–15), who, having also started as a Scientist 'B', enhanced the institute's research profile as director and renovated its laboratories.

When roadmen talked informally about life in the institute, they often made a soft distinction between those who had started low ('B') and worked their way up (the 'lifers') and those who came from consultancy or academic backgrounds to serve as directors (those 'parachuted in'). Cultural and attitudinal differences were identified between these two groups. Both, however, were brought together in regular turns of phrase such as the 'right kind of officer', 'men made for the role' and those 'who had [the] ability to pick [the] right person for the right job'. Many managerial roadmen evoked the skill of matching temperament to task in successful project implementation. Experienced roadmen often said that PMGSY was so great because it stemmed from the 'right kind of officers' occupying leadership roles and taking the programme forward.

Interviews gave signposts to the identities of the 'right kind of officers'. Speaking to them revealed a general zeal and passion for rural road building, but particularly for PMGSY. Former NRRDA director general Rajesh Bhushan, for example, described his role as delivering critical access to the poorest in the country. Other colleagues in the programme expressed similar sentiments, telling us that they were in positions of privilege to help. Mr D.P. Gupta, now an octogenarian, was a 'lifer'. He is highly respected as an engineer and has seen first hand the growth and development of road building in India. He was proud to have served in the Ministry of Roads, Transport and Highways and sees his contribution as a service to the nation. He choked with emotion when talking about the transformation brought about by PMGSY. He had seen schemes and fashions come and go, but the effects had been piecemeal and 'weak' when compared to what he was seeing today.

We asked the roadmen where the idea for PMGSY came from. Jugal Mohapatra and S. Vijay Kumar, also both former director generals of the NRRDA, separately directed us to a study published in 1999 by the International Food Policy Research Institute in Washington, DC (funded by the World Bank and others) that they told us had played an influential role. The paper, written by economists Shenggen Fan, Peter Hazell and Sukhadeo Thorat, argues in favour of building roads for rural development. They write: 'Additional government expenditure on roads is found to have the largest impact on poverty reduction as well as a significant impact on productivity growth. It is a dominant "win-win" strategy.'[13]

These authors were not writing in isolation. Previously, the World Bank had supported rural road programmes with the CRRI, working in Andhra Pradesh, and later in Gujarat, Punjab and Haryana. Most of the bank's experience had, however, been in Sub-Saharan Africa, where throughout the 1990s, increasing agricultural productivity was seen as the most effective way of reducing poverty. Correspondingly, in India, former Planning Commission member Abhijit Sen argued for the resources to increase agricultural productivity to reduce poverty. Sen pointed to the effects of increased spending between 1976 and 1990 as the principal reason for the reduction of poverty levels and subsequently argued that increased government expenditure during this period had also led to an expansion of rural non-farm employment.[14] Fan, Hazell and Thorat analysed the same data to similar conclusions, describing increased spending on agricultural research as 'another dominant "win-win" strategy'.[15] Increasingly, however, the World Bank's emphasis shifted away from improving agricultural technology to the improvement of rural infrastructure.[16] That was the zeitgeist within the organisation when Fan, Hazell and Thorat drew on all these strands to develop the economic model producing favourable outcomes for increased public expenditure on roads for rural development.

Mohapatra opens some of his own writing with quotes from other work by Shenggen Fan, which argue that the study of 'government expenditure and poverty in rural India has revealed that an investment of Rs 1 crore in roads lifts 1650 poor persons above the poverty line'.[17] He supports this further with evidence from an International Food Policy Research Institute paper about the 'productivity effect' of rural roads.[18] In both sets of writing, public investment in rural roads and agriculture research and development achieve the highest marginal returns in poverty alleviation, primarily through improving agriculture productivity. It is worth pointing out that the data on which these papers are based is taken from 1970 to 1993—whether the kind of modelling used then maps well into the post-liberalisation era is a pertinent question. Indeed, when Srinivas Chokkakula, the researcher leading the PMGSY strand of the project, asked Sukhadeo

Thorat about the impact of the piece, he was surprised it had been referenced as shaping PMGSY.

Another officer of the 'right kind' is Ashok Kumar, now a senior highway engineer with the World Bank. Kumar led research on rural roads at CRRI before joining the bank in 1999, at the height of its shift in emphasis towards rural infrastructure improvement. His role was to provide technical assistance for the development of PMGSY. Just before this move, he had written a doctoral dissertation at Birmingham University in the United Kingdom—one of the global centres in the production of knowledge about rural roads—on developing a core network of rural roads for India. The concept later became central to PMGSY's design.[19]

The idea was that instead of maintaining the entire network, the government should focus on the sections that brought most benefit and the simplest connections to larger roads. The model placed greater emphasis on connecting villages to towns via larger arteries than it did on connecting villages to villages. These ideas grew subsequently to become policy at the confluence of the historical groundwork done at CRRI on technical aspects of building rural roads and the World Bank's core objective of alleviating global poverty.

Kumar's work on the core road network grew out of research he had conducted at the University of Birmingham with H.T. Tillotson (died 2016), then lecturer in transport planning. Tillotson also conducted consultancy work for the World Bank on road modelling. Kumar and Tillotson's joint paper was presented at an international conference on low-volume roads organised by the American Transportation Research Board in Washington, DC in 1991. They put forward a methodology for 'generating optimum rural roads networks', seeing villages as '"unconnected nodes" to be connected to "root nodes"—either market centers or on the existing main roads which inter-connect the market centers ... the optimum rural road network emerges in the form of several rooted minimum spanning trees, minimizing the total costs'. Kumar and Tillotson saw that their proposed methodology could be used for preparing master plans; this optimum network could be 'generated from a minimum construction cost network by an iterative process which reduces the travel costs until these are offset by the consequent increases in construction costs'.[20]

Kumar also drew on an older model that he had helped to develop as a young man with senior colleagues from CRRI, including C.G. Swaminathan, who was then the director, which saw main roads as electricity cables, villages as electrical charges and markets as attracting charge.[21]

***

Within this brief reconstruction of the influences behind PMGSY, there is an evident convergence of the interests of development banks, hungry international consultancies and local road-building institutions. A small number of men has been shown to have produced enormously influential ideas that have travelled through institutions and across continents. In Gadkari's charismatic hands, abstract university models of connectivity and networks become political and nationalist instruments, linked to a strong rhetoric of transparency and efficiency that has accompanied the rise of the BJP in India: a win-win! The legacy of the Licence Raj (the system of permits issued by the government to regulate enterprise in India for much of the latter half of the twentieth century) and the notoriety of corruption in road contracts give the rhetoric of improving governance extra bite.

With PMGSY, there has been an attempt to depoliticise road building by emphasising process, technology and non-corruptibility. The standardised and national system of tendering, quality control, computerised records and rhetoric of accountability is presented as transforming road building into a bureaucratic science. The theory is: out with local whim, largesse and electioneering, in with a strong central state and infallible process.

Consequently, PMGSY developed largely as a technocratic and managerial set of systems for tendering and quality assurance—the mechanical and engineering processes receive much less attention. There were the usual mapping exercises, the development of apps and portals, and heavy brand promotion. Templates and standards were drawn up for every stage of paperwork and construction. The high levels of investment encouraged new networks of contractors, technocrats and knowledge producers. The creation of standard processes became the major achievement, combined with national training programmes for engineers and administrators. Above all, according to B. Rajender, who described PMGSY as a 'beautiful institutional arrangement', it was the ease of online monitoring that accounted for the programme's success. As he said at the Delhi roundtable:

> The beauty of this programme is online monitoring management account system [OMMAS], it's very, very strong, the backbone of this programme, and it is the main reason for the success of this programme. From the selection of roads, to the contractors, to payment, everything is done online, now even the road sanctioning is done online.

All this energy and beauty notwithstanding, I remained stubbornly curious—given the size and certainty of the programme and the evident political capital gains, as witnessed in the emergence of copycat projects—as to why there was so little writing about PMGSY.

I was met with blank faces when trying to introduce a critical note to conversations about the scheme. PMGSY was 'non-controversial'—what was possibly wrong with building roads in rural areas? The country has been waiting for this! Often, the language that came back mirrored the words used by the promotors of PMGSY, particularly the idea of 'connectivity'. As we have seen in relation to Kumar's core network ideas, with their emphasis on connecting villages to towns rather than to other villages, 'connectivity' (to what, and why?) is not value-neutral in economic or political terms, any more than the attempt to depoliticise the language of road building through PMGSY.

It seemed to me in repeated conversations that we were dealing with a truth so self-evident that otherwise critical minds did not see a question in the idea, at least in the way it was packaged as a particular form of claims and data. Building roads equalled progress and meaningful development, and so it was an obvious priority in India. Srinivas Chokkakula asked around among academic colleagues in Delhi for their response to the question of why there was no critical debate about PMGSY. Memorably, and influentially, he received a reply from a senior colleague: '[T]he uncritical responses may be due to the belief across the board, there is no counterfactual to building rural roads.'

Since then, I have often wondered how to respond meaningfully to this provocative assertion. This sentiment would not have gone down well with John Urry in the project's original roundtable. For him, at least in London, the promotion of mobility was pedalling a form of capitalism, not human development in a straightforward sense. To say there is no alternative to the roads version of mass mobility would be akin to saying there are no alternatives to any political regime, a view likely to be endorsed by those in power and those who do not, or cannot, see a need to distinguish between ideology and everyday consciousness.

Investigating the Evidence Behind Claims of Progress

If, given this history, 'counterfactuals' are difficult, then it might be simpler to address the 'factuals'. We start with the voices of roadmen and those who have seen roads built to their villages before moving to discuss the scant academic literature that outlines and assesses the evidence on what rural roads do to the places they touch.

'A human being has no value without a road,' people in villages told us. 'If our fate is linked to the road,' they said, 'then we will be happy in every way.' Or, more simply: 'If roads are good, then everything is fine.' Above all: 'It used to take hours to reach the town; now, with the new road, it only takes minutes.'

Engineers in provincial PWDs made similar points from a more formal, bird's-eye vantage point. 'The road is the route to resolving problems,' they explained. 'Roads are bringing confidence to rural voices.'

State government officials spoke with greater abstraction, seeing roads as linking people and markets: 'This rural road-building scheme enlivens the dynamic connection between the village and the market, the market and the highway, the highway and the nation.'

… and as establishing law and order: 'There was so much crime in the area before we built the road because the police could not get there; now, things are peaceful.'

... and as good policy-making: 'PMGSY is about efficient management, good quality, and transparency in implementation.'

Sitting at his well-worn desk in a national institution, one official claimed with welling pride that: 'This is the most important and successful government policy since Independence.'

For an employee of the ADB, far away from the tarmac in a world of spreadsheets and corporate networking: 'The bottom line is not about aspirations but fundamental needs ... It is the fundamental human need of people to have a basic road.' Enthusiasm brought poetry: 'Disbelief has become part of rural thinking; now rural roads are paving hope into villages as we make futures.'

It was not only the state officials who pointed out that new roads have made access to markets easier. Farmers who used to carry produce on their heads told us that they now take it to market in a tractor-trolley or truck, meaning fresh items can be transported for sale without drying up or being otherwise damaged on the way. The lowered price of transport makes rural produce better value in an urban market. In the other direction, roads reduce the cost of transporting building materials so villagers can build more and better-quality buildings. We were shown in most places we visited how land prices had risen, not only because of retail opportunity but because of the comfort and prestige of being roadside.

As well as boosting the economy by facilitating transport, the road itself is a source of income. Many rural men told us that they had been unemployed before the road came, but they now drive a rickshaw or taxi between the village and the highway. There were social and educational benefits too. Repeatedly, we were told that teachers are more likely to accept positions in village schools and turn up regularly if there is a road. Conversely, children are more likely to travel to town for higher levels of education. Access to hospitals improves and mortality rates, especially those associated with childbirth, decrease.

In his presentation to the roundtable in Delhi, B. Rajender made a strikingly similar list of claims about the impacts of rural road building:

> The first impact I could see was in education. It's heartening to see that especially girl student enrolment has gone up tremendously.

And number two, the medical facilities, accessibility. People used to die. Two thousand bridges were constructed so people could come and save their lives, and accessibility to medical facilities has gone up like anything. Third is the market, and you will be surprised to know that the cultivation of cereals has come down and vegetables has gone up most places. Fourth is teachers' movement. Earlier, teachers were absent ... they never used to go to some places, remote places and schools were without teachers ... The biggest thing is that crime has come down ... people can go and walk in the night—even the ladies, even at twelve o'clock in the night. These are the impacts.[22]

An early impact assessment from 2004 on PMGSY reported a spectacular range of benefits, particularly to farmers.[23] Earlier, farmers had found it 'difficult' to sell goods in the 'bigger markets'. The labour and time involved in transport reduced profits. Roads reduced transport costs and improved transport systems throughout the year, particularly during monsoon months. According to the report: 'Habitations are now using motorised equipment such as tractors, threshing machines for cultivation leading to a more efficient, time-saving and profitable process of cultivation.' Many families reported having purchased bicycles to carry dairy products to town.

Conversely, it had also become easier to transport materials such as chemical fertilisers, seeds and pesticides to villages. In some areas, there had been a switch from food crops to cash crops (such as ginger, jute, sugarcane and sunflower). 'In the post PMGSY road phase' (a wonderful turn of phrase from the report), there was also evidence of a change in cropping intensity as a result of increased agricultural trade, and new crops such as tomato and cauliflower had been introduced.

In addition to agriculture, PMGSY roads were reported to have brought job opportunities and avenues for self-employment. 'A lot of housewives' had started small-scale industries, making pickles, lentil cakes and puffed rice balls. There was a noticeable increase in the numbers of people heading to towns for 'odd jobs', such as selling wood, vegetables, dairy products and other locally made items. The report also noted the overall increase in access to health facilities and better birthing and antenatal care.

Improved roads resulted in higher school enrolment and attendance of both students and teachers. Many parents were more confident about sending their daughters to school unescorted, and more boys and girls were reported as attending higher studies and college education.

New rural roads had increased the frequency of visits by government officials and facilitated quicker access to police services, which had 'ensured an improved law and order situation in some areas'. A notable change, as observed, was that villagers' social networks had widened and the marriage alliance radius had increased. Women felt more comfortable travelling alone in buses and on bicycles, and many had reported having taken up casual employment.

The areas that had been studied described rapid changes 'from traditional to modern ways of life'. For instance, 'the phenomenon of neon light attraction has drawn the villagers to the town entertainments' and 'there has been increased use and ownership of television and other electrical gadgets'.

The states of Mizoram, Tamil Nadu and West Bengal reported the conversion of makeshift houses to permanent structures. All areas surveyed reported a sudden escalation in the price of land adjacent to PMGSY roads, which had in turn led to an increase in the sale of land for commercial purposes.

Depending on where in the world you are reading this, such arguments about access to services and facilities might sound familiar and sensible. But there are other ways in which roads feature in local judgements that are not simply practical or based on ideas of 'access'. In all the rural locations where we conducted research, people said that previously, girls had often refused to marry into the village because of poor roads. The presence or absence of a road is both a part of their reckoning about the economic situation that they would be marrying into—a lack of road is taken as a gross negative sociological signal about the progress or aspirations of a particular place—and an indication of the worth and attractiveness of possible marriage partners, a way to measure the man, his mentality and the kind of life the village offers. Marriage, too, could be read as a kind of market, but the point here is to emphasise the moral and emotional force of the road as a shorthand for understanding the nature and desirability of a place.

The authors of the impact assessment made no attempt to distinguish between PMGSY change and change that would have happened anyway. They saw rural roads ushering in a modernity premised on mobility, technology and participation in a national market economy. Roads were bussing tradition out of the countryside for good, breaking down gender roles and bringing an entrepreneurial spirit to the withering countryside.

When I started this research in 2010, a decade into the programme, there was little more published material on PMGSY. By 2015, there were half a dozen peer-reviewed papers on the socio-economic impacts of new rural roads. Three of these had been funded by the World Bank.[24] The others were dissertation studies, primarily by economists.[25] Further papers have been published since then, including the one that Shilpa Aggarwal presented in draft form at our second roundtable in Delhi.[26] This growing body of literature examines some of the strong and repetitive claims made for PMGSY. For example, there are studies on farm income and on access to medical and educational facilities. Overall, however, the dearth of published work is surprising considering the scale of investment. In contrast, the MGNREGS (with assumed proprietary ownership by the Congress-led UPA coalition) had received, and continues to receive, extensive and critical attention from scholars.[27]

Before taking a more detailed look at the literature on PMGSY, we should pay attention to the concerns raised by Aggarwal at the roundtable about this kind of analysis:

> Do roads lead to poverty alleviation? Unfortunately, in the case of this programme, I was not able to quantify the benefits. The one big issue with beginning to quantify road building … the impacts of roads are so all-pervasive. And they also go over such a long term that how do you even begin to say what is the benefit of the road?

Aggarwal's point about timescales applies to most studies of road building. Getting access to places and having long enough to conduct research before and after a road is built is generally difficult. Looking at price data before and after roads is also tricky because perhaps people consume new goods, or higher-quality goods, and have to start paying for new forms of transport and vehicles. Road construction itself brings new people and connections to villages, a so-called road effect—the 'all-pervasive' impacts noted by Aggarwal. She went on to suggest:

> You can probably say it in one dimension, say that roads led to a 3 per cent increase in the use of fertiliser … then farmer incomes rise and so on. So, on this metric, you can ask if roads are worth it or not. But to be able to say whether the road paid for itself, who knows? How would you ever begin to quantify it?

In her more recent, published work, Aggarwal is even more cautious in her conclusions on the uptake of fertiliser and notes other possible mechanisms, such as the easing of credit constraints. While acknowledging that 'data limitations preclude me from isolating the exact channels at play', she confirms, on the basis of her findings, 'an association between rural road construction and technology adoption in agriculture'.[28]

Aggarwal's study, like others on PMGSY, draws on a variety of datasets—information collected on a periodic basis, usually by the government, such as sample surveys and census data.[29] Many economists love nothing more than to debate the strengths and weaknesses of particular datasets. When American economist Sam Asher presented his collaborative work on PMGSY in Delhi to a room of fellow economists in 2016, most of the questions he fielded were about the data. There was little discussion of his finding, which was that the PMGSY scheme appeared to reduce agricultural employment by around 10 per cent.[30]

In a more recent policy brief, the same authors state more boldly: 'Rural roads had fewer positive effects on villages than would have been expected given the prior literature.' They add: 'We found no evidence that roads affected agriculture investment or production or household consumption.' In their view, the primary impact of new roads is to make it easier for workers to gain access to non-agricultural jobs outside their villages. They conclude:

Our research suggests that rural roads do not meaningfully facilitate growth of village firms, agricultural production, or consumption in the short to medium run. Roads alone appear to be insufficient to transform the economic structure of remote villages ... Our results make clear that transportation infrastructure alone is not going to lead to thriving villages.[31]

Data from PMGSY's wonderfully named 'OMMAS' (Online Management, Monitoring and Accounting System), when read alongside other datasets, show that new roads bring new crops and a shift from subsistence to commodity farming, suggesting better incomes for farmers.[32] The same study also recorded increased mobility of labour between villages, leading to better use of labour pools.[33]

Clive Bell, who was at the original roundtable in London, was funded by the World Bank to conduct research on PMGSY in 2010. He conducted follow-up surveys of thirty villages in Odisha that had previously been surveyed by Susanne van Dillen in 2001–2.[34] At the time of the original survey, only two of the villages had all-weather roads, while by 2010, nine further villages were connected with PMGSY. Bell concluded that, since the provision of an all-weather road, net output agriculture prices had increased by 5 per cent or more, fewer schooling days were being lost, and more timely treatment was available to the acutely sick.[35] In another paper, he suggests the expected benefits cannot be realised unless PMGSY roads, and larger roads falling outside the scheme, are maintained, suggesting that investment in PMGSY depends on investment on larger roads as well.[36]

As others have done, Bell highlighted the wide-ranging nature of the 'road effect' that extends further than the communities connected to the network. On the one hand, he argues, rural road building increases the range of employment that villages can offer and relieves the pressures on urban infrastructure due to a slower rate of migration. On the other hand, new roads bring an increase in accidents and pollution. All these effects, positive and negative, 'ramify through the whole system in ways that are complicated and hard to estimate'.[37]

The evidence on the public health impacts of new roads is similarly ambiguous. A study using data from 2005 to 2006 found no perceptible impact on infant and neonatal mortality or sex ratios due to the provision of PMGSY roads.[38] Other datasets have been used to demonstrate the increased use of preventive healthcare in villages following the introduction of PMGSY.[39] However, the authors of this study caution that the increase cannot be directly attributed to the improved physical access, because of other variables such as a general increase in awareness, improved reach of healthcare practices, and intensified social interactions—which can be only indirectly linked to the physical access afforded by a road.

Regarding the effect of PMGSY intervention on educational access, Aggarwal drew a varied picture at our Delhi roundtable:

> Now, I also found that households were reporting that their younger kids, between the ages of five to fourteen, were actually more likely to be in school, so in line with some of the things that have been said here about roads improving access to school and school enrolment. But then I also found that for older children, fourteen- to twenty-year-olds, they actually dropped out of school and started working.

In her published study, she quantifies the drop in enrolment for the older age group as 11 per cent, compared to a 5 per cent increase in enrolment in the younger group.[40] At the roundtable, she pointed out that the school dropouts were not working in high-end jobs, but rather:

> Low-level, low-skill manufacturing, or not even that, that kids were working in, simply because these jobs were now accessible and it was possible to work in these industries. And of course, it's debatable what the returns to education would be in rural India, so it made sense for kids to drop out of school and actually join the labour force right away.

Use of 'big data' complicates this picture yet further. Political scientists have used 'fuzzy regression discontinuity design' and comprehensive household and census microdata to argue that four years after road construction, the main impact of new feeder roads is to facilitate the movement of workers out of agriculture.[41] This study also shows that there are no major changes in agricultural outcomes, income or assets. Employment in villages expands only slightly. Even with better market connections, remote areas may continue to lack economic opportunities.

All in all, would you invest $50 billion on the basis of this evidence? It might be unfair, but many of those writing about PMGSY almost seem to be looking for evidence to demonstrate that the investment has had strong local effects, when in fact most conclusions point only to the incremental effect such action has on the integration of rural people into a petro-economy.

***

As we have seen, conversations about the benefits of rural road building are dominated by economists. Beyond the datasets, however, one might argue that cash crop production produces other forms of vulnerability and exploitation, or that roads do nothing to alter the quality of educational and medical services. It could be pointed out that increased daily wage migration has expanded the labour pool and hence reduced the price of labour, and that women marrying into the newly roaded village are simply contributing to a shortage of brides elsewhere, leading to a wholesale escalation in exploitative forms of marriage and dowry. It is also the case that money invested in roads has come at the cost of other things, notably health and education. Further still from the datasets, a romantic might make the case that the village did not need the civilisation of the town, or that cultural homogenisation was eroding the traditional ways people in India relate to one another.

In the 1970s and 1980s, a similar debate took place among development economists working in Nepal. Geographer Piers Blaikie published extensively on the subject with John Cameron and David Seddon, arguing that simply connecting two rural places with a new road would do little to alleviate poverty without 'radical improvements in basic productivity'.[42] They highlighted some of the adverse impacts of road building in Nepal, such as deepening the income differences between and within regions, and eroding local markets by flooding them with cheap Indian goods. Overall, they argued, road provision tended to accelerate processes that were already in place rather than creating entirely new impacts.

Others noted at the time that there were gendered inequalities produced by roads. For a while, these ideas influenced international development policy in Nepal, but they are now long forgotten. Looking back, nearly twenty years later, Blaikie, Cameron and Seddon reiterate their conclusions from earlier studies of the road-building programme of the time, which 'essentially serve[d] to deepen dependency and underdevelopment rather than alleviate it'.[43] More recently, a study comparing data from two rounds of the Nepal Demographic and Health Survey (2001, 2011) 'finds evidence of reductions in household deprivation' but observes no 'significant effects on the health and education indicators'.[44] The same study argues that roads will not alleviate poverty unless they actually reach 'schools and clinics with properly trained professionals'.[45]

A somewhat more optimistic conclusion was reached in a 2016 literature survey by a team of transport and infrastructure consultants. Reviewing studies from the Global South, they concluded that extending rural road networks typically has 'very strong positive impacts' on employment, income and consumption, and a 'quite strong positive impact' on health take-up, albeit with some negative impacts on the spread of infectious diseases.[46] Meanwhile, there is a 'positive to neutral evidence base' for impacts on other sectors such as agriculture and education.[47]

Over time, these debates come in and out of fashion like other trends in the literature and practice of international development. However, road building has been populist in India for at least a century and probably longer. Through PMGSY, the national government is able to take credit for local development, and in this sense the project has a strong political effect. The style and language of PMGSY reflects the self-presentation of BJP leaders: efficient, result-oriented and transparent. In the process, PMGSY is thus distinguished from previous road-building activity undertaken by the Congress party. In interviews with officials, it was often stressed with utmost pride that PMGSY was the first attempt to construct roads for 'transportation and mobility'. These were new paradigms—previous projects had been aimed at general notions of rural development and employment creation. Meanwhile, and in line with this shift in emphasis, the five-year plans and the Planning Commission have been scrapped in favour of the longer-term stability to be brought about by entrepreneurial and technological innovation.

Another rural road-building project was launched in 2016 under the broad banner of PMGSY: the Road Connectivity Project for Left Wing Extremism Affected Areas. The scheme was primarily oriented towards the mountainous states of the north. The assumptions are telling: 'The roads would also serve the strategic security needs of these areas, which have suffered from historical deficit in terms of infrastructure development, giving rise to Left Wing Extremism'; 'Increased road connectivity in these districts will lead to the exploitation of the latent socio-economic potential and socio-economic upliftment of the people at large, thus weaning away the youth from joining LWE [i.e. left-wing extremism] cadres.'[48]

Elsewhere, one of the most eloquent and troubling speeches I have seen on the effects of rural roads appears in a World Bank promotional film made in Rajasthan and Himachal Pradesh. The narrator describes people in rural India as 'waiting for opportunity'. The road is the 'basic response' to change rural India. These now familiar expressions are followed by the disarming words of villager Heerji Bhai from Meru Ka Guda:

> Until now we were just in a jungle, not knowing anything about others. Now, with the road, slowly we are getting a vision. We'll also become human like you. We were like cattle, knowing nothing. We couldn't get news from the city and knew nothing of city life. Now the road will give us exposure, with people coming and going. There will be contact. Slowly, the village is lighting up and we'll become human. We'll educate our children. They will travel and learn customs and what's happening in the world.[49]

In the preceding segment of the film, the narrator recalls how PMGSY is attracting attention 'due to the many examples of best practice, especially efficient management, good quality and transparency in implementation'. Heerji's words are intercut with close-up shots of yellow machines scraping and levelling the earth. The narrative is intended to be understood as a positive statement of change and improvement. Stand back, however, and Heerji Bhai's statements make for uncomfortable reading. He describes his own inferiority and inhumanity in relation to other invisible and hegemonic ideas, notably the civilising effects of the city.[50] For the areas of leftist extremism, the lack of roads has been seen by the government as a cause of anti-national politics. Likewise, the provision of roads is described as a corrective to draw people away from their bad habits.

The desolation of these statements finds a companion in Dipankar Gupta's thesis that the village has become a redundant economic unit.[51] In his view, the agrarian economy has waned in the face of rising rates of rural–urban migration, and the village has become a 'vicinity'. Along similar lines, others have suggested that the village has become a 'waiting room' for industrial labour markets.[52] Some see this as the development of 'regions' or an 'urban–rural continuum'. Echoing Gupta's 'vicinity' elsewhere in the literature, we also have 'sprawl', 'peri-urban', 'urban fringe', 'rurban' and 'exburbs', and the less familiar 'townizing', 'hermaphroditic' and 'in-between city'.[53]

The bias towards the urban in urban–rural thinking has also been keenly debated in development economics.[54] You will recall at the start of this chapter the unconscious metropolitan view that highways were not for rural people—why should rural people fund them? For anthropologists, this is a bias of culture and knowledge as well as resources, a form of metropolitan elitism so deeply intertwined with the politics of everyday life that it almost appears self-evident and 'natural'.

In fact, the imagined inferiority of the village relative to the city is one of the world's favourite just-so stories, a teleological fairy-tale, which orders both countries and individual life trajectories. It lurks in the storybooks we read to our children about prosperity and progress, and it inheres in classroom textbooks and other forms of authorised national history. The story of how the village became the city and the city became the centre of civilisation runs deeply through the films and novels of popular culture. The road is the key technology and intervention in this monumental edifice. The underlying structure of this thought, however, clearly has a much longer existence, stretching back to the urbane Roman, the

106

metropolis of Greece, the culture of the royal courts, East and West, and the European colonial traditions in India.[55]

This tale of progress is a neat story, which runs deep and explains how the most influential parts of the world came to be so. It has a compelling momentum, giving human life a sense of constant betterment and purpose, and focusing our gaze in certain directions while obscuring others. When we imagine what will happen next, the city only gets more city-like, condensing in form and enchantment: the so-called 'smart city' of the future. The village largely disappears from the story, as the future is given over to the market and mobility. The rural, with its inhumanity and decadent lefties, is networked out of existence. The rural gives way to Ecumenopolis, the continuous worldwide city imagined by Greek planner Constantinos Doxiadis. Heerji Bhai disappears.

... or so a response to PMGSY from outside India might have gone.

Inside India, however, the desire for roading the world is so strong that such abstractions cannot find a place in conversations with roadmen. In India, roadmen want, perhaps not explicitly, Heerji Bhai and his backward and superstitious ways to disappear. Very occasionally, I encountered a metropolitan romantic attitude to the innocence of past rural life. In the provinces, the view was clearer: villages need to change, and roads are the most efficient way of redistributing the grain heap. No missionaries, sages or prophets: roads. In the stories of India's roadmen, the country has reached a tipping point; there is no going back to the time of simple life in isolated villages. India is 'opening up', and peasants are forecast to become mobile producers and consumers.

GANDHI, NEHRU AND THE ROYAL ROAD
THROUGH THE TWENTIETH CENTURY

Before Independence, India's road network was relatively uneven, as building roads had not been a major priority for the British rulers. In this chapter, we will learn how the idea of the motor road was consolidated in India throughout the twentieth century by examining the words of two of the country's most prominent leaders, Mahatma Gandhi and Jawaharlal Nehru. Over the course of Gandhi's and Nehru's lives, roads and motorised vehicles penetrated not only India's landscapes but also its popular consciousness, remaking the boundaries between public and private, utility and leisure, and engineering and finance in the process.

Within this story are two largely forgotten but arresting ideas. First, in the 1930s and perhaps earlier, there was a widely held belief in India that the 'motor age' was already old-fashioned. It was assumed that the technological promise of flight and nuclear energy would propel the country over broken road surfaces, potholes and blocked culverts and into the future.

The second idea is that of the bullock cart as a quintessential symbol of slow-moving and rustic India. In some authoritative state histories, the bullock cart is 'India's first vehicle'. In the 1930s, a model bullock cart was excavated at Harappa, an important Indus

Valley settlement. The archaeological department of undivided Punjab dated the find to 2500 BCE and made a full-size replica. They assumed the model represented a technology that existed at that time, rather than a fantasy of the future. These assumptions about the cart's longevity are eloquently brought together in a government survey of bullock cart technology published in 1979:

> We know today how swiftly the human civilisation has plunged from gasoline propelled engines to nuclear devices and thence from jet age to the space age. Under such a back drop, bullock cart may appear as a queer survivor of the things of antiquity. Yet the first bullock cart must have not been a lesser wonder for the ancient man who lived in the caves. It is still a greater wonder that the bullock cart is surviving in this space age and its popularity has never declined at the least. This reminds us the fact that some elements of our culture and civilisation have lasting values.[1]

Throughout the twentieth century, there was a steady increase in investment in research on the bullock cart's technology and how it interacted with road surfaces. A few decades ago, the archetypal image of the road in India was a single strip of tarmac with wide shoulders of dirt on either side. This was not an accident, nor was it solely the product of constrained fiscal circumstance; rather, it was the culmination of decades of testing materials and designs to accommodate the wide range of speeds at which India was already moving. The shoulders were for bullock carts and passenger traffic, the tarmac for the motor vehicles—at least until the motor vehicle encountered another motor vehicle hurtling in the opposite direction, and one or other driver would yield by bumping off the tarmac and into the dust. In time, as traffic got faster and vehicles more numerous, these roads became dustier and increasingly dangerous for all travellers, both fast and slow.

The bullock cart was beloved as an 'appropriate technology', fitting the 'structure' of India. Gandhi and Nehru thought so, as did some of those who came after them. The bullock cart persisted in the twentieth century not because farmers were conservative and tradition-bound but because political leaders and government policies encouraged them to keep their carts in action. Roads purposefully facilitated the slow speeds and wooden construction of the cart. In the 1980s, attempts were again made to innovate the cart's design and make it more efficient.[2] Technology students up and down the country continued to make prototypes using lightweight and cost-effective materials.

There is no reason to think that the cart has not been used in India for many thousands of years. Today, however, both the certainty of the 1979 government report and the re-engineering of the 1980s look misplaced. The cart has all but gone, while potholes and blocked culverts remain. As the economy of India liberalised, average incomes rose and credit markets expanded, the cart has been rapidly replaced by motor vehicles, though not everywhere and not totally. This is a rémarkable moment in history: a technology that has served the ecosystem of agricultural India for a long time is fast vanishing; in many regions, it has already disappeared.

In the last century, the popular appeal of the motor vehicle has trumped both the age-old bullock cart and the 1930s over-egged promises about the takeover of flight and nuclear. India's motor age has lived on.

The Road to Nagpur

Railways came to India in the nineteenth century and changed the geography of the country by connecting different places and regions. The colonial government seemed to introduce railways for trade rather than passenger demand; one of the first tracks was laid to transport granite for road building in Madras in 1837.[3] Mass passenger trains came later in the century and soon became the principal mode of long-distance transport, with the rapid expansion of rail accompanied by fascinating discussions about the harmful effects on the human body of moving at high speed. Roads in British India were neglected in comparison, often seen as 'feeders' for the rail system and systematically run-down in the second half of the nineteenth century.

Nevertheless, there were many roads in India even during the height of the railway era. During the 1830s, the East India Company rebuilt the ancient Grand Trunk from Calcutta through Delhi to Peshawar. They constructed or upgraded routes connecting Bombay to Pune Camp and Agra to Madras. The company also built local networks of metalled roads for commerce and administration in certain regions. A PWD and civil engineering college were founded to educate surveyors and engineers about building and maintaining roads.[4] Periodically, a 'road–rail controversy' might be followed with plans to think more systematically about India's different forms of transport.

The first cars came to India in around 1900. The main contenders for the prize for the first across the line are a German Mercedes-Benz imported by an English merchant to Bombay and a French De Dion-Bouton owned by the ruler of Patiala in Punjab. Other cars found their way to Calcutta and Madras at about the same time. In 1901, Oldsmobiles were sold to Jamsetji Tata, founder of the Tata Group; Rustam Cama, an attorney; and Kavasji Wadia, who ran the famous Bombay Garage. Motoring became associated with British merchants, Indian urban elites and the rulers of the Princely States, many of whom went on to hoard large numbers of luxurious motorcars.[5] Bombay had its first taxicabs by 1903, and there were around 1,000 cars in the city by 1910. In the inter-war years, foreign manufacturing plants were established, including Ford and General Motors. Strong unions and unreliable supply chains prevented them from producing their planned numbers of vehicles.

With rising numbers of car imports after the First World War came a clearer demand for motorable roads. During the Second World War, the importance of establishing an 'indigenous automobile industry' became apparent given the disruption of supplies of machinery, parts, fuel and expertise. Thus, during the 1940s, Premier Automobiles Ltd (PAL), Hindustan Motors (HM), Mahindra & Mahindra and Standard Motors set up plants.[6] The car in India, as in most other parts of the world, had gone from zero to a feeding frenzy in a matter of four decades. Until this time, systematic road-building initiatives had been local rather than national in scope.

Between the wars, the government commissioned a Road Development Committee, also known as the Jayakar Committee after its chair. Their report of 1928 influentially outlined the history of roads in the country from antiquity to the present.[7] Indeed, this chronology of key moments in road building and policy set the standard, tone and structure for subsequent scholarship, institutional structures and language about roads. M.R. Jayakar, a lawyer from Bombay and first vice chancellor of the University of Poona, advised that road development ought to become a 'national interest', because the need was beyond the capacity of local bodies. He recommended the establishment of a Central Road Fund (CRF) supported by an additional tax on fuel (a 'cess'), as well as the formation of a semi-official body to pool knowledge and research on roads. Although the Depression of the 1930s led to the abandonment of a nascent plan for a national trunk road system, Jayakar's ideas were carried forward into the formation of the IRC in 1934.[8]

The IRC promoted 'scientific approaches' to improve earth, cement and concrete roads, and its early sessions concerned the latest developments in road design and technology, with teams of engineers sent to Britain and the United States for training and observation. Annual meetings repeatedly drew together engineers from across India, who consolidated knowledge, produced codes of practice and standardised units of measurement and specifications for road construction and signage. A testing site was established at Alipore, Bengal, to develop surface technologies for use in different climates and conditions.

The road surface was becoming a key focus of Indian roadmen. Although road building was closely allied at the time to increasing the efficiency of agricultural production, the new roads built for cars were ill suited for bullocks. For a while, cart traffic was discouraged due to its slow pace and the damage wreaked on the road surface. However, because of sheer numbers, it quickly became apparent that the unmetalled road and the bullock cart had to be incorporated into new road designs. The use of solid wheels on earth roads had been studied extensively in America, but nowhere had attention been given to the thin, hard, iron tyres of India's bullock carts. The novel challenge was to design a road at reasonable cost that would accommodate both the cart at lumber and the car at speed. The result was the quintessential twentieth-century Indian road: a raised strip of metalled material with wide earthen shoulders.[9] In this way, early concerns about the road and a political will to find solutions led to an engineering preoccupation or path dependency in road design that has outlasted need.

The watershed moment in the history of India's roads came a few years before Independence. The Nagpur Plan of 1943 established targets for national and state road building, notably a requirement for 16 km of road per 100 sq. km of land. It also classified national and provincial highways, major and minor district roads and village roads. Significantly, the engineers in Nagpur consolidated Jayakar's recommendation that road building should be a national interest rather than a provincial pursuit.[10] The course was set for roads to become matters and measures of government.

In Nagpur, the heady story of India's roads would collide with that of Hindu nationalism. The city plays an important role in the nationalist imagination as the centre of Akhand Bharat, greater and undivided India, a civilisational claim on territory that sometimes stretches as far as East Africa and South East Asia. Some nationalists campaign for the restoration of this lost glory, and arguably, the Look and Act East policy (Chapter 3) is a manifestation of this underlying ambition. Nagpur was also the birthplace of K.B. Hedgewar, founder of the Hindu nationalist RSS paramilitary group. In subsequent decades, the ideas developed by the Nagpur nationalists were to become mainstream, eventually taking Narendra Modi's BJP to power in the twenty-first century. Their ideology offered an alternative to the political dynasty of the dominant Congress party, represented in different ways by both Mahatma Gandhi and Jawaharlal Nehru.

Mahatma Gandhi

On 12 March 1930, Mahatma Gandhi, accompanied by a large group of Congress volunteers, embarked on a twenty-four-day march from the Sabarmati Ashram in Ahmedabad to the coastal town of Dandi in protest against the British monopoly and taxation of the salt trade. Along the route, swelling numbers of travellers and listeners gathered to hear his speeches. At the coast, Gandhi picked up some rock salt and famously announced: 'With this, I am shaking the foundations of the British Empire', thus launching the *satyagraha* (civil disobedience movement).[11]

Gandhi used the Salt March to spread a message; the spectacle drew crowds along the way as his collective movement gained momentum on the road. His staged action evoked traditions of pilgrimage and journeying, which were often also about self-discipline, sacrifice and the realisation of goals. Roads and journeys became integral backdrops for his protest. Drawing on the symbolic power of these motifs, Nehru described the march:

> And today the pilgrim marches onward on his long trek. Staff in hand, he goes along the dusty roads of Gujarat, clear-eyed and firm of step, with his faithful band trudging along behind him. Many a journey he has undertaken in the past, many a weary road traversed. But longer than any that have gone before is this last journey of his, and many are the obstacles in his way. ... It is a long journey, for the goal is the independence of India and the ending of the exploitation of her millions.[12]

Gandhi was born in 1869 in Gujarat, where he was educated, before studying law in London. Between 1893 and 1914, he practised law in South Africa, before returning to India. Over the course of his life, roads—as well as more general ideas of movement—transformed dramatically in India. As we have seen, a coherent and planned road network was not a priority during the colonial period, and roads played second fiddle to railways. Gandhi was born some three decades before the first motorised vehicles came to India. When he was assassinated in 1948, roads were under central government control and carried 300,000 vehicles.

Accompanying these developments were shifts in Gandhi's own understandings of what roads were and could be. His early references to roads are from a time when motorisation was embryonic. Then, he was thinking through morality and religion: the road was a path, the path of truth. As the decades came and went, his rhetoric developed to see roads as another instance of colonial oppression; however, he was also aware that roads eased pain and hardship. As the twentieth century matured, roads become techniques for government and, in many ways, they came to stand as an index of national development.

115

As these changes were taking place, Gandhi, along with others in India, learned the vocabulary of both road construction and freedom. He used roads as common metaphors for delicate problems, notably religious difference. He was torn between the development that roads bring, the servitude that comes with them, and their provocative association with personal refinement and choice. His critics saw him as backward-looking, perhaps misunderstanding his idiosyncratic views.

Gandhi varied his message on roads over time and before different audiences. On occasion, he spoke in favour of improving the roads— not to carry more cars, he said, but to ease the passage of bullock carts. As is well known, Gandhi's modernity contained elements of traditional India rooted in the idea of the village.[13] He had personally endured the discomfort of bad roads and understood how unpopular a universal argument against road improvements would be. During the 1920s, however, Gandhi started to describe roads as instruments of oppression to be avoided, his view becoming more trenchant in later years. From this perspective, the road was an element of a colonial system of production and extraction that had enchanted India into its own oppression.

Others have noted the road in Gandhi's writing: 'The road metaphor carries with it the idea of a destination. Roads both lead somewhere and never end … A road is a promise, an opportunity, and a challenge, a way out, and a way forward.'[14] Gandhi often used road language of varying complexity to represent personal and collective journeys in terms of struggle and morality, just as Nehru did in his description of the Salt March cited above. However, in Gandhi's speech and writing, the road is more. On the one hand, it is a space that makes visible racial and caste inequality—a clear stage on which symbolic and structural violence is enacted in full view. On the other hand, caring for the road had the potential to bring people together in collective labour, so that by improving their villages and environment, they also improved themselves and thus overcame the empire. As these two aspects of roads are brought together, the metaphorical and the material become key devices for non-violent problem-solving and resistance.

Gandhi's changing use of road language was presumably unconscious and directly reflected the increasing importance and institutionalisation of roads in India over the course of his life. His promotion of *swaraj* (self-rule) was dependent on travelling the country, and thus he experienced first-hand the hardships of the road and the inequalities of mobility. But even as he travelled, Gandhi called for a way of life that was in some key respects against mobility: self-sufficiency in the village, localism. These tensions and ambiguities in Gandhi's speech and thinking can tell us about the shifting meaning of roads in India's national and political consciousness in the first half of the twentieth century.

***

In 1907, while he was living in South Africa, Gandhi drew on the positive imagery of a 'path' linking truth, morality, civilisation and progress:

> Besides, it is a rule of ideal morality that it is not enough to follow the trodden path. We ought to follow the path which we know to be true, whether it is familiar or unfamiliar to us. In other words, when we know a particular path to be the right one, we should set out on it without fear. We can progress only if we observe the laws of morality in this way. That is why true morality, true civilization and true progress are always to be found together.[15]

Gandhi refined his idea of the path to truth over the years, contrasting it with other paths: '[W]e cannot achieve real *swarajya* [self-rule], by following the path of evil.'[16] Elsewhere: '[War's] path of glory is foul with the passions of lust, and red with the blood of murder. This is not the pathway to our goal.'[17] The moral path was to be one of sacrifice and determination: '[A]t long last a time does come when men begin to tread the path of morality consciously, deliberately with a determined will ... ready to sacrifice themselves.'[18] Gandhi's path also offered way-finding certainty: 'He who habitually follows the path of truth will know the right way at the crucial moment.'[19]

As early as 1911, the path had evolved into a road replete with engineered features:

> The first need of a man lost in a thick wood at night is light. He may then bide without fear till he finds the road. When he does

find it, he will take it straightaway. If he finds any institutions on the way, he will use them as bridges for crossing rivers and streams. If the bridges are in disrepair, he will examine them with the aid of the light and call attention to the cracks and other defects.[20]

As the footpath began to give way to the motor road, the technical language of road building as an expression of mastery entered Gandhi's rhetoric. In 1922, he described the task of improving communal relations between Muslims and Hindus in these terms: 'There still remain in our paths many deserts to be crossed, many forests, valleys and hills. The road has yet to be cleared, metalled and rolled.'[21] Here, the road is a metaphor for progress made in trying circumstances, the path itself becoming a guide through unfamiliar terrain, a symbol of possibility and hope.

As was common for the period, Gandhi also evoked the symbolism of the historic 'royal road', an ancient trail that was improved by the Persian king Darius the Great in the fifth century BCE. Having travelled the road, the Ancient Greek historian Herodotus wrote in his *Histories*: 'There is nothing in the world that travels faster than these Persian couriers.'[22] For Gandhi, the royal road stood for the religious dimensions of the path to truth: 'The royal road is the doing of one's appointed duty to the best of one's ability and the dedication of all service to God';[23] 'The royal road is for us to keep ourselves engaged in doing the duty that lies before us, and to be patient and hopeful that God will solve spiritual problems.'[24] Unfortunately, 'There is no royal road to the control of passions. Constant endeavour and constant waiting upon God are the two things needed.'[25]

Much later, in the last decade of his life, Gandhi returned to the road to illustrate the challenges of *swaraj*: '[T]he road to *swaraj* is steep and narrow. There are many slippery ascents and many deep chasms. They have all to be negotiated with unfaltering step before we can reach the summit and breathe the fresh air of freedom.'[26]

***

One of Gandhi's first consequential mentions of roads dates from 1906 during his time in South Africa, where he learned that roads were not always for everyone. He wrote extensively on the inequities of the British law that made it illegal for Indians to walk on footpaths: '[N]o Indian has the right to use any municipal foot-path, and may, at the will of the first policeman, be curtly ordered into the middle of the road.'[27] It is quite possible that these experiences reminded Gandhi of his childhood in Saurashtra, where untouchability was practised strictly.[28] These racialised legal frameworks codified exclusion and inequality and translated these codes into unequal rights to the road.

The question of access arose again in 1925, when Gandhi campaigned to open up roads, temples and other public spaces in Travancore in the south of India to Dalits (as former 'untouchables' were known). Gandhi wrote: 'The road must be opened. It has got to be opened. But that will be the beginning of the end. The end is to get all such roads throughout Travancore to be opened.'[29] In 1934, the government resolved to open all public roads and wells to all regardless of caste.

A few years later, roads also served to capture the challenges and opportunities facing village India in the struggle against colonialism. Rural development and road building were straightforwardly linked in a letter written by Gandhi in August 1941: 'Some attempt should be made to construct *pucca* roads in the rural areas. Rural development can be brought about at a very low cost if the vilagers [*sic*] lend a helping hand.'[30]

Playing on themes of hope, progress and challenge, in 1925 Gandhi described the roads in his native Gujarat. Local councils were gradually passing to men from the Congress party, which Gandhi believed would lead to an improvement in both roads and education. He thought the region's roads 'unsatisfactory' and 'dusty beyond description'. He noted: 'Villages have practically no roads. This is a great hardship both to human beings and cattle.'[31] Gandhi suggested that infrastructural growth was bound up with human development to the extent that the 'economic programme and moral progress go together'.[32] This integration of the moral and the material was a central part of Gandhi's *nai talim*, or 'new education'. *Nai talim* was constituted in opposition to the colonial education system and sought to establish a new social order grounded in dignified manual labour and the principles of non-violence.

During his *satyagraha* campaign in Champaran, Bihar, Gandhi linked his ideas about education with the possibilities offered by communal road building in villages: 'Instructions will ... be given to grown-up people ... about the advantages of joint action for the promotion of communal welfare, such as the making of village roads proper, the sinking of wells, etc.'[33] 'Bread labour', as Gandhi termed this form of work, was just that: labour for bread and no more. It was an idea developed through engagement with both the work of Tolstoy and John Ruskin's notion of the value inherent in craftwork and manual labour.[34] Gandhi conceived of bread labour as consisting in the sorts of community work that he believed were needed to renew the fabric of the Indian village, including its roads. This concept of labour premised on collaborative effort was key to Gandhi's ideas about cooperation and, by extension, the political power of civil disobedience.

Five years later, in a piece addressing village roads in 1930, Gandhi focuses on the potential that road-building projects hold for fostering an ethos not only of community but also of self-sufficiency, an attribute necessary for overcoming both colonial dependency and the dominance of the city. Writing in opposition to policies of urban industrialisation, Gandhi proposed a programme of cooperation at the village level that he believed would result in the alignment of individual and social interests. For him, '[t]owns exist to exploit the villages. The city culture does not therefore fit into the framework of villages.'[35]

In 1925, Gandhi visited Kutch, now a district in western Gujarat but then a Princely State. He was not fully welcomed and was asked difficult questions. Gandhi reports: 'One gentleman asked me in all seriousness whether I preferred tarred roads or cutcha [rough, unpaved] ones like those in Kutch?' Gandhi took the opportunity to clarify his position. His critics were finding it increasingly easy to dismiss his politics as 'backward'. Gandhi thought that railways or motorcars were not essential for human civilisation; however, the railways had come to stay in India and there was no point opposing them. He continued: 'I am for all roads being tarred ... In fact, tarred roads enable us to practise our *dharma* [religious duty]. How much suffering do uneven roads cause to animals? I also look forward to improvements in bullock-carts as well.'[36]

On the same tour, Gandhi said: 'Good roads are the mark of a well-organised government.'[37] The roads in Kutch were terrible, and his sideways remark was aimed critically at the rulers. 'It is the duty of both the ruler and the subjects to build good roads.'[38] 'Building good roads should be easy in Kutch, as the distances are short … In the first instance, the people should place this request before the ruler.'[39] The experience of travelling in Kutch gave Gandhi food for thought, as the tour left him weaker, lighter and shaken, 'owing to the very bad roads'. Looking back on his journey, he reflected: '[N]obody had bargained for the nature of the toil that travelling in carts, on rough roads, would mean for my dilapidated limbs.'[40] His original plan had been to 'holiday' in Kutch to recover after a long period of imprisonment and subsequent fasting.

Experience had shown Gandhi that rural roads were in poor shape and hard to traverse for men and for the cattle that drew carts. Gandhi saw that pulling heavy carts on poor roads meant drawing double the load. In his words: 'Butter is given away with whey and, moreover, the giver is branded a slattern.'[41] He reasoned that if roads were metalled, the wasted energy would be freed up. What, then, was to be done for these miserable roads? According to Gandhi, if the spirit of cooperation prevailed among the inhabitants, villagers could build metalled roads with little expense and add to the wealth of the village.[42]

***

Gandhi saw the poor condition of village India's roads as a reflection of the widespread experience of human suffering, particularly that of children who 'are cared for no better than the roads'.[43] His broader point was that the care and pride taken in maintaining the fabric of the village, including roads, was bound up with the nurturance and education of humanity. Moreover, the social process of renewing the roads, whereby each and every villager participates according to their capacity, could be seen as an act of sacrifice that fosters self-reliance and community spirit. In the context of British colonial rule, such a narrative drawing together community with the aims of human progress and social development spoke compellingly to the struggle for independence and self-rule.

Over the next few years, Gandhi made many speeches in which he attempted to motivate people to action by highlighting the poor condition of roads and water tanks. In Gaya in 1927, he told the crowd that he had 'never before seen such dirty roads in any part of India', going on to say that proper care for shared space was bound up with liberation.[44] He expressed similar ideas in Bardoli in August 1928: 'Do we want the *swaraj* of barbarism, freedom to live like pigs in a pigsty without let or hindrance from anybody? Or do we want the *swaraj* of orderliness in which every man and everything is in his or its proper place?'[45] Gandhi had motored from Wankaner to reach Bardoli, and he complained that 'the journey well nigh finished me. The road was so wretched.' 'Surely', he said, 'the Government cannot prevent us from repairing our roads if we want to.'[46]

During a visit to London in 1931, Gandhi expressed in an interview with *John Bull* magazine: 'I would build new roads—fine roads, that would benefit both man and beast. I picture the new India as filled with linked villages, happy in their industries.'[47] Yet even as Gandhi spoke about the positive transformative potential of well-kept roads linking India's communities, he also identified that, when connected to what he deemed the empty 'progress' of Western industrialisation, roads were possessed of a unique capacity to alienate humanity. Gandhi believed that economic progress with a focus on industry and cities was antagonistic to 'real progress' and was taking the country downhill, away from the path to truth. This position extended to transport and mobility:

It is not possible to conceive gods inhabiting a land which is made hideous by the smoke and the din of null chimneys and factories and whose roadways are traversed by rushing engines dragging numerous cars crowded with men mostly who know not what they are after, who are often absent-minded, and whose tempers do not improve by being uncomfortably packed like sardines in boxes and finding themselves in the midst of utter strangers who would oust them if they could and whom they would in their turn oust similarly. I refer to these things because they are held to be symbolical of material progress.[48]

Gandhi also regarded the growing number of motor vehicles in India as an imposition that was linked to the British imperial regime. To students in Surat, he said of colonial infrastructure:

> No matter how many metalled roads they build and what peace prevails in the country—we would rather have rivers of blood flow. Nay, even if we had to go without railways and ships and even if the administration were to break down, I would rather prefer that to the present condition.[49]

Similarly, during an interview in Lausanne in 1931, he was asked about public works and his ideas of local self-government. He replied that the Grand Trunk Road provided facility for millions of travellers and that the colonial government had built well-equipped hospitals and grand palaces for schools. However, the whole apparatus was crushing the nation, 'like the snake with a jewel but with poison fangs'. Gandhi concluded that British rule in India had stunted the nation and that 'the gentlemanly way' was to reject any of its privileges.[50] A decade or so later, he was more pointed: 'Hospitals, roads, railways are probably good in themselves but when they are instruments of evil they are to be shunned. They become snares.'[51]

Gandhi's agitation about inequality extended to the car. Visiting Suri in August 1925, he recounted his unease at being driven along a road with rows of poor people sitting on either side waiting for their meal: 'I felt ashamed and, had I not been afraid of being discourteous, I would have got down then and there and run away. What kind of an arrogant servant of the poor was this who rode in comfort in a car between rows of people eating?'[52] At Vizagapatam in 1933, as an illustration of inequality, Gandhi again invoked the image of his car passing along a road where Dalits had gathered to eat: 'Just imagine how you and I would feel if some insolent person drove his car through the road where we were taking our meals.'[53]

Gandhi thought carts should move at a natural speed, without motors. In correspondence with the industrialist Ishverbhai S. Amin of Baroda, Gandhi discussed the relative merits of the bullock cart over the motor lorry within the village sphere, concluding that the former was a productive part of a village agricultural system, the latter not.[54] In 1934, he wondered out loud whether the 'motorcar age' should be no more as India entered the 'aeroplane age'. Poignantly, he wrote: 'But all this rushing about is only for a while. Our legs, however, will remain as long as mankind survives. Those who are content with the natural speed of their legs remaining unimpaired will win in the end.'[55] By 1946, he had refined the message:

> You must make it a rule to prefer walking to using a conveyance. Motorcar is not for the millions. You will therefore shun it. Million[s] cannot afford even train journey. Their world is their village. It is a very small thing but if you faithfully adhere to this rule it will transform your entire life and fill it with a sweetness that natural simplicity carries with it.[56]

These words resonate with ideas of today's environmentalists, although, of course, the connection between burning fossil fuels and climate change had not been made at the time, and Gandhi's concerns were local. For him, cleanliness and order in the village were ways of generating a moral community with the resolve to deny colonial entrapment.

Gandhi's aim was freedom for India. While roads might provide benefits for the village community, they did so as conduits for a mode of economy that was exploitative and created dependency, and hence they were tools of colonial oppression. At the same time, his gentlemanly ways of non-engagement with the poison fangs of the viper rested on being able to travel and take his message to the people. His body was punished and pounded by bad roads, bumps, ruts, holes, dangerous river crossings, standing water and mud.

Gandhi's vision of India was pro-poor and pro-rural. He believed this way of life was part of the 'structure' of India and that to undo this, in part or wholly, with roads and urban- and industrial-oriented policy would be to sap happiness and satisfaction from the village and replace it with dependencies. After his death, his view of rural India had influence in post-colonial set-ups when village-level governance structures were implemented. Various community development schemes were created, which included road-building activities managed by village councils. However, as the decades have passed, the aim of rural road building has not been to connect villages to other villages as Gandhi had wished, but to connect villages to the highway network to 'open up' the village to the national economy. Today's roadmen, riding a wave of backlash against Gandhi, believe this to be a wholly positive course of action. Gandhi would be quite undone by the logic of those who run India today and would no doubt organise a non-cooperation movement with the aim of freedom.

Before we get to the roadmen of today, we will consider Nehru's ideas about roads, which, like Gandhi's, were holistic. To Nehru, roads were never simply engineered materials and landscapes but rather part of a system. At Independence, Nehru's government formed the road institutions that made modern India. He pushed ahead with networking the nation, building roads for industrial and military purposes. In this, he perhaps felt as if he had betrayed Gandhi, for there are signs in his speeches and writings that he was aware that things could have been done differently. He chose a state-led industrial path for India, and on occasion he might have doubted the decision. Given Gandhi's own views, there is some irony that under Nehru, tens, if not hundreds, of roads were named after him—Mahatma Gandhi Marg, M.G. Road and so on—in the decades after Independence.

Jawaharlal Nehru

Born in 1889, around a decade before the first motorcars arrived in India, Jawaharlal Nehru was a prominent leader in the independence movement with Gandhi and later became India's first prime minister, a position he held until his death in 1963. His government created a mixed-socialist economy with strong planning and PWDs, looking to both the USSR and the United States for guidance. Roads had been central to the work of his government, both as tools of development and for military and strategic purposes, especially in the Himalayas and north-east as India and China redefined their relationship.

Independence brought the Planning Commission, and with it the 5-year and 20-year plan. In all, ten quinquennial plans were implemented between 1951 and 2015, while the 20-year Nagpur Plan of 1943 was followed by Bombay 1961, Lucknow 1981, and a Road Development Plan in 2001 called 'Vision 2021'. The Nagpur Plan set the terms of the debate, suggesting a rapid expansion of the road network was required and inducting Jayakar's presentation of roads as sets of numbers and targets. Consequently, the first two 5-year plans (1951–61) set objectives for a vast project of road building, including the construction of 1,200 miles of 'missing links' in the highway system by an all-India cadre of engineers.[57] The third 5-year plan (1961–6) developed national highways to connect centres of population, with the World Bank extending a development credit for highway projects in West Bengal, Bihar, Orissa and Maharashtra.

In 1959, the second 20-year plan (1961–81) was produced, popularly known as the 'Bombay Plan'.[58] The main aim was to improve communication in rural areas; all villages were to be within 4 miles of a metalled road. At the 1959 Indian Roads Congress in Hyderabad, Nehru expressed hope that the engineers could find good local materials for the construction of much-needed village roads.[59] The Village Road Development Cooperative Scheme started in 1962 and aimed to develop feeder roads on a cooperative basis that would connect villages to markets or the nearest government road.[60]

Much of what Nehru had learned as a younger man during the independence movement influenced his ideas when in government. In the late 1930s, Nehru had outlined a vision for shared village labour in road building and other community development projects that somewhat mirrored Gandhi's views. Nehru saw this kind of work, particularly when undertaken by students living in cities, as a form of political education and civic duty that would offer young people training and an insight into the reality of the challenges that India faced. In 1952, as part of the first 5-year plan, the Planning Commission proposed that all 'medically fit' students between the ages of 18 and 22 should undertake a form of national service focused on community work, including road construction, irrigation and other kinds of manual work.[61]

***

In 1961, Nehru addressed a seminar on road transport organised by ECAFE in Madras, a body established after the war as part of the global reconstruction initiative. The seminar was part of the nascent plan to build a pan-Asian network of highways (Chapter 3). There, some three years before his death, Nehru reflected on what he had learned about roads and India over the decades through politics, his engagement with Gandhi and questions of rural and national development. In his clipped and epic style, he told the engineers and technocrats how the tradition of travel in India was an old one, chiefly connected with pilgrimage. The city around them, Madras, was studded with famous temples and places of pilgrimage:

> [I]t is quite extraordinary how they travelled over this land and thereby gave a sense of unity to the land. It was divided politically into kingdoms, but nevertheless, there was the basic unity. And persons who went from the south to Banaras and the Himalayas felt at home there more or less.

Nehru observed: 'All of us, of course, have something to do with roads.' For him, roads evoked modern amenities and methods, but also 'the caravan routes in the old days, when people crossed continents by these routes and by various means of transport, possibly camels'. He continued, marvelling at the genius of the person who had 'discovered' the wheel: 'I imagine that a very interesting and fascinating book can be written on the development of civilisation based on the development of road transport.' For Nehru, roads were good to think with, not only as metaphors or as development problems, but as a way of asking profound questions about the organisation of society: 'I find it difficult to imagine a country which is without roads now.'

In 1958, Nehru had visited Bhutan, and the experience lived with him. He found it extraordinary that three-quarters of the boys he met in a school there had never come across a wheel or a road (though they had seen aircraft). In Nehru's words: 'I was thrown back to a previous period of history in regard to transport by going to such places.' He was clear that the boys were not primitive, nor were they ill, poor or uneducated. They simply lived in a world with no motorised land transportation, suggesting that

127

alternatives to networking Asia with roads were practical if not imaginable possibilities.

The Bhutan experience made Nehru wistful for what perhaps could have been. Throughout the 1950s, he had repeatedly expressed nostalgia for the old ways, as buses and lorries, 'extremely ugly things', took over the roads.[62] However, it was now 1961, and India was changing fast. Nehru talked about the remarkable growth of motor transport and the constant demand for more and more. With understatement, he added: '[W]e have a large number of people living in this country and they are fond of going about.'[63] Like many things Nehru said decades ago, the sentiment would still be understood today.

Nehru had been concerned with roads from his early days in the 1920s in Allahabad, where he campaigned for better maintenance and financing of roads against the broad backdrop of city planning. This gave him exposure to the budgetary limitations of municipal governance and practical experience of the effects of increasing volumes of motorised traffic; as a result, he advocated for experimentation with materials so that a cost-effective and durable alternative could be found to metalling roads. Nehru was disturbed by politicians promising roads to the electorate as substitutes for a thought-out programme of political and social action. He also saw how the prioritisation of urban infrastructure over rural development entrenched existing social inequalities.[64]

As the freedom struggle gathered momentum in the 1920s and 1930s, Nehru deployed road imagery to talk about politics, likening independence to a road leading towards a future of freedom and opportunity. He worked closely with Gandhi, and some of his early metaphors resemble those of his mentor. Political junctures, where important ideological and practical decisions had to be made, became crossroads where comrades might have to part ways without rancour or ill will.[65] Like Gandhi, Nehru used the road in a positive way to emphasise tolerance, cooperation and equality, with the metaphorical road giving a sense of direction towards ideas of independence. He described India as being 'on the road to progress'.[66] 'Under the leadership of Mahatma Gandhi, the Congress and the country will march ahead again along the hard path of suffering and sacrifice which leads to freedom.'[67] He also used more elaborate road metaphors: 'The shackles of alien rule have been thrown off and the country has attained political freedom which is only a milestone on the road to progress and not the end of the journey.'[68]

After Independence, and Gandhi's death, Nehru's tone unsurprisingly changed as he began to speak about the challenges ahead. Laying the groundwork for the ongoing struggle for self-determination, Nehru used road and transport imagery to talk about the economic and industrial development needed 'to maintain our freedom and progress on the road to prosperity'.[69] He described how '[t]he road to industrialisation is being cleared removing all obstacles from the way'.[70] While for Gandhi the 'royal road' had been the path to truth, Nehru spoke about the 'royal road of socialism' that would lead India to progress.[71]

***

In 1952, Nehru inaugurated the CRRI in New Delhi, an institution leading experimentation in new techniques for building roads that remains at the forefront of road research today. Nehru spoke passionately at the institute's opening: 'I want you to understand the spirit behind these laboratories. The modern temples or mosques are these science laboratories where there is a search for truth and for the upliftment of mankind.' Nehru expounded the importance of the road network for alleviating poverty and furthering the cause of national development. He paid particular attention to rural areas, just as he had done in Allahabad, and called for the creation of roads designed to accommodate bullock carts. Like Gandhi, Nehru had a vision of India in which its first vehicle would be planned for, rather than planned away.[72]

In the same address, Nehru admitted: '[T]he more I travel in India, the more I am convinced that the most urgent priority should be given to the construction of roads because we cannot reach anywhere without roads.' He reflected on how the British had built roads to the foothills of the Himalayas to escape the summer heat but had not provided facilities for the population in the hilly areas. The British had also connected the cities but ignored the rural areas.

In Nehru's view, the aim should be to 'knit' together the villages all over India with roads.[73]

At the end of 1953, some decades after Gandhi made a similar point, Nehru attacked the idea that road transport was the path to modernity in a speech for the Associated Chambers of Commerce and Industry entitled 'Bullock-cart, Motor Lorry, Jet Plane and Atomic Energy': 'May I point out that even the motor lorry, however useful, is rather out of date? You do not refer to modern economy as the motor lorry economy. Modern economy is symbolised by the jet plane and atomic energy.' Nehru was interested in technology, but he saw that development in India required careful thought: 'I cannot superimpose a fifth storey on a house without laying the foundation, and building the first, second, third and fourth floors.' The problem in India was not the false division between a bullock-cart economy and modernity, but rather how to have the 'latest techniques so that they fit in with the structure of India'.[74]

***

Both before and after Independence, the way that Nehru got to know India was through travel. As well as helping him to understand more about life in the countryside for India's peasants, travel in rural India also taught Nehru about the power of roads as sites of protest and populism. In 1931, ditches were dug across the road leading to Baraipur in the United Provinces as villagers attempted to prevent him from hearing evidence about assaults on women.[75] The roadside was also an important space for political rallying, an issue that came to the forefront in the 1936–7 election campaign, during which time Nehru estimated that he travelled 22,500 miles (36,000 km) by road, coming into contact with several million voters along the way.[76] Nehru realised that limited road networks had an effect on election outcomes, writing in 1937 about how Congress's electorate was dispersed, rural and thus harder to reach than the urban populations who voted for the Muslim League.[77] The more roads, he reasoned, that his government built, the more people it could reach for political support. He did not seem to believe that building more roads was a royal road to more votes for the Muslim League.

After Partition, political instability led to high levels of violence and contestation on roads across the region, as millions were displaced and military forces on both sides moved in. Throughout this period, Nehru wrote to his allies and friends about the unfolding crisis in Punjab and Kashmir and its relationship to roads. These years underlined the strategic importance of the road network, and throughout the rest of Nehru's career, he wrote extensively about the connections between transport links, security and military strategy and their significance for India's relationship to Pakistan, as well as to China, Tibet, Bhutan and Nepal. The Border Roads Development Board (now the Border Roads Organisation) was established in 1960 in response to controversy around the Ladakh road near the border with Pakistan, and Nehru initially chaired the meetings himself.

The ways that natural disasters impacted roads and other infrastructure contained further important lessons for Nehru. Over the course of his political life, there were a number of catastrophic events in India. Nehru visited Bihar after the Nepal–India earthquake of 1934 and saw the problems caused to relief efforts by damaged roads.[78] He also visited the sites of an earthquake in Kutch in 1956 and of flooding in Orissa in 1960 to offer condolences and reassurance and oversee relief works. In these places of destruction, he saw that the work of roads is most visible when the road is broken and does not function. After an earthquake in Assam in 1950, he saw how the highways had been 'torn and twisted to take on an unpassable, strange and vertically wavy appearance'.[79] Nehru sent the army to rebuild the roads and bridges, a course of action that remains popular in India today in the aftermath of disaster.[80]

The politics of names arose in 1948, when Nehru warned against cheapening Gandhi's legacy by widely renaming streets and other public places after him. For Nehru, this mass memorialisation was crass, as it required no awareness of or dedication to Gandhi's fundamental teachings. Nonetheless, Nehru recognised the general value of renaming public space after Independence and, in 1955, he advocated the gradual change of road names in New Delhi to mark the dawning of the post-colony: Great Place to Vijay Chowk, Kingsway to Rajpath and Queensway to Jan Path. Responding to other suggestions, Nehru also felt it quite absurd to call Connaught

Circus 'Ashoka Sthan', not wishing to associate the great emperor Ashoka with something as mundane as a market.[81] The issue of road names also related to signage, and in July 1958 Nehru issued guidance to chief ministers that road signs be written in both English and the state language, thus easing comprehensibility for tourists and other travellers. In his request, he emphasised that despite their distinctions, for example in language, states must remain cognisant of their role in a cohesive India.[82]

***

In 1960, Transport Minister Paramasivan Subbarayan wrote to Nehru about establishing a highways corporation. The Durgapur Expressway in West Bengal was congested and the government had insufficient funds for an upgrade. There had been a discussion about raising a loan for these projects from 'private capitalists' or the finance ministry's Life Insurance Corporation. Subbarayan wanted to keep Nehru informed, because he knew that the prime minister did not like the private sector taking over anything already in the public domain. His suggestion was to set up a government corporation to control the highways and to let it levy tolls so that the loan could be paid off over 20 years. On the whole, Nehru thought this was a good idea.[83]

Nehru died in 1964, but the idea of establishing state-owned corporations to manage road arrangements with the private sector lived on through the troubled 1970s and into later planning periods, going on to blossom most powerfully in the last decades of the twentieth century. Nehru himself was perhaps moving out of time, his socialist values ageing in the glare of new headlights.

Roads, for Nehru, were a public good. From as early as 1933, he outlined his socialist vision for a transition from private roads and amenities to a wide range of infrastructure funded and maintained by the state, catering to the material, social and cultural needs of the people. Even into the third 5-year plan, there was a live debate about the relative merits of public and private investment in infrastructure. Nehru had a favourite speech on the subject, which he gave at least three times between 1959 and 1960. The most refined version was presented in Delhi to the inaugural UNESCO regional seminar on

Public Administration Problems of New and Rapidly Growing Towns in Southern Asia:

> Call it what you like, communalisation, socialisation it is; in older times almost everything in the city was private, roads were private, bridges were private, everything was private. Gradually these things, these public utilities become, come under public ownership, they are socialised; and I think it is a measure of the growth of the city, the progress of the city or town, how far its utilities have been socialised, and there are so many of them, always in your parks, in your lighting, in your cleaning and your schools, and how many things go on. All these are in an enlightened community under social ownership, not of private ownership.[84]

TOYOTA TO TESLA
ROAD BUILDING IS PRIVATISED

T.R.S. Kynnersley was a well-known road engineer in Western India throughout the 1940s. He worked believing that better roads brought better vehicles and better vehicles required better roads. He saw this as a cycle of progress that would lead to the situation seen in 'advanced countries', where roads were like 'billiard tables' passing 'over hills and dales' (he presumably had in mind a country where there were dales) and 'bringing education, health, wealth and happiness to the countryside'.[1] He was not alone in this vision, and we have seen how the first half of the twentieth century ushered in the motor road in India and intensified mobility. The motor road crept like a vine into the country, as bicycles, motor scooters, trucks, buses and cars increasingly became routine parts of life.

Many routes in India are of course much older, perhaps ancient, and tied to sophisticated ideas of security, trade and communication. Some parts of the country have their own road-building epics, in which the visionary, the pioneer or the jilted lover decrees to build roads in pursuit of their dreams or to keep fear at bay. Kingdoms of old had their own construction techniques, measures of distance and ingenious systems of extracting revenue.[2] The journey is established in the pious traditions of renunciation and pilgrimage. The narratives of religious books entwine geography and movement with the lives and struggles of heroes and heroines. The idea of *yatra* or pilgrimage is widely understood to mean that the journey itself is as important as the destination, and the hardships of travel are forms of devotion and loyalty.[3] In short, ideas of routes and travel have been progressively etched into India's soils, mentality and ethos.

Through the twentieth century, politicians built on these older ideas and used travel to discover the country and to touch the electorate. The late twentieth century brought economic liberalisation, as the relatively closed economy was swiftly 'opened up', the state rolled back and new forms of symbolism were mixed with the staples of religion and politics.

Lord Ram Drives a Toyota

In 1990, L.K. Advani, president of the BJP, brought together new and old ideas about religion, pilgrimage and automobility in his infamous Ram Rath Yatra (chariot pilgrimage in honour of Lord Ram). His chariot (*rath*)—resembling those of the gods (not of old but of television serials)—was a decorated Toyota light goods vehicle that carried him from Somnath in Gujarat through Central India to Nagpur, north along SH31 in Madhya Pradesh and through Ratlam to the temple town of Ayodhya in Uttar Pradesh. Along the way, Advani gave passionate speeches about Hindu god Lord Ram and the lost glories of Indian culture. He urged the crowds to join him as he raised awareness of the disputed site of the Babri Mosque, which, he claimed, was built on the site of Ram's birthplace in Ayodhya.

As the psychoanalyst Sudhir Kakar observed:

> Like a pond choked with lotus storks during the monsoon, this religious-political exercise was replete with symbols. The symbolism began with the 'chariot': a large lotus, the symbol of the BJP, was painted on the front grille of the Toyota. The Lotus is one of the most Hindu of the universal symbols and is ubiquitous in India's religious iconography.[4]

Advani's chariot became known as the 'juggernaut of Hindutva' (the ideology of Hindu nationalism). As this political-mythological theatre hurtled through the countryside, the populism and dramatic staging of his journey received tremendous attention. With hindsight, it was an extraordinary thing to have done by any measure. It was successful in polarising the population and brought about widespread communal disturbances: at Ratlam, Advani left fighting between Hindus and Muslims in his exhaust fumes. The *yatra*, riots and general unrest in the country culminated with the public demolition of the mosque in Ayodhya two years later, as the manufacturing of antagonism between Hindu and Muslim communities became a political staple in the BJP's consolidation of power.

Most scholarly effort has been spent trying to untangle the religious and mythological messages of the Advani show.[5] In addition to these, the choice of a Toyota was itself a form of shrewd commentary on the politics that Advani opposed, as represented by the India that Nehru had created. Advani was promoting the BJP by connecting nationalism, territory and automobility. For him, there was no trudging bent-backed and staff in hand along the side of dusty roads or addressing crowds in flyblown railway stations. His was not only a campaign about birthplaces and buildings but an intervention in how to do politics and to think about what India was due. Advani modernised campaigning; his messages were commentary on the complementarity of Indian traditions and neo-liberalism—and, importantly, both were fused with mobility, speed and fuel.

Advani was part of a movement that rebelled against the politics and legacy of Gandhi and Nehru and their Congress party. He considered them to have left the country in a 'backward' condition. He saw Gandhi as having been against progress and Nehru as having adopted the socialism that had slowed and then suffocated India. Advani's was a revolution against the India that had tried to build its own cars. Advani's route, message and vehicle were also rich with meaning, as protectionist and command policies that had dominated the Indian economy began to be rolled back and new brands and technologies appeared for the first time.

Shortly after Independence, Nehru's government had decided to take control of automobile manufacturing. In 1952, the Tariff Commission put an end to the assembly of cars in India made of foreign parts to restrict the market and encourage indigenous production. The Americans—General Motors and Ford—left India in 1954, leaving a few products under licence. Indian companies were permitted to produce three models of car and medium goods vehicles and one heavy truck. Indian capitalists could only meet this challenge by continuing to look overseas, given the lack of indigenous engineering, design and plant capacity. In consequence, most of the new vehicles were based on older American and European models.

Technical collaboration between the Indian company Tata and Mercedes-Benz produced diesel trucks in 1954. The following year, Ashok Leyland began the manufacture of Comet trucks. Mahindra & Mahindra manufactured jeeps based on an American model. Standard Motors, under an agreement with the Union Motor Company, assembled Vanguard cars, producing the Standard 8 and 10 models. In the early 1960s, the company produced the two-door Standard (Triumph) Herald. Between 1971 and 1977, the company manufactured the Gazel, a car designed in India and 'inspired' by the Triumph. PAL first assembled the American Dodge DeSoto and Plymouth; between 1962 and 1998, they produced Italian cars from Fiat under licence.

The big story of the early years after Independence was Hindustan Motors' production of the Hindustan 10 and 'Baby Hindustan', the former based on the British Morris and the latter on the Morris Minor. In 1957, an entire tool line of the Series 3 Morris Oxford was transferred to India and production of the famous Ambassador car started in 1958. Models produced in India included the Mark 1 to 1V range, Nova, 1800 1SZ and the Avigo. In 1985, HM brought in a 1972 Vauxhall Victor, transplanting its ageing Ambassador engine—the Contessa was born, a lumbering heavyweight of the Indian motoring scene. In time, and for different reasons and associations, Ambassador and Contessa models became the best-known cars, as favourites of governments, heroes and gangsters. Unlike other manufacturers, Hindustan Motors managed a national profile, with a widespread distribution network for parts and marketing. However, the company's monopolistic tendencies later made it synonymous with technological backwardness and the entrenched corruption of the government.

Surya Ram Maruti Technical Services Private Ltd, a private company, was first launched in 1970 to provide technical know-how for the design, manufacture and assembly of 'a wholly indigenous motor car'. The company went into liquidation before the decade was out, mired in various high-level financial controversies. A few years later, Maruti Udyog was born to make a people's car for middle-class India, and by 1982 it had a joint venture with Suzuki, at first to import vehicles. Production in India commenced in 1983 with vans and small cars, as component manufacture was gradually also shifted to India. With the further liberalisation of the industry, as well as the more general economy in 1991, Suzuki increased its stake and today has the largest share in the Indian car market.

The Maruti–Suzuki cars were something new in India—and they emitted progress as well as fumes from unleaded petrol. They were lightweight and relatively economical to run. The low purchase price meant that even with import tariffs they were competitive against the heavy and thirsty Ambassador. Gradually, liberalisation allowed other Indian interests into the market; the reforms then widened further to include more joint holdings and, later still, foreign manufacturers. The winds of change ran quickly though the sector, as the promised potential of a large and increasingly prosperous population attracted the global motoring industry. Thus, Toyota began to sell vehicles that could be converted into political props to use on the stage of Indian politics.

It was not only religious and nationalist slogans emanating from Advani's symbolically overloaded caravan: Toyota was sending messages too. The firm's logo consists of three calligraphic ellipses. The inner ovals symbolise the hearts of customer and company, overlapping in a mutually beneficial relationship of trust. The outer oval signifies the world, embracing Toyota. The spaces between the ovals are the 'infinite values' of the brand: superb quality, value beyond expectation, the joy of driving, innovation, and integrity in safety, the environment and social responsibility. Perhaps over-thought, the result also resembles the letter 'T' of Toyota.

The Planning Commission: From State Planning to Liberalisation

The Planning Commission was formed in 1950 with Nehru as chairman; it was closed by BJP Prime Minister Narendra Modi in

2014. The commission produced 5-year or quinquennial plans to determine the most effective and balanced use of the country's resources. The changing language of the commission over this period reveals the refinement and intensification of the road-building programme: projects were devised with greater ambition and confidence, as the endorsement of the government and the spread of technocratic vocabulary transformed road building into a national obsession. When read across the decades—as I will do swiftly below—the plans demonstrate huge growth and the gradual commodification of roads and travel.

By the time of the Fourth Plan (1969–74), roads had become an 'overhead investment': literally, something that could not be imported and that was basic to economic and national activity. The Committee on Transport Policy and Co-ordination emphasised the 'development of various modes of transport as complementary services in such proportions and combinations as will meet the total need of the community at each stage at minimum cost to the economy'.[6] India had the lowest mileage of road per cultivated acre of any country, with large areas having no roads. Just 11 per cent of India's half a million villages had 'all-weather roads'.[7]

The Fifth Plan (1974–9) therefore focused on the provision of rural roads as part of the Minimum Needs Programme (MNP), set up to improve the living standards of the poor and through which the state would also oversee the delivery of primary health and education to rural areas.[8] The MNP envisaged provision of all-weather link roads for villages with populations of over 1,500 and for 50 per cent of the villages with a population of 1,000–1,500 within a decade. In the case of hills, tribal, desert and coastal areas where population was sparse, villages were to be clustered to assess the need. The scheme was anticipated to 'link' 20,000 villages during the Sixth Plan period.

The Sixth Plan (1980–5) responded to the continuing growth in mechanised road transport, which had risen from covering 23 billion passenger-kilometres in the first planning period to 250 billion passenger-kilometres in 1979. 'Missing links' had to be filled; 'blockages', namely local tax collection points, had to be removed. Overall, this 5-year plan echoed the concerns of the third 20-year plan drafted in Lucknow in 1981, which reclassified roads and set new targets for rural road building.[9] The energy crisis of the 1970s had restricted the availability of diesel, and so fuel efficiency and speed limitations for diesel vehicles were introduced. Cycles and bullock carts were to be utilised to their full potential.

The Seventh Plan (1985–90), with Rajiv Gandhi as prime minister, looked forward to the millennium as a target to make India a technologically progressive economy. The road network was expanding at 4.5 per cent and traffic by 6.8 per cent annually. In 1984, one in three villages had no road 'connection', and effort was directed to construct the missing links. Just under half the road network had a 'proper surface'. The pavement width of most was single lane with broad shoulders for bullock carts. As for national highways, 30 per cent of their length was single lane, the composition of which was 'extremely deficient with poor riding quality and unsafe operations'. There was a growing mismatch between traffic levels and capacity. The result was severe congestion, fuel wastage and higher operating costs. 'Upgradation' and 'rehabilitation' were the political words of the moment, shorthand for productivity, faster travel and 'energy conservation'.

The Eighth Plan (1992–7) came on the back of the IMF's bailout of India on the condition that the country open up to market forces and competition, including car manufacturing.[10] Public sector investment was rolled back, and the system of licences controlling production was removed. Rural road building was again intensified. It was then anticipated that most of the villages with a population of 500 and above would be connected by all-weather roads by the turn of the century.[11]

The National Highway Authority of India (NHAI; tagline: Happy Highways) was set up in 1988 and fully operational by 1995. It experimented with road projects under the PPP build-operate-transfer (BOT) scheme, aiming to provide 'passenger oriented wayside amenities' and raising money through non-taxable bonds.[12] These experiments led the way to the 1995 amendment of the National Highways Act of 1956 to encourage 'private participation in the development and maintenance of the National Highway network'. Private entrepreneurs could develop and operate road projects, collect and retain user toll fees and regulate the traffic on those roads.[13]

The Ninth Plan (1997–2002) was to coincide with India's fiftieth year of independence, but it was delayed.[14] The older concerns with 'missing links' and 'poor rural connectivity' remained, but 'four-laning' and 'deregulation' were now the headlines. It was boom time, with high rates of GDP growth as the government cautiously pushed 'economic decentralisation' and 'private initiative'.

Atal Bihari Vajpayee, then BJP prime minister of the NDA government, captured the transforming mood:

> Experience has shown that economic growth has not necessarily led to commensurate improvements in the social indicators, which are a measure of the quality of life of our citizens. Such social infrastructure needs to be provided by the government as part of its social responsibilities. But in these areas as well, decentralisation is of the essence for effective and responsive delivery of the services.[15]

The priority during the Ninth Plan was to consolidate the existing network rather than to expand its length. But even with such conceptual restraint, hyperbole crept in, with a plan for 'black topping' the entire length of state highways and major district roads with traffic of more than 100 commercial vehicles per day. The plan also proposed the rehabilitation of '50 per cent' of weak and narrow bridges with heavy traffic, and '20 per cent' of the state highways were to be widened—including the construction of missing links. 'At least 100 bypasses' were required. The work was branded as the National Highways Development Project, the first phase of which was to be the Golden Quadrilateral: four and six lanes connecting the four major cities of Delhi, Mumbai, Chennai and Kolkata. The Golden Quadrilateral was launched in 2001 and completed in 2012, some six years behind schedule, as India's largest single road-building project. Branded infrastructure had now also arrived in India.

Funding for road projects remained difficult since public utilities produced little surplus and the government did not have access to capital markets for equity or debt. Consequently, in a significant move, the road sector was designated an 'industry' to facilitate commercial borrowing.[16] Tolls were introduced on high-density traffic corridors and the major bridges to raise funds.[17] Tax concessions were offered to private investors, land acquisition and environmental clearances 'simplified', and highway land protected with special legislation. BOT contracts were extended to bypasses, bridges and 'four-laning'. Experiments were also undertaken in the privatisation of maintenance and management to 'secure the benefits of competitive price and quality'.[18]

The fourth 20-year plan for roads was branded as 'Road Development Plan Vision: 2020'. Its major concerns were funding, tolls, privatisation through incentives, capacity and the construction of roads in rural areas. Within this big wheel, the smaller wheel of the Tenth Five-Year Plan (2002–7) described infrastructure as 'integrating the national market' and 'promoting global competitiveness', with an emphasis on mobility through the NHDP's highways and on accessibility through the PMGSY and its rural roads.

The targets continued to escalate, accruing still more digits. In 2005, the Committee on Infrastructure, chaired by the prime minister, proposed four-laning 10,000 km under NHDP Phase III; two-laning 20,000 km of national highways under NHDP IV; augmenting highways in the north-east; and six-laning and development of 1,000 km of expressways in selected stretches.[19] The plan also cleared the ground for still more forms of PPP to attract investment and innovative ways of working on India's roads, including a more systematic toll policy.[20]

Strong economic growth continued, and the Eleventh Plan (2007–12) aimed to harness this effervescence to promote sustainability and inclusiveness, particularly for weaker sections of society.[21] Alongside concerns for social equity, the planners also dutifully pointed to the shortfall in the quantity and quality of roads and their neglected maintenance, suggesting the need for more. Roads that had been built, they said, during the last two plan periods were sub-standard.[22] Private sector investment was further encouraged and made easier by the publication of new manuals for procurement and contract work. In rural areas, the 'Bharat Nirman' (2005–9) aimed to improve 'connectivity' through all kinds of infrastructure. Under this umbrella, the rural roads of the PMGSY were to 'connect' all habitations (a planned 66,802) with populations above 1,000 (500 in hilly/tribal areas) with all-weather roads.[23]

A new Master Plan was proposed for the construction of 15,600 km of controlled-access expressways, and the formation of an Expressways Authority of India was discussed, but came to little.[24] A special effort was made to speed up road connectivity in Jammu and Kashmir, the north-east and other Special Category States, particularly those affected by 'Left-Wing Extremism'. Most influentially, both national- and state-level highway programmes aggressively promoted PPPs for toll roads on a BOT basis.

The Twelfth Plan (2012–17) recorded that out of 76,818 km of national highways, 23 per cent had four lanes (then above standard), 54 per cent had two lanes and 23 per cent had a single lane. During the Eleventh Plan, 10,000 km of highways had been completed, and a similar length was planned for the Twelfth. Spending on improving and building roads rose from 5 to 5.45 per cent of GDP. Special mention was made of the crucial role of the Madhya Pradesh and Gujarat road development corporations in upgrading state highways using the central government's 'Viability Gap Funding', a subsidy of up to 20 per cent of the total project.[25] Again, distinct effort was put into building roads through troubled areas and those with a proven disloyalty to the project of Indian nationalism. The Planning Commission further clarified contract and construction codes with the publication of new codes and concession agreements.[26] A Model Concession Agreement for operations and maintenance of 'tollable' roads was taken up to ensure their effective upkeep.

In the early years of this century, the meaning of roads became strongly aligned with the language of the market, project management and consumerism. Roads left behind the engineer's concern with surface materials and the bureaucrat's worry with public finance, evolving instead into assets, commodities and forms of consumption. The idea of 'corridor management', for example, changed thinking about roads and responsibilities, and new industries and expectations emerged: systems to manage road property and furniture, mechanisms for dealing with incidents and accidents, and the implementation of traffic and engineering upgrades.

144

Concerns about road safety brought in new objects such as crash barriers, road signages, delineators, road studs, median railing, thermoplastic markings and the plantation of shrubs in the central reservation to reduce the glare from vehicles travelling in the opposite direction. New forms of road patrol included the deployment of round-the-clock vehicles to attend accidents and cranes to tow away damaged and wrecked vehicles—reminders that things did not always flow smoothly. Truck stops and tea stalls on hard-packed urine-soaked earth gave way to the plastics and ceramic tiles of 'wayside amenities', restaurants and shops, destinations in themselves and places of leisure.[27]

***

In 1951, India had a counted population of 361,088,090 and 300,000 vehicles on 399,942 km of classified road. In 2011, India had a population of 1,210,726,932, and in 2015 had 210,000,000 vehicles on 5,603,293 km of classified road.[28] In 1951, there were 903 people and 1.3 vehicles for each kilometre of road. In this decade, there were 216 people and 37 vehicles for each kilometre of road. Therefore, in gross terms, between 1951 and the latest census data, the population increased by 335 per cent, vehicle ownership by 70,000 per cent, and the length of roads by 1,402 per cent.

India's 5- and 20-year plans build on the older language of the Jayakar Committee and Nagpur Plan from the first half of the twentieth century to establish classificatory practices or conventions that correlate population size of villages to road-building targets, often with a comparative eye on other countries. As with other classificatory practices, the use of targets takes on a particular style by implying and stressing need: preceded by generalised country-wide statistics such as those above, the target becomes a self-evident national requirement. Over the years, the 5- and 20-year plans became blueprints for political engagement and infrastructural communication with the electorate that outlived the Planning Commission, and national statistics gathered at an unimaginable scale would become the imperative and justification for local action.

As we saw in Chapter 5, the early twentieth-century political language of Gandhi and Nehru used the road to illustrate freedom and liberation. The condition then of the country's roads meant it was easy to create common bonds through a shared experience of hard and difficult journeys. Independence brought the Planning Commission, introducing new goals and ideals: the target, missing links and laning. Gandhi's path to truth was now another country from another era. The failed promises of the nuclear and flying ages, the unwieldiness of the licensed economy and the promotion of the bullock cart also contributed to the unique character and style of Indian roads, loved by many, embarrassing to others. Over the decades, as the realities of tarmac and fuel became embedded, the road metaphor changed from one of dreams, future promise and sacrifice to that of service provision, logistics and contractual detail.

The language of road building has long been a shared form of public communication in many parts of the world. Seemingly without thinking twice, Gandhi readily employed both technical and engineering vocabulary in his daily lexicon, as well as broader ideas of the territorial conquest that comes with building roads through rude countries. In more recent years, the terminology of road management has entered the public domain, to the point that some of the common PPP models, such as BOT and OMT (operate-maintain-transfer), are understood in India as household terms. The promotion of such ideas in the public domain helps to generate interest and buy-in to road development projects. It also reinforces the idea of innovative governments drawing on imported ideas and separating the 'technical' from 'political'. The strong focus on contractual terminology thus promotes the rhetoric of transparency that has also been encouraged in India by the World Bank and other institutions.

In 2009, Congress politician and then union minister in charge of highways K.H. Muniyappa announced that the government of Gujarat would build a 'heritage route' commemorating Gandhi's momentous Salt March. Planned in two stages, the proposal was to resurface and widen the extant road tracing the route in the first instance, and then upgrade it to a two-lane road complete with paved hard shoulders, bridges and bypasses. Alongside work on the road, the 2009 plan included development of the places where Gandhi had rested overnight, turning the route into a site of heritage tourism. In 2016, a prominent newspaper ran with the headline 'Soon, Drive Down the Path Gandhi Walked', 'retrace this 410-km journey in your car, your foot firmly on the accelerator'.[29] In the article, technocratic visions for the road—'two lane', 'paved hard shoulders', 'bridges' and 'bypasses'—are given as much space as the original purpose of the march. Gandhi's defiant journey against colonial oppression, on foot at 10 miles per day, had been turned into a mainstream route of mobility and leisure.

That Advani went to Ayodhya in a Toyota was no accident: it was his statement on the ills of protectionism and a rejection of old-fashioned and second-hand technology that made India subservient and inferior to Euro-America. Would the Babri Mosque have been demolished in 1992 had Advani travelled in a Hindustan Ambassador? In the event, Advani's colourful campaign, a symbolic lotus painted on the front of his chosen vehicle, ushered in a new wave of support for the BJP. Though the liberalisation of the early 1990s would probably have happened regardless of which party was in government, the BJP's blend of Hindu nationalism and free-market policies, while safeguarding the cow, would let the bullock cart go.

Nehru's role in establishing and inaugurating the CRRI in Delhi has been erased from promotional literature and official history. Despite such silencing, as the BJP have wrestled history from the Congress through ridicule and the creation of their own mythologies, there remain continuities in how roads are envisaged and talked about. The target—the golden principle of the 5-year plan and a key electoral promise—remains, albeit recast as a comment on efficiency and 'can-do' attitude rather than reflecting the power of the state. The hyperbolic language of planning that crept in during the 1980s remains too, arguably intensified by the latest generation of roadmen, who, since the 1990s, have also recognised the potential of infrastructure branding and the association of roads with leisure and consumption. The metropolitan concern with the miserable countryside has hardly changed since Gandhi and Nehru were bumping along rough tracks. Each 5-year plan raised concerns about rural roads. Politicians have repeatedly re-invented the road, if not the wheel.

The work of the Planning Commission was of course never written to be read as a story of intensification, acceleration and infinite growth in the way that I have used the material here. The result of my reading is teleological: seventy years of more, bigger and faster roads and increasing private investment. Missing links are the fantasy objects of road builders' endless dreams—single, double, four, six and now eight lanes, the interval between each expansion shrinking as each one increases the amount of traffic. 'Gaps', 'connections' and 'laning' are infinitely renewable forms of political logic, and so there will always be further opportunity for expansion until the whole of India is covered in motor road.

Georgieva Drives a Tesla: The Role of Development Banks

Alongside drafts for the future of India in documents produced by the Planning Commission, there is also the parallel story of development banks—a story largely written out of published plans. Speaking at the 'Transforming Transportation' conference at the World Bank in Washington, DC in January 2019, Kristalina Georgieva (then one of the world's most influential road builders as then CEO of the International Bank for Reconstruction and Development, an arm of the World Bank) described in her plenary speech how excited she was about 'new mobility':

> I am excited because I'm one of the early adopters of electric vehicles, I drove one in Brussels and I have my Tesla charging right now down in the garage of the bank. But I'm mostly excited because when we talk about new mobility, we actually talk about the most critical goal of the World Bank, and it is eradicating poverty.

The collision of luxury cars and poverty notwithstanding, Georgieva's words reflect the central idea used to explain road building across South Asia today: growth and prosperity as key to poverty reduction.[30] The Washington conference is a big deal, one of the highlights of the roads conference circuit. While the theme of the moment is 'sustainable transport', here delegates were also reminded of how shifts in development and governance priorities, often visibly led by the World Bank, now mean that new and improved roads are viewed as primary instruments of poverty alleviation and governmental reform.

Financial institutions like the World Bank, itself created at the 1944 Bretton Woods Conference, grew up alongside the independent countries of South Asia, and their fortunes are intertwined.[31] The language and ideologies of such organisations dominate the scene and have a fundamental influence on the region's roads. National governments, by comparison, excepting some notable acts of rebellion, seem to play supporting roles, mimicking the institutions' language and adopting reform measures imposed through loan conditions.

The transformation of the interests of the Planning Commission from state to market, for example, directly reflects the ideologies embedded in loan conditions. This entanglement is exemplified by the spread and adoption of PPPs in India. In Pakistan, the geopolitics are different and have been since Independence; here, international competition for influence has led to a competitive funding market for infrastructure borrowing. In both contexts, however, the promotion of infrastructure as an 'asset class' (remember that in the Ninth Plan, the road sector was designated an 'industry' to facilitate commercial borrowing) has been a crucial element of the story. This shift toward liberalisation is elaborated below, with attention given to the narratives of roadmen themselves, bringing our history of roads through people and plans up to the present day as we bump back on to the surface realities of roads in contemporary South Asia.

The World Bank established a resident mission in New Delhi in 1957. The ADB came later, first lending to India in the 1980s and opening a resident mission in 1992. In Pakistan, the offices of both banks are in Islamabad and have focused on transport as an area of strategic development. The current mission of the World Bank is to eradicate extreme poverty, as described by Georgieva and outlined in the institution's tagline (End Extreme Poverty and Promote Shared Prosperity in a Sustainable Way). The ADB's current public presentation of its mission is also found in its broad tagline (Prosperous, Reliant, Inclusive, Sustainable), in addition to providing loans, technical assistance, grants and equity investments to promote social and economic development.

In Pakistan, the ADB actively promotes roads through the language of 'corridors' and 'multimodal connectivity'. Campaigns such as 'Connecting Places, People, and Profits in Pakistan' stress the urgency of the bank's work: 'Roughly 2 percent of GDP is lost annually because of an inadequate transport system in Pakistan.'[32] The gravity of the claim deflects attention from the bombastic figure. Xiaohong Yang, head of the ADB's country mission, describes the bank's role as providing 'a safe, affordable, efficient, durable and environment friendly means of transport'.[33] In essence, this means building roads and improving railways.

For example, the Faisalabad-to-Khanewal stretch of the M-4 in the Punjab was completed in 2015/16 with financial assistance from the ADB. A film by the bank lends legitimacy to the project with local voices from 'Charaghanabad Village', who marvel at the changes the road has brought:

> Zameer Hussain: Before the motorway our village was quite deprived and backwards. Since the construction of the M-4 our village has become prosperous … In fact, people from other areas are coming and looking to settle here.

> Chaudhry Yassin: Because of the motorway we now have gas in our village and housing societies are coming up. All this development and construction work is also providing jobs for us, as well as the financial capacity to upgrade our homes.[34]

Meanwhile, the World Bank began to loan money for improving the network and management of roads in West and East Pakistan in the 1960s. America was the largest contributor to the pool of available money. In 1964, the World Bank financed and subcontracted the upgrading and realignment of the road between Karachi and Hyderabad.[35] Roads and transport management systems were studied during economic missions in 1961 and 1962. In the same years, a comprehensive transportation survey of West Pakistan was made by the now defunct Transportation Consultants Inc. for USAID, the overseas development wing of the American government (tagline: From the American People). At the time, the Communications Wing (Buildings and Roads Branch) of the Communications and

Works Department of the provincial government in West Pakistan was responsible for roads. The organisation was seen as outdated and lacking capacity, so further American consultants were given the work.[36] In Washington, it was noted that '[t]he United States along with other free-world donors of aid is vitally interested in the development of Pakistan and the survey report will be a continuing source of valuable information in the consideration of many project proposals requiring external funding'.[37]

The study was supported by the US army on the assumption that '[t]he economic resources of a nation cannot be efficiently and satisfactorily developed and used without economical and timely movement of goods and people'.[38] From then on, the World Bank consistently invested in roads and institutions in Pakistan, with the Highway Project entering third and fourth phases.[39] Throughout the 1980s, the World Bank issued further loans to lower transport costs, develop capacity and efficiency, improve safety and 'ensure continued adequate mobilization of revenues from road users'.[40] This century, the World Bank has continued this work using the language of 'phased improvement' and 'rehabilitation of the network', upgrading— again—the projects for which it loaned money in previous decades.[41]

In short, the economic Cold War in South Asia left distinct marks on transport planning, in terms of language, orientation and institutions.[42] Early on, West Pakistan—whether because of the influence of the army, or the challenging stretch of geography, or the interests of the first consultancy firms—became a place of 'difficult logistics', a theme that was carried through the 1980s and is still, as discussed above, reflected in transport campaigns by development banks in the country.[43] The World Bank, with strong American support, became influential in Pakistan. USAID continues to build roads in the country, raising slogans such as 'Pathway to Prosperity'. The Kalat–Quetta–Chaman road in Baluchistan was opened in 2016. USAID states:

> A road is not just a way to get from one place to another. Roads create opportunity. They connect farmers to markets, traders to buyers, children to schools, and travelers to destinations … This road is a concrete expression of the United States' commitment

to help bring peace, stability, and prosperity to Pakistan. It is testament to the far-reaching benefits of a decades old partnership, as it will serve the people of Pakistan for generations to come ... The daily stream of trucks barreling down the road are a sign of new possibilities.[44]

Who could argue with USAID's view that roads create opportunity? Or with Zameer and Chaudhry's view of the ever-accelerating good life in 'Charaghanabad Village'?

This is the same accelerating good life that has allowed the World Bank to loan money at interest to the government of Pakistan to upgrade the same highways four separate times since the 1960s. Building roads has become a national project, as well as the ongoing rationale for international friendships, aid relationships, institutional entanglements—and usury.

Roads, Roadmen and the Public–Private Partnership

Development banks have played influential roles in the deregulation of economies in South Asia through pedagogy, lobbying and loan agreements. Economies of the region have 'opened up' to the market (just as a road 'opens up' a village, in the language of roadmen), a process through which 'foreign' investment and enterprise have been permitted into spaces that were previously restricted.[45] Since the late 1980s, the World Bank and allied institutions have promoted infrastructure as an 'asset class', a commodity that can be invested in and profited from, again moving away from infrastructure as a public good.[46] With this marketisation of infrastructure came the promotion of the PPP. The ADB and the World Bank run offices across the region to support and enable greater private investment to generate economic growth; with PPPs came legions of consultancy firms, who, in turn, introduced new working methods and international networks.[47]

For roadmen, this initially led to a dramatic improvement in status and visibility, as new money supported their work. In the simplest form of PPP, the state paid competing private contractors to build roads. More complex arrangements included different forms of partnership in construction, maintenance and revenue collection.[48]

Importantly, in many such arrangements, the state guaranteed a return on the investment, with inflationary protection built in.

As part of the internationalisation of road building in South Asia, some of the most common forms of development aid to the region in the last few decades have gone towards growing the knowledge and institutional mechanisms that are required to run PPPs.[49] Road engineers, who had always been in the business of issuing contracts, now became partnership managers, as international consultants explored new markets and infrastructural opportunities that arose as South Asia opened for business.

Many roadmen were initially great enthusiasts of PPPs, pointing to the ways that finance, capacity and expertise were injected into their profession. In the 1990s and early 2000s, the accompanying semi-privatisation of road-building agencies, particularly in India, gave them greater freedom and powers 'to get things done'. Roadmen recalled attending training courses in exotic locations (I personally attended one in Waterloo, just south of the River Thames in London) to learn a new road-building vocabulary mapped on to a set of managerial practices: 'concession', 'concessionaire', 'output focus' and 'asset ownership'. The business of 'making roads' was pushed out of their offices and into those of aggressive private contractors, as many of the roadmen became brokers between local and global concerns.

In the longer term, however, many PPPs in South Asia have been loss-making, despite optimistic initial projections, and have been bailed out with state revenues. Now, looking back on that heyday at the turn of the millennium, roadmen described how liability had been pushed into the future, how responsibility for loss usually remained with the state, and how concessions were given away at bargain rates to attract investment, amounting to a transfer of state or public wealth to the private sector. Even if concessions turned out to be loss-making in the longer term, in the shorter term many road assets acquired by private companies subsequently changed hands on the open market for more than the initial purchase price from the state.

Given this backdrop, during the research, roadmen in India increasingly saw themselves in a moment of flux and uncertainty. The realities of road funding deficits began to emerge, but the language and practices of the development banks had not moved on. PPP arrangements began to appear unviable, given the evidence of real losses on real roads. In their minds and conversations, the project to 'road' India, where this failing was most particularly evident, was stalling, although in reality the mechanisms that had allowed for the unsustainable credit boom were still functioning as before.

At the same time, the political demands to build more roads were increasing day by day. For the roadmen, the bonanza that had brought fame and wealth had begun to lose its lustre, as debt had become the overarching theme of their working lives. To quote a confusing but evocative metaphor provided by a government engineer from Central India: 'You know ... a giant wave of interest crashed over our offices, affecting the lives of everyone outside, but leaving us safe inside to carry on our work when the waters receded. Of course, it was not as simple as that! Now we are paying the price!'

In Central India in particular, the roadmen employed by the government-owned company that intended to funnel private and development bank finance knew the game was over. Still, at the same time, state- and national-level politicians continued to announce more new roads as political battles intensified between a bullish and hungry BJP and a defensive Congress party. Finance remained available, even if the promise of longer-term profits from roads built ten years ago on a 25- or 30-year concession had already been exposed as over-inflated hyperbole. These roads increasingly demanded expensive maintenance, which put new pressures on the purse strings. The research began to reveal a lag between experience on the ground and the policy direction of major institutions; oil tankers with momentum could not change course swiftly.

These tugs put the roadmen in a double or triple bind. They had generally loved the freedom and possibilities that cheap money and exposure to the winds of the market had given them. They were proud of the excellent roads they had built in the bubble. But despite these liberating experiences of privatisation, roadmen knew that something would have to give way, and many now defaulted to the ethos and resources of the state as a protective and sovereign guarantor to save the day. The roadmen had become Janus-faced.

As one roadman put it (and I paraphrase), the ambiguities of the development experience made them see how their affairs with the market had opened horizons and made new worlds possible; however, they could also now tell that the homely surety of the state had endured and that it might even forgive them the mess to keep things ticking along. This man wanted to maintain both wife and mistress.

Having said that, I also sensed that some of the roadmen simply did not care about losses. Debt was a long-term problem that would ultimately fall to others to sort out. Loss was not their personal or even their professional problem, and regardless, importantly, they would carry on building roads because the country needed them. The road project transcended the immediate balance sheet and the longer-term demands of debt. The red budget line or defaulted loan were often forgotten with the help of the election cycle and debt consolidation mechanisms. When held against such trivialities, roads were a majestic project that would live on with the nation long after the stresses and strains of their offices had been forgotten.

International Investment and the Promise of More Roads in Pakistan

On the ground and in offices in Pakistan, there were glimpses of other processes and different power relations playing out as China had disrupted the road market. Khalid Chauhan, who had previously worked in the higher levels of the government, oversaw some of the research in Pakistan. He returned to interview a former colleague. When they worked together, the officer had been in high demand; he occupied a good office near the main secretariat. Khalid recalled his fresh looks, as if he were in complete command. In the intervening years, the country's Planning Commission was renamed the Ministry of Planning, Development and Reforms and given a new building, perhaps to bring it into line with Chinese nomenclature. All projects relating to highways, railways, ports and aviation were approved in these offices.

Although the building was new, the office ceilings were in poor condition, with a couple of tiles missing and others water stained. The officer, too, was now worn out, overstretched, with little time for himself. In his office, three customary chairs for visitors stood in front of a table and leather sofa set, the latter used for special guests and to break up the monotony for the officer of sitting in one place. On the table were piles of ordered files, suggesting a backlog, and a plastic lunch box containing curry and two pieces of chicken, beside which were a couple of chapattis. The evidence suggested that the officer had not had time to eat his lunch, and it was already mid-afternoon.

The officer was reluctant to talk about his responsibilities. Instead, conversation turned to health: '[T]hat one I can't figure out, but I have control of diet and walk too much.' He had a heart problem and had undergone angioplasty; two stents were put in. He was now regularly using medicines. The arrival of the Chinese on the scene had increased the amount of work that passed through his offices, but it had also decreased his significance. His office had to process paper, and lots of it, but decision-making and consultation powers had been passed to offices and officers that interfaced directly with the Chinese investment.

Elsewhere in Islamabad, the National Transport Research Centre occupies an unkempt plot in an elite neighbourhood. Unusually for a government building, there was no security, not even a visitors' book. Offices were piled high with files and documents. Unlike the planning ministry, these offices were untidy because there was too little work. Khalid's host smiled when asked who the director general was: 'For many years now,' he said, 'whosoever is close to retirement or has six months or so of his service remaining is posted here as DG. They say: "Help me get through my last six months."' Now, additional responsibility had been given to a 'lady officer' who sat in the main building of the Ministry of Communication. She only came to the centre occasionally. Our host thought this appointment was another sign that their work was not valued. The institution was an old and venerable one, an 'antique piece'. The research they undertook was of a certain time and was being supplanted by technology and ideas from China.

In both the ministry and the centre, road-planning projects generally originate with prime minister's directives as political promises rather than the fulfilment of research-based needs. This means, effectively, that politicians announce new roads, and research institutions have to respond rather than produce their own strategic road plans. Roadmen saw this as 'adhoc-ism in action'. Dusty offices and leaky ceilings suggested that the actual administration of road building was being neglected, even if roads are a high national priority. The demand for roads was described as 'all in the pocket', those with political power more likely to benefit. The tasks that filtered into research institutes were mandatory feasibility studies, but the planners, sociologists and environmentalists we met who worked on these projects felt their work was of little worth. Final decisions had already been taken and they had to complete the paperwork to produce that outcome. They had become actors within a perfunctory performance dictated by political will and the capture of funds with ties from development banks.

In the centre, conversation moved to the power of roads. One man, rising to the occasion, said: 'Civilisation travels by road. If you will build road then it will happen.' Another said: 'Overall, the narrative was that religion is something which brings us all together in Pakistan. Now it seems, as PM also stated, that roads lessen hate and brings the provinces closer.' Another chipped in: 'I have been working in Baluchistan and I have seen that when the road was built, it gave people the confidence to move. The people started using buses, the mobility increased. Then it started affecting culture. So yes, it will affect a locality.' Another: 'Road building is a *shauk* ['interests' verging on vices] for this government. There are two or three ways to bring change. Through new structures, through improving the human agency or some say through both simultaneously.'

Throughout Pakistan, roadmen were interested in talking about China and national integration. The most sweeping set of interventions from China is packaged under CPEC, an investment promise of tens of billions of dollars for ports, industrial parks, power projects and roads. Quite tangibly, CPEC began to change narratives in Pakistan. Back in the Ministry of Planning, Development and Reforms, Khalid was told that

in terms of stability, it is making a difference. The assured investment is coming. Confidence has increased. Pakistan's future is better, no doubt about that. Traditional donors used to attach strings and conditionalities that have now been relaxed. These are good signs. Plus, there will be competition. They don't want the Chinese to have too much. They don't want to lose the space. One of the tangible benefits of CPEC and the assured investment has been the greater political leverage to the government.

In the past, loans or grants from the banks were relatively small, but now, to the astonishment of many, overseas investors were showing an interest, including Japanese banks that were 'more generous and are willing to give more grant money on their own initiative ... if they make things difficult then we can call it CPEC and this might make them more generous'. In these offices, another overworked officer also said: 'Now planning is regaining leverage. There is a change in behaviour. The narrative is changing. When there was aid dependency, the traditional donors would put conditions; now they are attempting to gain space.'

The informal message was that international competition to lend money in Pakistan was creating markets for loans. The government could play one lender off against another. This, of course, had a history dating back to Independence, when competition between China, the UN and the US was already evident in road politics and 'aid'.

***

This journey has brought us firmly back to where we started this book: the present, the here and now of roadmen, whether that be stresses and stents, or riding the feel-good wave of excessive funds for which accountability lands above their heads. Either way, roadmen today generally feel they have little influence; others determine whether there is no time or too much time for lunch.

Through the twentieth century, motor roads spread like intensifying glaze crackle across the map of South Asia. This continuing project of road building has been driven by practical, imaginary and political momentum, but it is also directed by finance and international relations and the ripples of national and provincial politics. In India, the hegemony of development banks has given roadmen resources with which to build; in a sense, however, the market remains limited. In Pakistan, with more overt international competition, the result is 'adhoc-ism' and shopping around.

I heard words of frustration from roadmen all the way from Brussels to Delhi about how their discipline and knowledge were frequently hijacked by rash political gestures. Despite their strong professional ethos, roadmen felt as if they were in-betweeners, sitting in offices between the government and the people, between idealistic plans and complex landscapes. Their potential to road the Subcontinent efficiently, making use of their knowledge and expertise, was endlessly derailed by political bluster, unpredictable struggles for finance and difficult terrain.

EMPERORS OF THE ROAD
MR MOTORWAY AND MR FLYOVER

We will now turn to the trajectories and antics of a new set of roadmen: those in politics, who, as seen in the previous chapter, are considered by the roadmen in offices to be pulling the strings. Two such politicians, Nawaz Sharif in Pakistan and Nitin Gadkari in India, are particularly notable in this story, having played with both the danger and the promise of roads.

South Asia came late to the idea of road-networked nations, as the colonial government had other priorities. Since Independence, there has thus been an urgency and perceived need to compensate for the lack of roads in both India and Pakistan, with roadlessness seen as an indication of backwardness and deficiency. In this context, two strong political personalities elected to take on the project of road building as a sure way to win currency and power.

Mr Motorway: Nawaz Sharif

Nawaz Sharif served as Pakistan's prime minister for three non-consecutive terms as the leader of the Pakistan Muslim League (Nawaz) (PML-N) party. Hailing from a family of industrialists deeply involved in national and regional politics, Sharif was the first to make the idea of the 'motorway' in Pakistan into a reality and established a distinct political brand focused on road building and infrastructural promise.

In the early 1990s, Sharif's first government began work on the Peshawar–Lahore–Karachi motorway, then called the 'Trans-Pakistan Motorway'. This project was part of a programme to upgrade roads to 'international standards' and was managed by a highway corporation newly opened to private finance.[1] Sharif inaugurated the work and renamed the road network as the snappier 'Pakistan Motorway', recalling the story of a man who wanted to find his way to 'Shah-ran-i-Sultan Abdul Hameed Bin Badees Road' but could not find a passer-by who would stand still long enough to hear where he wanted to go.[2]

The route incorporated the M-2, which connected Islamabad to Lahore; inaugurated in 1997, it was the first motorway in South Asia and part of Asian Highway 1 in the United Nations' AHN. Many pioneering and innovative engineering methods, including the use of state-of-the-art software, were used in the construction of the highway. A Sri Lankan engineer who had worked on the road as a young man told me that it was built to a specification that could land military planes. The M-2 pointed to the future, to the possibility of a Pakistan internally networked and connected to its neighbours with highways. Even the service stations were built to high standards, intended to cater to middle-class consumers who valued American fast-food restaurants and the accompanying imaginings of global citizenship.

The opening of the M-2 in November 1997, a few months after Sharif's election to a second term after a stint in opposition, was a public demonstration of the prime minister's achievements. Not only was the road completed; it was also beautiful, brought a new standard and quality to the country, and sent powerful messages to Pakistan's neighbours about the country's upwards trajectory. It marked a high point in Sharif's career as a politician—roadman, and he repeatedly referred to the project as an example of what he could achieve if given a mandate.

**

Before the CPEC infrastructure projects began in 2013, Sharif dominated road talk in Pakistan. In the mid-1990s, roads were associated with mass corruption in the popular imagination. Sharif turned this around, connecting motorways to the political struggle against the misuse of funds. He took this even further to argue that roads were in fact instruments of fiscal stability; in October 1997, facing a default on an IMF payment, Sharif thanked Allah for giving Pakistan the capacity not to default. He began to speak openly and aggressively about fighting high-level corruption and promised a 'pleasant revolution in the life of the common man', for which the country would need better government finance and foreign investment. In this vision, Sharif saw himself as setting in motion the development of Pakistan, and road infrastructure was central to the project: 'To accelerate this process, we worked day and night to complete the motorway which, Allah willing, would be opened for traffic next month. These were the foundations which we laid through hard labour for building a prosperous future.'[3] Speaking to a crowd of thousands at the opening ceremony of the M-2 three weeks later, he said the motorway 'will prove to be a milestone for Pakistan's development and prosperity'.[4]

Many years later, when work was due to begin on a PPP to 're-carpet' and modernise the M-2, Sharif reflected: 'When we first started this mega project, our government was toppled, but we completed it when people again elected us in 1997.'[5] His observation captures the sense that moments of conflict and struggle in his career were linked to the development of infrastructure, setbacks in his political trajectory marking junctures at which road construction faltered, while in turn his road-building announcements intensified at times when he was in difficulty. The opening of the M-2, for example, came in the wake of charges for contempt of the judiciary. Sharif had accused the chief justice of overstepping his authority after a Supreme Court ruling had found unconstitutional his attempts as prime minister to ban legislators from changing political parties.[6] This confrontation was the start of the fractious relationship Sharif would have with the judiciary, which, in 2017, ultimately led to his disqualification as prime minister.

In the Ministry of Planning, Development and Reforms, a man with decades of national experience relates to us that Sharif himself had 'coined' the concept of the motorway as far back as 1988, when he was chief minister of Punjab and Benazir Bhutto was prime minister. At the time, the government of Punjab wanted to build a motorway between Lahore and Pindi. The Planning Commission blocked the move on the grounds that it was unnecessary and there were insufficient funds. Additionally, with the Grand Trunk Road running parallel to the proposed motorway at 40 to 50 km away, they argued that it would be better to rehabilitate the existing network than to put money into new infrastructure. In a nutshell, Sharif's plan lacked economic and business sense.

Nevertheless, when Sharif came to power as prime minister in the early 1990s, the bureaucracy was put to work. The motorway was a symbol of his 'dream for Pakistan', with a clear preference for the elite of his native Punjab: 'They dream of travelling across the motorway in their Pajeros [high-end Mitsubishis], eating McDonald's burgers and Kentucky Fried Chicken along the way. The ones with a rather desi outlook expect "progressive" Nihari and Tikka outlets to dot the highway.'[7]

Sharif regarded the Planning Commission's methods of working as slow and cumbersome, and it was eventually side-lined completely in the development and maintenance of the country's motorways. In 1991, the NHAI, a body then headed by the prime minister, was created in order to 'speed up the process' and 'to have full control of the project'. The Planning Commission thus had no say in proposed changes to the M-1, a motorway that would connect Islamabad to Peshawar; Sharif's original plan for six lanes was reduced to four when Benazir Bhutto returned to power in 1993, then restored as six by Sharif in 1997. Unsurprisingly, there remains professional scepticism within the Planning Commission today about the rationale for the M-1 and the M-2.

In April 1998, the year after the Lahore–Islamabad motorway (M-2) was opened, Sharif began to direct resources to the country's wider road network; Rs 50 billion in loans went towards the construction of motorways from Pindi Bhattian to Faisalabad and Karachi to Hyderabad, as well as for the four-laning of the Grand Trunk Road between Peshawar and Karachi.[8] There was a buzz about roads in Pakistan, and the pace of announcements and inaugurations accelerated. In the summer of 1999, on a trip to Sheikhupura in Punjab to lay the foundation stone for the Hiran Minar interchange, Sharif spoke about the benefits that the M-2 would bring for tourism and the local economy.[9] He also used the occasion to confirm to the public that the Islamabad–Peshawar (M-1), Pindi Bhattian–Faisalabad and Karachi–Hyderabad motorways were being constructed on a BOT basis through PPPs that he claimed would have 'no monetary burden on the national exchequer'.

A few days later, Sharif travelled to Kohat, a city in the Khyber Pakhtunkhwa province, to inaugurate work on a tunnel there. At a cost of over Rs 6 billion, the Kohat tunnel was seen as a quicker and safer alternative to the existing road over the mountain. Claiming that 'ours is a strong government' and speaking of his desire to transform Pakistan into a 'developed country', the prime minister said that the completion of the Indus Highway and the M-1 would 'introduce revolutionary changes in the country'.[10] These bold claims came two and a half months before Sharif was deposed by General Pervez Musharraf in October 1999.

In the wake of the coup, army authorities investigated Sharif and his brother Shehbaz for allegedly using public money to build a road connecting the Sharif family estate to Raiwind Road on the outskirts of Lahore. During the investigation, it was reported that, under the supervision of Shehbaz, money had been diverted from a range of other projects, including irrigation works and rural veterinary dispensaries, a school-building programme and the Punjab regional budget for 1998–9.[11] The roads that Nawaz Sharif had built to serve his dairy farm and industrial complex were of the highest order. The Sharif family had also purchased vast swathes of land at low prices before the route was announced to the public. These were serious allegations, pointing to an organised and planned abuse of office. Given Sharif's existing reputation for using the promise of motorway modernity when the political heat was on to display his commitment to the country, it was perhaps due to the corruption charges' focus on roads that they did not simply go away but dogged him for the next eighteen years.

***

In 2013, Sharif won a third term as prime minister, having pledged during his campaign to build a motorway from Peshawar to Afghanistan to usher in a new era of development and cooperation between the countries.[12] He soon announced that China and Pakistan would develop their relationship through a programme of extensive infrastructural works; initially valued at $46 billion, the CPEC would continue to grow in worth from then on. In August 2013, Sharif described CPEC as the 'future of the country'.[13] At this stage, CPEC work on the Peshawar–Lahore–Karachi motorway was contracted on a BOT basis through PPPs. Planning Minister Ahsan Iqbal commented that the government alone would be unable to fund the construction, suggesting that Pakistan did not itself have sufficient resources to build roads already promised by politicians.[14]

At a government meeting in May 2014, Sharif heard that work on the Lahore–Karachi motorway was due to begin by the end of the year, and that a budget had been allocated for the Faisalabad–Khanewal M-4 section of the road. Of these developments, Sharif proclaimed in now-characteristic style: 'We have embarked upon the road to progress and projects initiated by our government will usher the country in to an era of prosperity.'[15] In a further meeting in August, Sharif directed work to begin immediately on the motorway, saying that the project was a continuation of the PLM-N party's economic road map first drawn up in the 1990s.[16] The M-4 section of the Lahore–Karachi motorway was opened in November 2015, in a ceremony attended by Punjab Governor Rafique Rajwana.[17] He used the occasion to make assurances that motorway projects across the country were being managed transparently, emphasising the 'development boost' that infrastructure projects would offer.

At the end of November 2014, Sharif broke ground on the construction work for the Hazara Motorway (M-15), a 180-km stretch linking the Burhan Interchange in Punjab with Haripur, Havelian, Abbottabad, Mansehra, Shinkiari, Battagram and Thakot in Khyber Pakhtunkhwa province. In front of a huge and well-organised crowd, Sharif denounced his political rivals and announced a cut in the price of fuel. Even before the works began, however, the cost of the road had spiralled.[18]

The M-15 encapsulates both the need and the frivolousness that characterise Pakistan's motorway journey. The road had a logic to it: serving as a southern extension to the KKH, it connected other roads, and as part of an economic corridor, it also allowed for the creation of industrial parks and a 'dry port'. However, because of the unstable, hilly terrain, the route was expensive and difficult to engineer, and despite the investments made, the result is far from perfect. This road was constructed during our research, and we were able to trace the products of the crushing, matching and asphalt plants as they became a road. Along the way, there were battles in the courts and newspapers about the process and equity of land acquisition and compensation. There were also objections to the route because its final alignment traversed steep country, arguably making it inefficient for freight transport.

Although the route was an extension of the KKH and frequently considered to be part of CPEC, its first phase was also financed by loans from the ADB and grants from the UK's Department for International Development (DFID). Thus, Chinese-branded infrastructure was in fact supported by UK overseas aid and a multi-lateral development bank. The new road served these interests in that it was envisaged as 'the missing link' in Pakistan's transit routes. Xiaohong Yang, ADB country director for Pakistan, said the M-15 was 'an important step towards positioning Pakistan as a trading hub between Western and Central Asia by transforming adjoining towns and industrial zones into economic corridors'. Joanna Reid, head of DFID Pakistan at the time, said:

> The expressway will connect Pakistan to its neighbors and important cities like Abbottabad, Haripur, and Northern region with the motorway network … UKAid is pleased to have helped the Government of Pakistan provide better, safer, and faster transport connectivity so women, men, and children can access opportunities, markets, and basic services and develop their local economies.[19]

Phase I of the M-15 connected the M-1 at Burhan to Havelian, while Phase II takes the road further north and into higher mountains. Khalid Chauhan conducted interviews with people along the road, who expressed views both for and against the development. He met those who had protested against land acquisition and low levels of compensation. Through these interactions, he saw clearly that highway projects split farms and communities and had little to offer to those who lived on the other side of the boundary fence. The road became an exclusion zone, built for the greater good of the nation. Those in its path were asked to make sacrifices and to live with the new inconvenience.

The road also produced a great deal of social media coverage. As people followed and recorded construction at road level or with drones from above, dramatic cuts in mountains and the clearing of massive open swathes of land for interchanges provided striking imagery. In one film, music blasts over footage of the as-yet-unopened highway, Chinese-manufactured plastic green grass glinting in the September sun: 'Allah, as I look to nature's beauty, dazzled am I, knowing everything comes on you, the Lord Most High.' In November 2021, driving along the completed road, Khalid Chauhan also marvelled at its engineering, crisp road markings, well-lit tunnels and signs proclaiming, 'Long Live Pak-China Friendship.'

That the road evokes such positive feelings of awe and wonder is something that Sharif well understands and has capitalised upon. The level of investment, the skilled techniques of the road builders, the clean and calm lines of the concrete, reassuring signs, crash barriers, clear fonts and smooth surfaces, not to mention uncongested and clean carriageways, all make people want to share images of the road, saying, 'Look, this is Pakistan, can you believe it?'

***

On 11 March 2015, in Nooriabad, an industrial town in Sindh, Sharif laid the foundation stone for a 139-km-long six-lane motorway between Karachi and Hyderabad, envisioned as the first phase of a road in four sections linking Karachi to Lahore. Rs 42 billion in funds had been approved by Sharif for the project in July 2014.[20] At the ceremony, the prime minister said that he hoped the construction of motorways would help promote national harmony and solidarity and reiterated once more the link between the continuity of his government and the success of infrastructural projects:[21] 'We also had started construction of motorway in 1991 and it was built from Peshawar to Islamabad and from Islamabad to Lahore. What happened in 1997 is no more a secret, everyone is aware that after the removal of our government all these projects were abandoned.'[22] In the same month, Sharif made a trip to Sialkot in Punjab to lay the foundation stone for a motorway linking the city with Lahore. He returned in August 2016 to break ground once more, announcing a further subsidy of Rs 23 billion for the project.[23]

Throughout his last term, Sharif continued to point to his expansion of Pakistan's road network as proof of his successful governance and development of the country. In May 2016, on the campaign trail in Mingora in Khyber Pakhtunkhwa, a stronghold for Imran Khan's Pakistan Tehreek-e-Insaf (PTI) party, Sharif said: 'Some people keep saying they will come out on roads. Well I am building roads on which you can protest.'[24] In May 2017, in Layyah, Punjab, Sharif announced that his government would build a bridge to link the city to the Indus Highway, a 1,264-km-long four-lane motorway, also known as National Highway 55 (N-55), that was built between 1981 and 1985 and connects Karachi to Peshawar.[25] The prime minister went on to say that enemies of the country were opposed to projects being undertaken as part of CPEC, his words drawing a link between the realisation of infrastructural promise and loyalty to the nation. The heat was on.

Sharif had by now been badly burned by the Panama Papers, the 11.5 million documents leaked from corporate service provider Mossack Fonseca. The papers linked three of Sharif's children, Maryam Safdar, Hasan Nawaz Sharif and Hussain Nawaz Sharif, as well as in-laws of his brother Shehbaz Sharif, to offshore firms based in the British Virgin Islands.[26] These revelations led the government of Pakistan to launch an inquiry into all nationals named in the leak. When a five-member judiciary found that Sharif's family were unable to account for wealth in offshore companies, he was disqualified as prime minister by the Supreme Court in July 2017.[27]

Less than three weeks after his disqualification, Sharif set off on the Grand Trunk Road from Islamabad towards his home and political stronghold, Lahore, in protest at the court's ruling. Accompanied by massive crowds, the former prime minister rallied along the 2,000-year-old trade route, taking night halts at Jhelum and Gujranwala on the way. In Rawalpindi, on the first day of the rally, he complained to those gathered that 'no prime minister in Pakistan has ever been allowed to complete his term. This joke has been repeated for 70 years and Pakistan can no longer bear it. It's an insult to the voters.'[28] Sharif travelled in a bomb-proof vehicle especially designed for the journey and was flanked by security; this 'rally on the move' was a muscular display of not only his political power but also that of the road itself.[29]

A year later, in July 2018, Sharif was sentenced by Pakistan's National Accountability Bureau to ten years in prison. His daughter and son-in-law were also convicted on corruption charges relating to four luxury flats in London. Released in September that year after his sentence was suspended, Sharif was returned to jail in December 2018 following a subsequent conviction for holding investments beyond his declared assets.

That Sharif turned to the construction and celebration of roads as a defence against the taint of corruption at this most vulnerable point in his career speaks to the role that infrastructural imagination has played in his politics. Before being named in the Mossack Fonseca leak, Sharif was riding a wave of infrastructural promise ahead of the 2018 elections. Inaugurations and announcements of new highways and other projects came thick and fast. Construction of a metro line for Lahore and a new airport for Islamabad had begun, and Sharif himself had pledged a 'bullet train' between Karachi and Peshawar, as India was building one between Ahmedabad and Mumbai.

Nawaz Sharif is not the only member of his family to understand the power of infrastructural politics: his brother Shehbaz, who served as chief minister of Punjab in 1997–9 and then again in 2008–18, also deployed road building and big infrastructure as a political strategy. Shehbaz is known for the Lahore metro and bus systems, but he also built extensive overpasses and underpasses when the craze ran through urban government circles across South Asia.[30] In 2014, a survey found that Shehbaz Sharif's provincial government was the most popular in the country.[31] Even after the Panama leaks, Nawaz Sharif and the PML-N topped Gallup polls in November 2017.[32]

170

The new prime minister, Imran Khan, based his campaign on the idea of building a 'naya' or 'new' Pakistan. Given Sharif's capture of the agenda and language of infrastructure, Khan had to distance his vision for the future from that of his rival. He said that a new Pakistan would not be built on roads alone; instead, he emphasised housing and health. In explaining Khan's politics, a social planning officer for the government put it like this:

> Whether Pakistan is new or old, people's needs are good food and shelter and clothing. It can't be done with roads. When people will be prosperous, 'new Pakistan' will be formed. We can't say 'new Pakistan', we have the 'same Pakistan' which was made by Quaid-e-Azam. In reality ... 'new' or 'old' Pakistan is the same, save for the fact that with the passage of time, technology is changing. Technology is changing and so is our country changing.

Sharif had often countered this Naya Pakistan rhetoric, clear that he and his party were the ones to bring about real change through infrastructure. Back in 2016 at Sangla Hill, Sharif told the crowd:

> [t]he map of Pakistan is changing with the China–Pakistan Economic Corridor. Go look at Gwadar. Go look at Balochistan. Then go and look at Khyber Pakhtunkhwa [PTI heartland] ... They said they would make a Naya Pakistan, but we are the ones building Naya Pakistan there. We are the ones making road and power projects there ... Look at the Pakistan of three years ago and compare it to the Pakistan of today ... Pakistan is with Nawaz Sharif.[33]

Mr Flyover: Nitin Gadkari

'The road man', 'Roadkari' and 'Flyover Minister', as of 2022 Nitin Gadkari is the incumbent minister for national roads in India.[34] Over the decades, he has made a career from building and talking about roads. From his days in student politics in Nagpur in Maharashtra to central government in Delhi, ideas about nationalism, development and road infrastructure have been bound with increasing sophistication in his action and rhetoric.

In different phases of his career, Gadkari has constructed urban flyovers, highways and rural roads. Under his initiative and oversight, government road-building projects have become demonstrations of efficiency and commitment, where their traditional legacies had been corruption and broken promises. Roads are the central feature of Gadkari's politics, shorthand for the performance of politicians and parties. They have become the mechanism through which he has successfully built networks of support through public inauguration ceremonies. Finally, he has used roads as a way of talking up India's technological prowess in the hierarchy of nations and of thinking through international relations in the region.

One of Gadkari's trademarks has been to announce the daily construction rate of four-lane highways in India, accompanied by staggering targets. In April 2018, at an optimistic press conference to mark the start of the new financial year, Gadkari stated that '[o]ur target is to build more than 45 km of roads per day. I won't be surprised if we touch 50 km of roads per day.'[35] On 20 September 2018, in an address to the J.P. Morgan India Investor summit, Gadkari committed his ministry to a target of 40 km per day by March 2019, tweeting his success at having achieved 28 km per day in the 2017–18 fiscal year. As 2018 ended, the rate of road building stood at 23 km per day, with Gadkari vowing further action and admitting that he was falling behind: 'I had fixed the target of 40 km per day but I was not able to achieve that.' In January 2019, civil servants at the Ministry of Road Transport and Highways explicitly requested anonymity when saying that they were at around 32 km for the 2018–19 year so far, somewhat short of their target.

The figures are both questionable and mind-boggling. Such statistics are difficult to calculate, even with the machinery of a national government behind the sums. Does the figure include state as well as national highways? How is the completion of a kilometre stretch on a continuous highway determined? How does Gadkari's claim that the previous government's construction rate was 2 km per day compare to government data suggesting an average of 16 km per day at the end of the 2013 financial year? Moreover, 32.8 km per day is nearly 230 per week, 12,000 per year and approximately

340,000 in total until Gadkari's target date of 2050—slightly less than fourteen times around the circumference of the globe.

In these seductive statistics, there are no setbacks, landslides or bitter tears of forced displacement. There is no repetitive and expensive maintenance, unwelcoming geography, tactical insurgency or unequal demand. There can be no questions about what the end game might be or how such an agenda might fall foul of a global politics of carbon emissions. Such huge numbers leave no space to ask what anyone would do with so much road. How many new cars and journeys would these new roads generate? What would fuel them? To ask such questions is to miss the point: the roads themselves have become measures of national success.

The strategy is populist and nationalist, if not entirely logical. Gadkari appeals to the Indian love of numbers, which flourishes alongside his own 'addiction to hyperbole'.[36] Gadkari's party, the BJP, has often been described as 'pro-business', and Gadkari has a reputation for being a 'blunt talker' and a 'no-nonsense businessman-politician'. Friends in India repeatedly tell me that 'he is one minister who takes his portfolio seriously', and that consequently, 'roads in India are developing very fast and properly'.

These qualities help differentiate Gadkari from leaders of the past, who were tied up with bureaucracy and dynastic legacies. His monikers instead point to quick thinking, shrewdness and the uneasy kind of trust that successful business requires. He has learned to use experience gained from political engagement to serve commercial interests and vice versa. For example, after breaking up one of the Mumbai fuel mafias, he opened an ethanol plant himself and used his office to promote the product as an alternative fuel to keep India moving. In the early days, these worlds were tightly entwined, but after a series of public scandals, he has effectively separated Gadkari the politician from Gadkari the entrepreneur of agricultural by-products.

Along the way, Gadkari's projects have introduced new ways of thinking about finance and infrastructural sovereignty to the country. He was public works minister in Maharashtra when some of the first and ultimately failed experiments with public–private finance were conducted in the name of the Mumbai–Pune Expressway. Since that time, various public–private finance models have become routine, and the global production of infrastructure as an 'asset class' has become part of India's story.

As Gadkari has risen through the ranks, his achievements have become India's achievements. Throughout, his loyalty to his hometown of Nagpur has not wavered, and a great deal of his political time has been devoted to promoting the city and enriching the lives of its inhabitants. A huge economic development project, the Multi-modal International Cargo Hub and Airport at Nagpur aims to locate the city as the distribution centre of the country, and Gadkari has encouraged the construction of roads in particular directions in pursuit of this aim. His extraordinary success overall is not only due to the natural promise and rich symbolism of the road: rather, in his political lexicon, roads have brand names and are marketed as national products. Gadkari not only builds roads: he talks about them loudly and frequently.

***

Gadkari grew up and was educated in Nagpur in Maharashtra, a city that in 1943 was home to India's most influential conference of road builders, which set the standard and tone for twentieth-century road development. It is also home to the RSS, and Gadkari grew up close to the headquarters of the organisation. He remains associated with the RSS today, and its Hindu nationalist politics and strong notions of social service have stayed with him throughout his career. He has also maintained close links with Nagpur, as well as a house there, and is known as 'Gadkari saheb', 'Nitinji' or 'Nitin bhau' in the city.

Gadkari was a student activist during the Emergency in the late 1970s, supporting Jayaprakash Narayan's movement to oppose Indira Gandhi and active in the student-led Akhil Bharatiya Vidyarthi Parishad (All-India Student Council, commonly ABVP). He graduated in commerce and with an LLB from the University of Nagpur, after which he moved from being a student politician to join the youth wing of the BJP and became its president for Nagpur. He first contested and won the Nagpur seat for the Maharashtra legislative council in 1989, retaining the constituency until 2014.

From early on, Gadkari took an interest in infrastructure and development issues in the city.[37] He spoke out against the corruption of state resources relating to rice and coal contracts and lobbied for the investigation of corruption within the Nagpur Improvement Trust.[38] As an opposition politician, in the early years he was tenacious and persistent in organising walkouts in the state legislature over allegations of poorly run sugar cooperatives.[39] He kept a watchful eye on government plans for orange-processing plants in Vidarbha, the region of Maharashtra in which Nagpur is situated, again taking a leading role in cross-party walkouts.[40] He was also keen to demonstrate his social conscience, donating Rs 7,500 to the *Times of India* Relief Fund in 1993.[41] He promoted his work ethic and willingness to address populist questions, once claiming that he had sent 200 letters to ministers in the government on which he was awaiting a reply.[42]

In 1992, the BJP's national leadership backed calls for Vidarbha to become a separate state. Gadkari said the committee appointed by government to study the imbalance between different regions of Maharashtra had not taken sufficient account of the important role that well-run cooperatives and industry could play in development. In 1993, Gadkari raised vigorous slogans and walked out of the state legislature to draw attention to the secession demand.[43] This was followed by a *bandh* (strike) in Nagpur on 20 December 1993 during which Gadkari was arrested.[44] In the following year, he led further walkouts against the lack of support for farmers in the region.[45] There was something prescient and humane in these protests, since the rate of suicide among farmers of Vidarbha would rise in the years to come and gradually emerged as a national tragedy.

Gadkari also aligned himself carefully with nationalist causes, leading a protest against novelist Khushwant Singh's 'derogatory' comments about the historical hero of modern Maharashtra, Chhatrapati Shivaji Maharaj, in the news magazine *India Today*.[46] He also protested against the arrest of journalists in relation to accusations over the Babri Mosque dispute at Ayodhya and was involved in a cross-party protest about parts of Kashmir being excluded from a map of India.[47] Gadkari chose his battles carefully and in line with the national priorities of the BJP. In his worldview, the values and

175

nationalism of the party were not matters of politics or choice but of common sense, representing a default position and a framework on which other realities could be built.

***

The first mention that I have found by Gadkari of roads came in 1991, with a 'calling-attention notice' in the local council through which he questioned delays to the Nagpur ring road. Gadkari mocked the PWD minister's claims that he would apply for funding from the central government for the project, pointing out that the road did not meet central government specifications and therefore that no funding would be forthcoming.[48] Even then, it appears as if Gadkari was well versed in the role of road standards and governance.

In 1995, Gadkari became minister of the PWD in Maharashtra in the government of Manohar Joshi, a coalition between the BJP and Joshi's party, the right-wing Maharashtrian regionalist Shiv Sena.[49] A month after taking office, Gadkari went on a media offensive to promote the construction of expressways: 'I have been hearing for the past ten years about the state government plans to construct these expressways. Now that I am in office, I will see to it that these projects go well beyond the drawing board stage.'[50] He announced a global tender process for the construction of an 84-km six-lane expressway between Maharashtra's capital Mumbai (then Bombay) and Pune: 'To begin with, the four-lane expressway will be built and later it will be expanded to 6 lanes ... The travelling time between Bombay and Pune will be reduced by 45 minutes.' The hyperbole with numbers and the promotion of future expansion had begun.

Gadkari also announced his intention to privatise the construction of roads in a 'big way'. Crucially, those developing the roads were to be permitted to recover the cost by levying tolls. The language and sentiment might seem innocent, but Gadkari was in fact at the cutting edge of a dramatic change in how roads were built and how the government could plan to get things done. The state then had very little experience in privatised infrastructure, and many initial assumptions from that time now appear naïve, as two decades of public–private finance have since hardened the country to new realities. Gadkari appeared conscious of the pioneering nature of his Mumbai–Pune Expressway: '[A]s this will be the first and the largest privatised highway scheme in the country, we want to make doubly sure that all transactions are transparent and competitive. We are aware that this scheme will act as a pilot project for all such future schemes.'[51] The project would involve many fascinating twists and turns, as the government learned the perils of private finance, the difficulty of rapid land acquisition and the powers of protest.

On the latter subject, Gadkari took another forceful stand. Hammering home the point that he was going to work hard on the road network, he gave repeated press conferences to say that he would not brook delays from, for example, environmental protesters. Environmental protest in Western India was not new at the time, but it had recently gained currency following agitation over the construction of the Narmada Dam in Gujarat. The use of law as a campaign tactic could bring construction projects to a halt in a tangle of slow-moving courts and procedures. Gadkari's early line on such protesters was strong:

> Those raising objections on environmental grounds are antinational elements … They do not want any development. I would like to ask these persons to go to the remote areas of Gadchiroli [to the south-east of Nagpur] where people lead a subhuman existence because of a lack of proper access … There can be no development without an efficient network of roads. The environmentalists should realise this. I am afraid that the environmental protection act is thought to be used as a no development act.[52]

He later refined his message. In 1997, speaking at the 'Infrastructure: Vision 2000' conference in Mumbai, he said:

> The role of environmentalists is like that of villains in Hindi movies … Eccentric environmentalists, with the help of courts are claiming that they have the support of the people who would actually benefit out of the infrastructure projects … I am not against the green movement, but this kind of extremism will have to go.[53]

The underlying logic of Gadkari's emerging mission was simple: roads are development. Pitching development against the environment aligned with his politics of 'common sense', as a pro-business and soft Hindu nationalism. Coupling this with pervasive rhetoric and bureaucracy focused on 'transparency', then associated in equal measure with the World Bank and the RSS, he had set in motion a cluster of ideas that quickly found receptive ears in other parts of India.

The value and practice of transparency is now everywhere in spaces of governance. However, in the late 1990s, in co-opting a discourse linked to efficiency and 'computerisation', Gadkari grasped the string of a rising balloon. Today, transparency is not simply to be equated with a culture of candour in the road world: rather, transparency tends to mean that publicity materials for public consumption are stripped of underlying research, simplified and generalised. Working methods and specialist knowledge common among roadmen are edited out of documents because they are seen as the cause of potential misunderstandings when given to the general public.

PMGSY (see Chapter 4), where Gadkari's career was heading by this time, took the bureaucratisation of transparency to a new level of formality and process. The publication and display of templates, timelines and working methods on the internet, supported by automated portals with quirky names, has been presented as removing human, therefore political, and, by implication, corrupt practices. Making documents, maps and animations available is not of course the same as telling the story of the activities that took place to enable the production and appearance of these artefacts. Here, transparency arguably becomes a distracting focus, a mask perhaps. Transparency is presented as a positive form of governance, a step forward, that counters some negative aspect of the past. Transparency as an ideology can only work if what is revealed is already known or feared—in this case, the road building practices and culture of past governments.

If transparency is an act of displacing the past, then it also has a difficult effect on the future. The future becomes hard to conceive when so much information is available, masquerading as all there is, while disguising other kinds of relationships and activities. Transparency has been called the 'neoliberal dispositive'.[54] Facts, claims and numbers out of context point to a just-so future in which corruption, self-interest and competition do not feature. The bones or materials displayed in the name of transparency can be assembled to produce creatures that have no resemblance to road-building offices or actual contractual procedures.

Gadkari adopted language that presumably spread through South Asia with inter-governmental and international organisations and engagement with the World Bank through transport planning in Mumbai and the early stages of PMGSY. Consequently, given the man and the times, there is a compelling overlap between the language of governmental transparency and the anti-corruption rhetoric of political Hindu nationalism. Both are about undoing the past and opening up the future with fixed parameters. On the public stage, Gadkari brings these ideas together with a 'can do' attitude, a spirit of ingenuity, forbearance and doing what has to be done— an appearance made opaque by the language and demonstration of transparency.

In 1996, the government of Maharashtra formed a committee of ministers and key civil servants to determine policy guidelines paving the way for the administrative sanction of private infrastructure.[55] This placed Gadkari and the PWD at the heart of the state government and close to Maharashtra's most influential figures. One of the group's key recommendations was to give tax concessions to infrastructural projects as an incentive.[56] At the same time, Gadkari went about modernising the PWD, introducing networked computers to prepare plans for bridges, flyovers and buildings, as well as video-conferencing facilities. Developing his straightforward language of openness and excellence, Gadkari says of this time that: 'All projects that I undertook as PWD minister were carried out with utmost transparency, adhering to the highest standards of integrity.'[57]

Even as he moved up through Maharashtra politics, Gadkari retained his interest in Nagpur. In 1995, he held a press conference to investigate the suitability of the city as an international logistics hub.[58] Subsequently, Ghulam Nabi Azad, a Congress national minister, commissioned an air cargo complex in Nagpur, which soon set off a pitched battle between Congress and BJP supporters over who was responsible for having led the initiative.[59] In March 1996, the Shiv Sena state government signed a memorandum of understanding with Simplex Infrastructures (tagline: Rising to the Challenge) for a feasibility study,[60] and in 1998, the central government, by now familiar with and sympathetic to Gadkari's work, approved proposals for the Multi-modal International Cargo Hub and Airport at Nagpur.[61] The story of the project is a long one, granted Special Economic Zone status in 2006, and has subsequently attracted considerable transport and logistical investment.

***

There is a popular story about Gadkari going out to buy a television and coming back with a new model of infrastructure finance. He found himself asking why roads could not be constructed with an investment recovery pattern similar to the monthly instalments model that allowed him to buy the television on credit. Its elements being somewhat interchangeable—in some versions, the television is a fridge—the story has often been repeated as a straightforward illustration of Gadkari's plain thinking about hire purchase arrangements for road building (even if its model is misleading).[62] In its simplicity, it also represents a populism for which Gadkari has become known. The can-do attitude that he developed in the face of 'expert' and 'professional' criticism as Mr Flyover in Mumbai has been refined into an anti-intellectual, almost anti-expert stance in later years. In Gadkari's vision, it is time for 'progressive politics' or the 'politics of development'; to be clear, this progressive politics is the provision of water, electricity, education and roads—above all roads.[63]

When Gadkari took over the PWD in 1995, there had already been extensive debate about different models of private sector participation in infrastructure. For Gadkari, a watershed moment came in 1996 when, after a visit to inspect development finance in Malaysia, he established the Maharashtra State Road Development Corporation (MSRDC) and took the role of chairman. The MSRDC, owned by the PWD yet insulated from its functioning, became the vehicle for PPP funding, a model later adopted in other states. It also made waves at a national level: when the prime minister's Council on Trade and Industry established a special subject group on infrastructure, which was now becoming a hot topic in central government, the group's chairman, influential industrialist Ratan Tata, paid a visit to Mumbai to learn of the work of the MSRDC. It was through MSRDC offices that Gadkari led the famous Mumbai flyovers project, in which fifty-five were built based on a system of toll revenues, and implemented the Mumbai–Pune Expressway. The flyover craze was described as a 'magnificent obsession', as innovative as it was controversial for promising to decrease congestion in the city at the cost of considerable displacement and investment.[64]

Gadkari also saw the power of infrastructure within the election cycle and began to urge that projects be completed in advance of elections.[65] Importantly, Gadkari claims, he raised money for these projects (more so with the flyovers than the expressway) on the capital market and diverted the budget allocated for the PWD to rural road development, thus giving the state resources to work in the most backward districts. There is some doubt about the veracity of this claim because BJP promotional literature had earlier stated that the money had come from soft bank loans.[66] Gadkari was then still learning the language of PPPs and was less careful with his words than he was to become in later years. For example, talking at a conference on infrastructure investment in 1997, he said: '[A]ctually you can also invest your black money into infrastructure and get white money out of it. Please don't take this as an official request, but those of you who have black money invest in these projects and give every justice to the people of Maharashtra.'[67]

The logic of privatisation in Western India at the end of the last century was thus: state funding is limited; private enterprise will be attracted to revenue and profit; urban road infrastructures are potentially profitable if tolls are levied; therefore, we must create mechanisms for private firms to levy tolls; this will free up the money the state was to spend on roads for other areas. Gadkari saw merit (and possibly votes) in the re-direction of these funds to rural poverty alleviation and infrastructure. In this move, he had refined his original anti-environmental message that 'roads are development'; now, not only were roads development but building roads with private finance freed up additional resources for other types of development work. The turn to the private sector permitted the state to address core questions of poverty and construct the types of infrastructure that would not attract private investment because there was no profit.

In Gadkari's view, the benefits of PPPs also extend to the promotion of India's traditional cultural values, as he sees them, including an old spirit of Indian entrepreneurship that was supposedly damaged by Nehru's government. The PPP model is a way of rekindling talent supressed by decades of socialism and protectionism: private parties need to be stakeholders in progress and development and PPPs harness entrepreneurial talent to develop the economy.[68]

In 1997, Gadkari started to say that 'America is rich because American roads are good.'[69] Variations of this quote have been on his office walls and in the frontispieces of his publications ever since. As he adopted this mantra, his local messages on roads began to diversify. He saw the possibility of renting out space under Mumbai's new flyovers and began to promote the technology of the new toll plazas as places of consumption and relaxation.[70] The first BOT project was announced as complete in the same year—the Thane–Bhiwandi bypass, 'completed in record time'.[71] Gadkari spoke with growing confidence about forging ahead with road projects in Mumbai that did not have approval of the central government, particularly the Bandra–Worli Sea Link, a cable-stayed bridge to connect two of the city's suburbs.[72] He began to lead conversation on the diversification of fuel through the use of compressed national gas following 'discussions' with corporates.[73] In 1997, work finally began on the Mumbai–Pune Expressway, with the ground being broken by Shiv Sena founder Bal Thackeray in a ceremony presided over by BJP General Secretary Pramod Mahajan, Maharashtra Chief Minister Manohar Joshi and Gadkari. In 1998, 70,000 trees were cut down to make way for the Mumbai–Ahmedabad Highway in advance of the alignment being made public—taking lessons from their earlier mistakes, Gadkari's road builders had acted swiftly to avoid delays brought about by the inevitable protests of environmental campaigners.[74]

Gadkari soon began to talk about the rapid transformation not just of Nagpur or even Mumbai but of the whole of Maharashtra. By early 1999, he was said to be outperforming the other BJP leaders of the state and was awarded the 'Bombay Bhushan' for having transformed the city through his determination.[75] He announced three further expressway projects, claiming that the Sena–BJP government had built more flyovers in four years than the Congress party had in forty-five.[76] In January 1999, Home Affairs Minister L.K. Advani and Manohar Joshi appeared with Gadkari at a series of infrastructural inauguration ceremonies in Mumbai.[77] The industrialist Ratan Tata, who had recently visited Gadkari in the MSRDC, spoke at the inauguration of the Vashi flyover, claiming that he would 'usually run away from inaugurations and ribbon cuttings' but had come on this occasion because Gadkari was 'a man who knows how to get things done'.[78] On a trip to Mumbai to hold talks with Shiv Sena, Pramod Mahajan, a leading BJP minister, took time out to inaugurate the Mahim flyover.[79] In 1979, Mahajan had been one of a select batch of RSS cadres co-opted into the newly formed BJP to promote the party. Organised and articulate, he would go on to be influential in the party's success and had a flat in the same complex in Mumbai as Gadkari.

By May 1999, Gadkari entered a new period of confidence, buoyed by these distinguished endorsements and powerful new friends. Everything was going well: road widening, resettlement, traffic diversion and the privatisation of infrastructure provision, but Gadkari's ambitions were bigger still. On Mumbai, he is quoted as having said: '[M]y aim is to save this city, which is already spoiled beyond control.' Shrugging away responsibility for controlling the automobile industry, he stated that '[m]y job is to create infrastructure'.[80]

But for the inhabitants of Mumbai, the costs of Gadkari's projects for infrastructural expansion were starting to show. In the run-up to the 1999 elections, Gadkari was facing increasing public resistance to the toll regime, eventually introduced in the city to pay for the flyovers. He responded in typical fashion saying that the agitation was politically motivated and argued that Mumbaikars were not against tolls but wanted a more efficient collection system.[81] The monsoon was heavy that year, and rain played havoc with the excavations required for flyover construction and temporary road surfaces. Large parts of the city were a mess, snarled with slow-moving traffic and lots of mud.[82] Public pressure mounted, as the logic and distribution of the toll regime came in for further scrutiny. As the rain continued, the Maharashtra Rajya Truck Tempo Tankers Bus Vahatuk Mahasangh called a strike from 1 August.[83] Slum-dwellers and fishermen affected by the proposed coastal road in the city also began to agitate. The hype hit the speed-breaker of reality. Gadkari responded to criticism by saying, 'if you need a good service then you should learn to pay for it. Nothing comes cheap.'[84]

***

In October 1999, Gadkari became the leader of the opposition in Maharashtra, the BJP and Shiv Sena having failed to form an alliance despite Mahajan's attention to these traditionally tense relations.[85] Gadkari's rule of the PWD came to an end and he fell back into opposition politics, making a fuss about the price of onions and legislative procedure. Maharashtra was now being governed by the Democratic Front, a coalition of Congress and a breakaway faction called the Nationalist Congress Party (NCP), under Chief Minister Vilasrao Deshmukh. The new state government turned to discrediting the previous one, making public news of a large financial deficit, aimed at casting shadows of doubt over Gadkari's achievements. Consequently, the central government, under A.B. Vajpayee's BJP-led NDA coalition, began to take more interest in the infrastructural politics of Mumbai.

Undeterred, Gadkari took on a new role at the national level when he was appointed chair of the NRRDC in January 2000.[86] They set out to 'blacktop' the country, and Gadkari's soundbites changed again. 'It is as if a Boeing plane crashes in India daily,' he said, in response to being told that 300 infants die every day from lack of access to proper medical treatment in the absence of pukka (permanent) roads. Gadkari estimated that 126,000 km of new roads would be needed to prevent these plane-loads of infants dying.[87] Thus, having already fought against World Bank interference with his flyovers in Mumbai, Gadkari took on what had been a World

Fig. 1: The Road Network in India in 1911. *Passage Through Passages.*
Brunei Gallery Exhibition: London, 2020.

Fig. 2: SH31 Gantry, Madhya Pradesh, 2018.

Fig. 3: The cover of *Indian Roads*, June 1938. The publication was issued by the India Roads Congress twice a year. The cartoons evoke a timeless message on the passage from chaos to order: roads carry our imagination to a better future.

Fig. 4: Means of Transport. Illustration by S.S. Brijbasi and Sons (Delhi, date unknown).

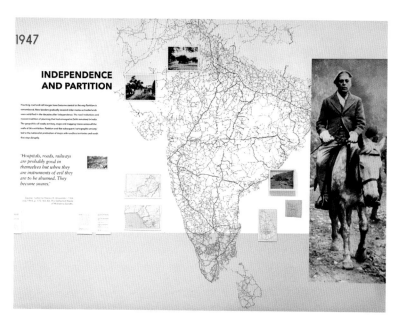

Fig. 5: *Passage Through Passages*. Brunei Gallery Exhibition: London, 2020. To the right, India's Prime Minister Nehru on Gangtok-Nathula Road to Tibet.

Fig. 6: Bullock cart (postcard, date unknown).

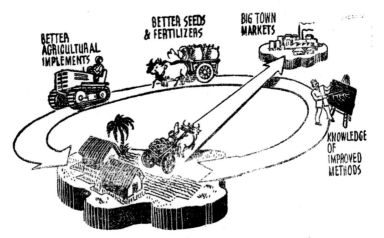

Fig. 7: Illustration of the effects of rural roads on agriculture.
T.R.S. Kynnersley. 1945. *Roads in India*. Bombay: Tata Sons Limited.

Fig. 8: Illustration of the
connections between
villages and services
made by rural roads.
T.R.S. Kynnersley. 1945.
Roads in India. Bombay:
Tata Sons Limited.

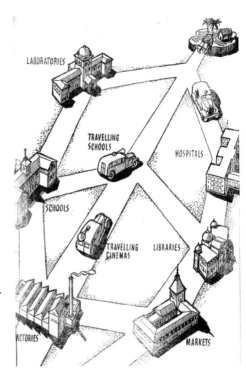

Fig. 9: Kynnersley's influential message. T.R.S. Kynnersley. 1945. *Roads in India*. Bombay: Tata Sons Limited.

Fig. 10: Roads and the wonders of India. T.R.S. Kynnersley. 1945. *Roads in India*. Bombay: Tata Sons Limited.

Fig. 11: 'Men of Steel' illustration by C.H.G. Moorehouse in Minoo Masani. 1953. *Our India*. Bombay: Oxford University Press.

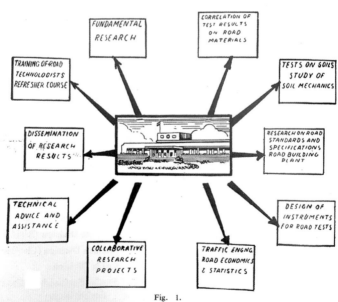

Fig. 12: Illustration of the role of the Central Road Research Institute. *Indian Roads Congress*, Silver Jubilee Edition, 1960.

Fig. 13: India Proposed Expansion of the National Highway System. *Silver Jubilee Souvenir 1934–1959.* New Delhi: Indian Roads Congress, 1960.

Fig. 14: Advert for the free road-building service offered by the Concrete Association of India. *Indian Roads Congress*, vol 16, 1951–2.

MESSAGE

I send my good wishes to the Indian Roads Congress on the occasion of its completing twentyfive years of its activities. Roads are of high importance in India and, therefore, the science and practice of road-building should be studied carefully. New methods are being evolved in other parts of the world and perhaps we are a little backward in utilizing them. We cannot always copy the expensive methods of rich countries. We have to devise our own ways of doing things more cheaply and yet effectively.

Jawaharlal Nehru

Fig. 15: Letter from Prime Minister Nehru. *Silver Jubilee Souvenir 1934–1959*. New Delhi: Indian Roads Congress, 1960.

Fig. 16: Goggomobil brochure (circa 1950s).

Fig. 17: Hindusthan advert.
MARG, vol. 4, 1950.

Fig. 18: General Motors
India Limited advert.
MARG, vol. 4, 1950.

Fig. 19: Fiat advert.
MARG, vol. 4, 1950.

Fig. 20: Mobiloil advert.
MARG, vol. 2, 1952.

Fig. 21: Tata-Mercedes-Benz advert. *MARG*, vol. 12, 1959.

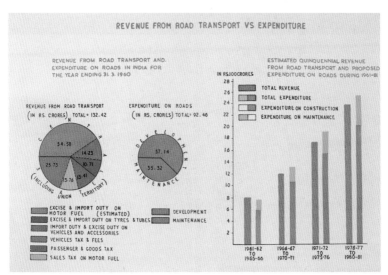

Fig. 22: Revenue from Road Transport and Expenditure on Roads in India for the Year Ending 31.3.1960. *History of Road Development in India: A Brief Account of the Genesis and Development of the Indian Road System.* New Delhi, Central Road Research Institute, 1963.

Fig. 23: Images of road work. *Passage Through Passages*. Brunei Gallery Exhibition: London, 2020.

Fig. 24: Stills from government-sponsored films about roads. *Passage Through Passages*. Brunei Gallery Exhibition: London, 2020.

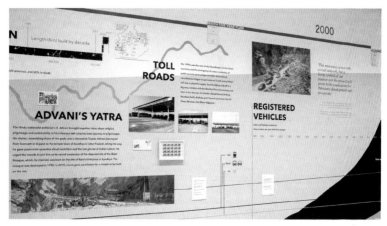

Fig. 25: Advani, privatisation and the growth of an economy on the move. *Passage Through Passages*. Brunei Gallery Exhibition: London, 2020.

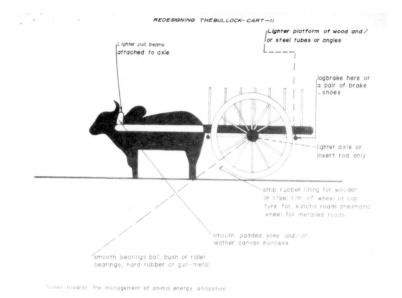

Fig. 26: Notes Toward the Management of Animal Energy Utilization. In N.S. Ramaswamy, 1979. *The Modernization of the Bullock-Cart System and the Management of Animal Energy Resources.* Bangalore: Indian Institute of Management.

Fig. 27: A roadside eatery 'cut' to make way for 'four-laning', Madhya Pradesh, 2013.

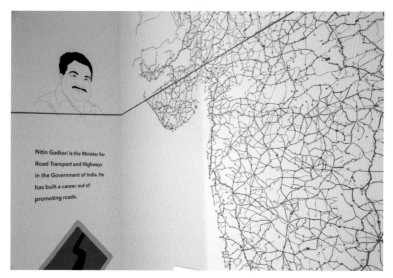

Fig. 28: Nitin Gadkari and the expanding road network. *Passage Through Passages*. Brunei Gallery Exhibition: London, 2020.

Fig. 29: The journey through Sindh towards the border with India. *Passage Through Passages*. Brunei Gallery Exhibition: London, 2020.

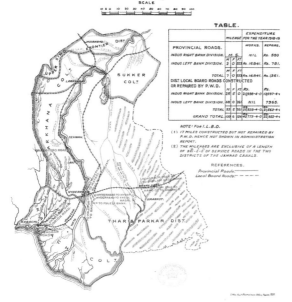

Fig. 30: Road map of Sindh, 1920.

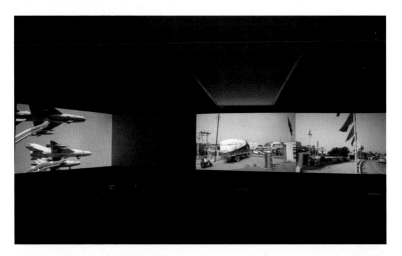

Fig. 31: The journey through Kutch to the border with India. *Passage Through Passages*. Brunei Gallery Exhibition: London, 2020.

Fig. 32: 'Madhya Pradesh'. *Economical and Statistical Atlas of Madhya Pradesh*, Directorate of Economics and Statistics: Bhopal, 1958. The SH31 runs roughly parellel to the border shared with Rajasthan and then turns southeast after Ratlam.

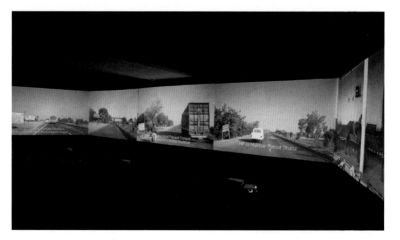

Fig. 33: SH31 Madhya Pradesh. *Passage Through Passages*. Brunei Gallery Exhibition: London, 2020.

Bank project and moved the rural road scheme to the government of India in the form of PMGSY.

Meanwhile, in Maharashtra, relations between Gadkari, now in opposition, and the personalities of the ruling state government were becoming rancorous. In Mumbai, the BJP launched a *rasta roko* (road block) on the Western Express Highway in protest against the rising cost of living under the Democratic Front.[88] The Shiv Sena–BJP alliance led a call for presidential rule—suspension of state government by central government—to be imposed.[89] In response, the state government launched new investigations into concrete roads built in Nagpur while Gadkari was in charge of the PWD, with the aim of exposing Gadkari's alleged corruption.[90] Mumbai's flyovers also became an easy target, as congestion still dominated city life. There were calls for lower speed limits and anxiety shifted to pollution, as questions were raised about the development model underpinning Gadkari's somewhat piecemeal vision for urban transportation. Perhaps most damningly of all, the new government announced that statues and inauguration ceremonies, which had been the foundation of Gadkari's strategy to gain the highest levels of patronage, would no longer be part of road-building programmes in the city.[91]

In reaction, Gadkari goaded the state government by launching a website to detail and present evidence of its corruption, targeting the chief minister, Vilasrao Deshmukh, with accusations of irregularities.[92] In the face of the allegations, Deshmukh dissolved the Nagpur municipal corporation in March 2001.[93] Gadkari went on to claim that the Democratic Front government was neglecting Nagpur and the Vidarbha region.[94] In June 2001, he alleged that the arrest of seventy Nagpur councillors on corruption charges was an act of political vengeance.[95] When the state registrar served a dissolution notice against the board of directors of the BJP-controlled Nagpur Nagrik Sahakari Bank, Gadkari retaliated by claiming the state government had 'sabotaged' the local implementation of the national rural road-building scheme, which 'amounts to injustice to people'.[96]

In November 2001, the Bombay High Court announced that Deshmukh had acted improperly by dissolving the Nagpur municipality and reinstated the corporation. Gadkari demanded Deshmukh's resignation and led walkouts every time the chief minister rose to speak.[97] He also mockingly arranged for sweet boxes to be delivered to legislators and journalists, each of which contained a small bag of rice and a tape recording of Deshmukh engaging in an allegedly irregular deal over a rice mill.[98]

In February 2002, in the run-up to the municipal elections, Deshmukh countered at a rally in Nagpur: 'You can't lay claims to be a pioneer in development activities by building four roads and a flyover ... Mr Gadkari may have built a flyover in the city for the benefit of car users, but the Congress has always strived for the poor slum-dwellers and the common man.'[99] Gadkari campaigned on crutches, having fractured his thigh in a road accident in September 2001. Many of the senior leaders who had become friends with Gadkari through the infrastructural inauguration ceremonies flew into the city to create a coalition with Shiv Sena. In these ways, both roads and Nagpur became central to Gadkari's politics as displays of prowess and as means of tactical warfare between the government and the opposition.

***

In November 2004, Gadkari was appointed president of the BJP in Maharashtra, a post he held for two terms while Deshmukh's Democratic Front continued to govern.[100] Gadkari kept a low profile in this new role, focusing his efforts on discrediting and undermining Deshmukh and his government. This included staging various protests to bring attention to the plight of Vidarbha's beleaguered farmers, 1,025 of whom were reported to have ended their lives in a single year. Gadkari formed a cross-party campaign group in response and invited Deshmukh to a TV debate, asking the chief minister to account for having 'pushed Maharashtra back by 10 years in business and development'.[101]

Aside from his rise within the party, these were not good years for Gadkari. He found himself dogged by scandal after scandal, starting with the death of his personal assistant in mysterious circumstances in 2004.[102] In the same year, he also faced a charge of violation of the Electoral Code of Conduct for raising political slogans in the district magistrate's office in Nagpur,[103] and in 2005 he was arrested following a BJP-led agitation against electrical load shedding in Nagpur.[104] In August 2006, income tax investigations were launched into both Gadkari and his Purti Group company.[105] Gadkari deflected criticism by claiming that Manish Mehta, a former director at Purti who had left in 2003, had been the subject of the investigation.[106]

Perhaps the most difficult scandal emerged in May 2009, when a 7-year-old girl, Yogita Thakre, was found dead in a car belonging to Gadkari near his home in Nagpur.[107] The autopsy revealed a number of injuries, including the suggestion of sexual assault, and concluded that the girl had been smothered and her dead body placed in the car.[108] Police launched a murder investigation, during which confusion emerged about which car the body had been found in, with Yogita's mother and sister identifying a different car from the one listed in police records.[109] Stories of blackmail began to swirl around the case, with Gadkari saying, probably correctly, the storm was encouraged by his political rivals.[110] On 19 June, police announced that the car at the centre of the investigation was owned by Sudhir Dive, managing director of the Purti sugar factory.[111] Despite the tragedy of the death, the case disappeared.

Gadkari's involvement with issues of road building and infrastructure was by now limited to occasional comments on the decisions of the MSRDC, the state road-building corporation that he had inaugurated as PWD minister.[112] Speaking in February 2005, he claimed the MSRDC had been 'emasculated' by the Democratic Front government because it had been so closely associated with his own rise and success.[113]

By November 2009, it became clear that Gadkari was going to be given the national presidency of the BJP, now in opposition at the national level to the Congress-led UPA coalition under Manmohan Singh.[114] Gadkari's RSS credentials and association with Nagpur were seen as positive attributes, as soft Hindu nationalism and development politics moved to the centre stage for the BJP at a national level.[115] Some saw Gadkari as a replacement for Pramod Mahajan, who had been shot dead in Mumbai by his brother in 2006. The Gadkari faction, however, held Mahajan responsible for the 'Congressification of the BJP' and took the opportunity to leave

187

behind those closest to him, a course of action seemingly approved by the RSS.

In his home state of Maharashtra, Gadkari's elevation received more sceptical coverage. The *Times of India* crowed: 'To build flyovers is one thing, but to lead a vast organisation like the BJP is a different task altogether.' The deaths of Yogita and Gadkari's personal assistant once again came to the surface, and questions were also raised about Gadkari's effectiveness as a state-level leader over the last few years—he was seen as a *mofussil* (small-town) politician.[116] The BJP had not grown or prospered, nor had it made a dint in the popularity of Congress. The uneasy relationship with Shiv Sena, which had dominated right-leaning politics since the mid-1990s, could also have had more fruitful outcomes.

Still, in December 2009, Gadkari ascended to the party presidency, proud to fill the position that in the past had been held by his political heroes A.B. Vajpayee and L.K. Advani.[117] In this new role, his horizons began to change, as he came to learn what India's society and politics looked like—and how to boost the BJP's vote share—across its many other states. The way he overcame his own limitations and appealed to varied electorates was to speak the universal language of roads.

***

Gadkari's rise to power was premised on ideas abouts roads and development, intimately woven around his loyalty to Nagpur. When, after winning the seat in the 2014 national elections, he took up his current position as road transport and highways minister within Modi's BJP-led government, the focus of his vision had to broaden. He needed to draw on nationalist history and take inspiration from other figures whose lives and works resonated with the kind of country and philosophy he wished to promote.

In his book *India Aspires: Redefining Politics of Development* (2013), co-written with Tuhin Sinha, Gadkari outlines his vision of development. According to Gadkari, the biggest impediment to equitable prosperity in India has been the absence of 'political will'.[118] The chain of 'political blunders' that ensued after Independence rested upon the first prime minister's 'flawed understanding of the concept of development'.[119] Nehruvian socialism empowered state institutions 'to such a disproportionate level' that it became 'the biggest impediment to our growth and progress of the nation'. In particular, a top-heavy state and patronage killed off the country's competitive edge. The Industrial Policy Resolution of 1956, which reserved seventeen industries for the public sector, and the emergent licensing system led to a monopolistic and bureaucratic system of production and distribution. Together, these policies and attitudes impeded economic growth and gave the state a particularly clumsy character and set of burdensome administrative qualities in the imagination of the population.

We can see in Gadkari's language that there is a longer-term aim focused on changing the functioning and qualities of the state and the expectations of the population. Consequently, much of this discourse focuses on discrediting past politicians and ideologies, as well as rivals in the Congress party, who, in name at least, represent these older political traditions, while simultaneously creating a new language and promoting new ideologues.

The simple fact that the right has had so little time in power in post-colonial India has meant that the heroes of their movement and politics are relatively obscure when compared to those of Congress— something that Gadkari and others have worked hard to counter.

During his years at college in Nagpur, Gadkari was drawn to the work of the RSS cadres and the ABVP. He was inspired by their ideas of humanity and nation-building. He also learned about K.B. Hedgewar, who founded the RSS in Nagpur in 1925, with the intention of promoting the concept of a united India rooted in Hindu ideology. These early influences gave Gadkari particular views about patriotism, social service and culture and justice in India, which have become the foundations of political action. Gadkari also names as sources of inspiration RSS activists and later BJP leaders Kushabhau Thakre and Vijayaraje Scindia, both of whom were born in provincial Madhya Pradesh and operated firmly out of Central India, where the RSS had worked hard since its inception to establish a strong base for support.

Gadkari claims that it was in the 1970s when he began to realise that there was something amiss with India's approach to development.

Innovative solutions were needed to eradicate abject poverty, which for him would mean the provision of basic necessities, ensuring that everyone gets an opportunity to rise in life. He recalled the vision and sacrifice of Dr Syama Prasad Mookerjee and Pandit Deendayal Upadhyaya.

Mookerjee was the founder of the Bharatiya Jana Sangh party (BJS), one of the precursors to the BJP, in 1951. He was opposed to religious appeasement in the name of vote bank politics and favoured free-market economics rather than the socialism of Nehru. He also favoured a uniform civil code for the personal laws of both Muslims and Hindus and campaigned for a ban on cow slaughter and the end of the special status given to the troubled state of Jammu and Kashmir. In 1953, he launched a protest against the prohibition on Indian citizens settling in Kashmir and the permit system that regulated their transit and settlement. He was arrested the same year and died in custody under mysterious circumstances. Whatever the actual cause of his death, for many, his demise became martyrdom and the cause of endless speculation.

Gadkari's other great influence was Upadhyaya, who developed the concepts of integral humanism that eventually formed a central part of the intellectual and moral genealogy of the BJP and as such are Gadkari's direct political inheritance. Upadhyaya argued that India's development should be rooted not in Western secularism but in *dharma*, the universal laws set out in ancient Hindu texts, leading the Hindu right wing to promote him as a nationalist philosopher and freedom fighter. The sovereignty of *dharma* and Upadhyaya's corresponding mistrust of a powerful state are being enacted through the structures of PPP schemes and the neo-corporatist ethos that Gadkari has brought to infrastructure and the ruling party, first in Maharashtra and later at the national level. In some ways, infrastructure finance has been a successful mechanism through which state functions can be rolled back, and the involvement of private enterprises in road building provides fertile ground for the implementation and promulgation of integral humanism.

Now in central government, Gadkari has intensified his familiar tactics and broadened his ambitions: he has revitalised the conversation about building a bridge between India and Sri Lanka;

launched the Bharatmala Pariyojana (tagline: Road to Prosperity), 65,000 km of highways to be constructed by 2022 around the border of India; and developed road-cum-airstrips in Rajasthan, a highway project to connect the Char Dham Hindu shrines in Uttarakhand, and endless expressways, including Delhi–Katra, Delhi–Meerut, Delhi–Bombay, and more recently, Bombay–Nagpur. Gadkari has also commented extensively on India investing in the Chabahar free trade zone and port in Iran as a means of providing trade access to Afghanistan, Russia and Europe, thus circumventing Pakistan.

***

Generating political capital with roads is not a new game. However, Gadkari and Sharif have excelled in political careers based on the promise and delivery of roads. Their work coincided with the expansion of funding opportunities, the rise of an international mobility-development paradigm and the simultaneous globalisation of the industry.

Gadkari learned on the job, gradually refining his messaging as he developed new tricks and saw the great potential of roads for both popularity and patronage. Developing a reputation as 'a man of action' interested in roading India, he has also been allowed to smuggle, almost unnoticed, a hard-line RSS Nagpur Hindu nationalist agenda to the heart of central government. In Gadkari's Delhi office are the framed words attributed to John F. Kennedy: 'American roads are good not because America is rich, but America is rich because American roads are good' (a sharpening of the words he first used in the PWD in Mumbai). The quote hangs just below a large plastic Hindu swastika, red against a white background. While there might be nothing unusual about him in Modi's India, Gadkari often appears not to be a politician at all; his guise is more that of a public servant, a problem-solver, who is in his post to perform a role without politics. His mask slips sometimes, of course, most obviously when he is asked about communalism and the civilisational nature of his country.

Gadkari is obsessed with numbers and perpetuates the traditions of targets and classificatory practices of the Planning Commission, while still managing to make it sound as if he is saying something fresh and new. Though he became known for Mumbai's flyovers, he has used all sorts of road schemes, from expressways to rural roads, and has not tied himself to one form of infrastructural persuasion. In contrast, Sharif was Mr Motorway. He, too, took a provincial obsession into the national frame, and, like others before him, used his product, the motorway, to spread his vision literally and metaphorically throughout Pakistan. The journeys of Sharif and Gadkari do not mirror one another, although they have certain traits in common: claim-making, persistence and the association of roads with national transformation.

Sharif was from the industrial elite of Punjab; consequently, his message was delivered with confidence from the outset. In contrast, Gadkari started in the back streets of Nagpur and worked his way up, learning about roads and politics as he went. When both men were riding high, they take us to a new level of ethnography: roadmen who, without a digger or level in sight, are the most powerful believers, proselytes and champions of the cause.

In both countries, roads have become political battlegrounds and important sites for inauguration ceremonies and campaign trails. Visionary and charismatic leaders have exploited the moral and anticipatory potential of roads for their own popularity and electoral success. In the region, roads are perhaps among the few electoral platforms that have near universal support. Key to their success has been their 'depoliticisation': building roads has been made to look like the common-sensical action of a humanitarian and compassionate government. The emphasis on technology, standards, process and the public performance of a role has contributed to the idea that roads are value-neutral and that strong governance removes the corruption of the political. On paper, roads are for everyone, excluding no one on the basis of religion, caste, ethnicity or even political persuasion; in practice, this might not be the case, but the dream and promise are available to all. And yet, despite this electoral allure, I think there is more to this than electioneering strategy or straightforward populism.

The great road builders of contemporary South Asia embody decisive action and a certain attitude to office and power. They have become particular 'types' of people, not role models exactly, but exemplary persons in their devotion to a cause. Their determination and fight to will roads into existence, against the odds of faltering finance, difficult bureaucracy, restrictive legislation and bumpy geography, represent masculine struggles on all fronts. With finance, they are mercurial; they shrink and streamline the 'cumbersome bureaucracy' of past political regimes; they manipulate legislation to think anew the scope of the public and the private; with machinery and concrete, they straighten up the landscape and conquer nature. The medium is the message, the path of the twentieth century gives legitimacy, and populist dreams allow all of this to fly.

The nation-building project of both countries is indexed by the capacity to construct roads and to harness the kinds of dreams of the future that roads spawn. Building roads is not simply to connect a village to a highway: rather, these men see it as connecting villages to the economy and to the forward thrust of national modernities. Roadmen are the dream-makers, gift-givers, their ministries glamorous and leading the way in reforming the processes of 'doing government'. 'Computerisation', 'latest technology', 'fast-track' 'implementation', 'BOT'—these are not just commonplace terms but carry with them tremendous emotional sway, and, importantly, hope.

8

THE BORDERLAND'S NEW ROADS
NATION-BUILDING AT THE MARGINS

Over the last few chapters, we have seen how roadmen are subject to political whims and how politicians whip up road magic through rhetoric, ceremony and promise. However, if we leave the offices of both political and engineering roadmen for the open road, we soon find that other messages about the nation's territory, identity and values begin to emerge along the route.

In 1947, a line was drawn down the western side of British India that would divide the new, independent nations of India and Pakistan. The different trajectories and ideologies of these two post-colonial states can be read through the stories of their roads: while Pakistan built its roads with the assistance of US-dominated institutions and China, India placed greater emphasis on self-reliance, with only some traces of international intervention and money. Seven decades of division have thus created very different countries and characters, and the two states have publicly been at loggerheads ever since Partition, their respective nationalisms, in both secular and religious periods, tending to demonise the other. Notably, their borderlands remain disputed and contested terrain, with occasional military skirmishes and acts of terror adding fuel to a complex psycho-dynamic drama.

We now take journeys in both India and Pakistan oriented by the mirror-line of the border. Roads have facilitated movement, and as people of the region have increasingly consumed different ideas, so too the road has become a medium of conveying distinct forms of identity politics. Signboards and hoardings litter the spaces by the side of the road, encouraging certain ideas and positions. These adverts do not only exist to sell toothpaste: they also advance ideologies about historical authenticity and national identity. In both India and Pakistan, the road is a way of promoting and consuming notions of citizenship, orientation and selfhood. The 'selfie point' and the memorial become ways of locating travellers and tourists within a particular national register.

The first journey takes us through the Kutch District of Gujarat in Western India and leaves us gazing along with tourists and pilgrims at the closed border with Pakistan. The second journey traces a similar route through eastern Sindh in Pakistan towards the border with India. On the first, we go with the flow authorised by the Indian state; on the second, we travel against the current, fighting the structures encouraging us to turn back to Karachi rather than continue towards India. The symmetry is figurative, not an exact method.

In Gujarat, the road to the border takes us through a nationalist theme park rich with symbols and signs pointing to the wrongdoings of the past and the hope that Hindu nationalism offers for the future. Such messages are not entirely orchestrated, but the tropes of contemporary Hindu nationalism dominate—of the nation, sacrifice and strength; anti-Gandhi, anti-Congress and anti-Pakistan. In the Rann of Kutch, the heavily marketed wild ass and flamingos are more than petty distractions, making patriots and true believers of those tourists plying the region's roads until they end.

In Pakistan, on the other side of the oh-so-beautiful no-man's land, mining is just getting underway, some thirty or forty years after the first big coal mines opened in Western India. Signs here are more rudimentary and speculative than in India, but a distinct process is recognisable, as petro-modernity is brought in with the coal road. First, the population will be rehoused, counted and ordered; they might be encouraged to take paid employment, play football or have their Hinduism tempered. In this future, the road will take them to

Karachi, a magnet for work and play. Then, the tide and direction of travel will turn, and either the state or the local population will build suburbs and theme parks across the region. Roads have the power to do these things. Roads structure the nation's narratives, reflect its identity and enact its priorities.

In showing how fertile roads can be as political projects, these two road journeys return us to the legacies of Gadkari and Sharif. Both men have been likened to the *Sher* Shah Suri, the ruler who expanded the Great North Road or Grand Trunk Road across the Subcontinent in the sixteenth century. Over the years, as we have seen, they both came to use the promise of roads with increased alacrity and refinement. As previously with Gandhi and Nehru, the biographies of Gadkari and Sharif reflect the language, aspirations and technology adopted by each of their countries in the post-colonial period, revealing different sets of development priorities and governmental messages.

India was first to exploit lignite, or brown coal, and gradually domesticated a rude country with border tourism and nationalist messages, memorials and sentiments. In Pakistan, by contrast, lignite mining is only just beginning. The names of new airports and hospitals are tentative, not yet conveying either a national or a regional message with confidence. Security forces remain highly visible, and experiments to resettle wandering populations with loyalties that are simply not compatible with nation-building projects are just underway. But while Pakistan's political promises are ambitious and uneven, they are often extremely successful. Pakistan discovered the rhetorical strength of the 'motorway' before such hyperbole found a way into India, where headline promises for massive new road projects tend to be made on more comprehensive policy foundations. In this sense, the political set-up and history of democracy and leadership in each country broadly reflect the story of its road building. Roads, their evenness and distribution, or otherwise, reflect national character.

On the Road Through Gujarat

The road heading west into Kutch and towards Pakistan is close to my heart. I have travelled that road for over twenty years and written extensively about the country and its landmarks.[1] As I crossed the bridge over the upper reaches of the Gulf of Kutch from Saurashtra, my mood would usually lighten, set free by the open promise of the sea and the peculiar safety of India's resolute border with Pakistan, the final limit of a vast country. At the town of Bhachau the road forks, the branches merging again after 80 km, just before Bhuj, the district headquarters. Although the southerly route via Anjar is more reliable, I generally preferred to turn right on to State Highway 42 (SH42), risking delays and unpredictable surface conditions, because of the quiet the road used to bring. After Bhuj, further west, the population thins out and gives way to remote power, chemical and cement plants. There are pilgrims and tourists, an airbase, Border Security Forces, Sir Creek, and then, finally, Pakistan.

My preferred route from Bhachau to Bhuj dissects the plain where many saw an opportunity after the earthquake of 2001 to create what they thought would be the best of all possible worlds. The place had been thoroughly done over by the earthquake, brought almost entirely to ruin, and there was an urgent need to imagine a new future. Development and reconstruction projects along the road were in high demand, while the less-visible hinterlands did not receive the same level of attention or investment. Some advertised their campaign with signs; others used concrete to get their message across. Many of those who came attempted to 'civilise' the villagers with both metropolitan and religious ideas from mainstream Hinduism. The BJP was then in power in both the state of Gujarat and central government, which gave them a long leash to impose their values and ideas on the countryside. Consequently, Hindu nationalist terms and messages gave villages new life.

Change was swift and profound. In the late 1990s, a single strip of tarmac bordered by shoulders of compacted earth had passed through an almost empty landscape. Most villages were hidden in the country beyond the road. Now the landscape is littered with factories, the road has been upgraded, and villages have sprung up on its verges, sucked out of the countryside by the magnetic enchantment of tarmac.

We come to one such new village, Indraprastha or Navi (new) Dudhai, about 30 km from Bhachau. The tangle of rubble, caste interests and history in old Dudhai proving too complicated to unravel, this new site was established on the main road. This is the work of Rashtriya Swabhiman ('Pride in the Nation'; tagline: Dedicated to Humanity), an organisation founded by Sahib Singh Verma in the 1990s. Verma had been an activist for the RSS and went on to a political career, notably serving as chief minister in Delhi and later as head of the labour ministry in the national government.

While in Delhi, Verma had led an unsuccessful campaign to rename the nation's capital as Indraprastha, the magnificent capital of the warring Pandavas in the Hindu *Mahabharata* epic and thought by some to have been located on the site of New Delhi. Where he had failed in North India, in Gujarat he had a free hand, and the roadside reincarnation of Dudhai became Indraprastha, or 'city of Indra', the ancient Hindu lord of heaven.

In this spirit, Verma wanted the village that he was creating in Gujarat to be a model for others to emulate, inspired by his personal philosophy for the nation. In his view, successful development was to be fostered through the promotion of self-sufficiency and self-reliance. While the words might echo the sentiments for which Gandhi is well known, Verma's means and creed are quite different. His ambition was global power for India, and he believed that this would be achieved through the embrace of technology, strength, education and disciplined religious and cultural purity.

In the early months of the project, Verma would visit frequently to oversee construction work. Later, he installed a retired colonel to oversee proceedings and discipline the villagers. I met the colonel many times, and he was always welcoming. We would spend hours talking in the village's library, where Verma's portrait hung on the wall, flanked by other national heroes, the contours and lines of their faces traced in blood extracted from Verma's followers. Gandhi was absent, an unwanted face in this new world.

On the outskirts of Indraprastha, Verma constructed a monument to those who perished in the earthquake, naming it Tiger Hill. On top of a small hillock, a plaque with the names of the dead is set into the foundations of a pole for the national flag. The hill is positioned between the village and the wilderness, beyond which it is easy to imagine Pakistan, just as the Tiger Hill from which the monument derives its name lies between India and Pakistan in the disputed border region. The bloody battle for Tiger Hill, adjacent to the Srinagar–Leh Highway in Kashmir, was a turning point in the border skirmishes between India and Pakistan in 1999. Soon after the Indian army captured the summit, media showed images of the tricolour fluttering in the mountain breeze. The Indian soldiers who lost their lives became martyrs; now, in a recycling of those sentiments, the earthquake victims also became martyrs for nationalist revivalism.

Scattered around Indraprastha were other slogans in Hindi: 'True love alone generates the sentiment of sacrifice'; 'Everything is possible with self-confidence, true labour, and strong will'; and, in English, visible from the highway, 'Purity is power.' Verma's elite brand of nationalism and sacrifice was knowledge-led, Sanskrit-based and premised on the myth of the traditional Indian village. The benefactor created the settlement as he saw India: diverse but hierarchical and Hindu at its core, with potent signs of contestation, conflict and martyrdom on the periphery.[2]

***

Dholavira is not on the main highway, but it is notable and popular with tourists because of a major Harappan archaeological site nearby. After the earthquake, the village was adopted by BJP General Secretary Pramod Mahajan. Mahajan, a high-profile MP and party leader, had given close support to L.K. Advani during the Toyota procession from Somnath to Ayodhya. The stunt, as we know, was part of the campaign to build a temple to the Hindu god Lord Ram on the spot where a sixteenth-century mosque then stood. From this and other experiences, Mahajan understood the important place of imagery, journeys and roads in the making and cementing of political messages.

In Dholavira, as in Indraprastha, the status and resources of a national ministerial position flowed into rural Gujarat in the name of a private trust. In this instance, Mahajan's relief funds for Dholavira were channelled through Rambhau Mhalgi Prabodhini, an organisation that focuses on social improvement through discipline and political leadership. Positioning itself as the 'enabler that elevates' the innumerable 'well-meaning individuals struggl[ing] in the dust laden streets' to become leaders 'for development of the nation', the trust was established in memory of Rambhau Mhalgi, an RSS politician from Maharashtra who served in the national parliament on and off between 1957 and his death in 1982.[3]

Like Nitin Gadkari, Mhalgi was influenced by Deendayal Upadhyaya, who developed the BJP's philosophy of integral humanism, a critique of communism and capitalism based on the 'core values' of Indian civilisation.[4] To Upadhyaya, the Congress party and others had damaged India's indigenous politico-religious philosophy through the blind adoption of alien Western concepts, such as that of the secular post-colonial state. Upadhyaya thought that the Independence movement should instead be based on Indian cultural values, what he called 'Bharatiya culture', which he equated with 'dynamic Vedic religion'.[5] Drawing on foundational texts of Hindu philosophy known as the Upanishads and other sources, Upadhyaya concluded that the ultimate principle of this culture was the operation of *dharma*, broadly defined as a universal and eternal system of rules or 'innate laws' within which all sentiment in India was bound. Rather than enforcing a separation between the secular and the religious, the state should be run on the basis of *dharma* and encourage ways and means of achieving both material and spiritual progress. This philosophy of *dharmic* sovereignty provided the political, intellectual and moral underpinnings of the reconstruction of post-earthquake Gujarat some twenty years ago, and Mahajan's use of names, messaging and active proselytes in Dholavira was intended to promote and cement these ideas.

In the signs and monuments on the road between Bhachau and Bhuj, a map of non-Congress Indian nationalist politics in the mid-twentieth century emerges, of which Verma, Mahajan and their own political genealogies are influential strands. In a more general sense, the networks and connections forged by youths spent in the RSS and adulthoods in the BJP become apparent to the outsider through the noticeable cronyism of reconstruction and inaugurations.

In Kutch, these figures saw the possibility of revitalising a twentieth-century politics that had not been as successful in India's early post-colonial decades as that of Congress, which held uninterrupted power at the national level until 1977. Put rather simply, Congress's legacy was branded on all of India's statues, street names and institutions; now in Gujarat was an opportunity for the BJP to make their own. They breathed new life into older ideologies from opposition politics by making villages out of them along the road, where they would be visible and influential to those motoring by.

***

Further west, on the outskirts of Bhuj, the road passes close to a grand replica of Parliament House in Delhi, described by its creators, the Ashapura Group (tagline: Touching Lives Every Day), as the 'very first 4-D Memorial where you can relive the entire journey of Indian Independence in life-like 4-D technology'.[6] Unlike in Verma's library, there are several statues of Gandhi, including one over 6 metres tall. But here, too, India is conceived in Hindu terms, as Bharat Mata (the national mother deity), with the model parliament's interior hosting a golden statue of the goddess on a chariot driven by four lions.

Very soon after leaving the replica parliament, we pass the life-size monument to the women who repaired the bombed runway during the war with Pakistan in 1971. The Indian jets gleam; the single Pakistani aircraft is rusty. Bhuj—the headquarters of the district and seat of the former kings—is now bypassed by traffic heading out further west on pilgrimage, business or border tourism. When the road was first constructed, it brought joy and awe to those who had suffered in the ruins; I used to play cricket and picnic on it with friends at the weekend. Now, it has been taken over by traffic and the humdrum and dust of suburban life.

Locals mirthfully call the road north out of Bhuj 'the Ayub Khan Highway', as it was constructed for the Indian military when the general was in power in Pakistan. It heads into flatlands known as the Rann, to securitised bromide factories and garish safari camps. The route also takes us to the summit of the famous Kalo Dungar, or Black Hill, a site for 'enemy tourism'. Visitors can ride camels, or they can hire binoculars from multilingual touts to train their lenses on invisible others. Honeymooners pose for photographs. The empty landscape perhaps only adds to the psychodrama of staring at the geography of Partition. The vista is beautiful, an awesome spectacle, its imaginative possibilities both greater and less terrifying in the absence of any actual Pakistanis. Border Security Force soldiers in their camouflaged tents in the sand below are the only visible signs of life—another memorial to war, another sign of recent symbolic colonisation.

SH42 exits Bhuj to the west, heading towards Rohar and the other villages where Gandhi suffered the effects of poor roads on his way from and to the coast in the 1930s (as narrated in Chapter 5). Still further west, lignite mining and electricity generation took off in the 1970s. Open cast mines feed power stations with dirty coal. Behind metal gates is a massive housing colony, built over forty years ago for the workers who came to produce power for the nation. Back then, it must have stood out as a beacon of modernity in an otherwise parched, poor and pastoralist land. The colony had smart houses, schools, health facilities and exercise gardens, a suburban oasis in the wild borderlands.

The colony was named after Shyamji Krishnavarma, a freedom fighter who strongly and violently opposed British rule in India. Born in Kutch into a Gujarati mercantile caste in 1857, Krishnavarma proved himself as a Sanskrit scholar in Bombay and went to study law and to assist a professor of classical Indian languages at the University of Oxford. Later, he enrolled as an advocate in Bombay and went on to hold senior administrative positions in a number of Princely States, including Ratlam in Central India, before leaving India for good in 1897. He settled in Highgate in North London, and in 1905, he formed the Society for Home Rule in India and opened a hostel for Indian students called 'India House'. He started a journal, *The Indian Sociologist*, which carried his opinion on the colonial occupation, arguing for political assassinations and armed struggle.[7]

After the 2001 earthquake, the rebuilt airport and new university in Bhuj were named after Krishnavarma, and a memorial complex was constructed in Mandvi, his birthplace.[8] The resurrection of Krishnavarma's memory and values aimed at dislodging an obstinate and difficult Gandhian political legacy in Western India.

For much of his life, Gandhi was associated with Congress, and many of his ideas became synonymous with what the party stood for: non-violence, economic self-sufficiency and cottage industries, anti-communal and pro-poor. Gandhi's image continues to represent sacrifice, national freedom and personal conviction of the highest order. His qualities and associations are impossible to simply discredit, so fundamental are they to the history of modern India. Speaking against Gandhi is still often seen as speaking against the nation, however unfashionable some of his ideas have become.

As we have already seen, however, Verma's nationalist portrait gallery at Indraprastha excluded Gandhi, and the political ideas that Mahajan brought with him into Kutch were explicitly anti-Congress and anti-Gandhi. For at least forty years, Krishnavarma has been promoted as the counterpoint to Gandhi and to a waning vision of Gujarati identity corrupted by colonialism. Earlier this century, during the rule of Narendra Modi as chief minister in Gujarat, this campaign intensified and Krishnavarma's face was promoted on tens of thousands of posters: a new visual icon for a different politics. He was heralded as a fitting hero for a new Gujarat, whose revolutionary ideas on freedom for India derived from the classical language and literature of Hindu civilisation. Krishnavarma's political creed, it is claimed, although radical, was fundamentally rooted in Indian traditions and religious understandings.

On the surface, Krishnavarma was an ideal discovery for the BJP, since his profile and personality seemed the counter to everything the party argued had gone wrong with India in the twentieth century. He opposed the Congress party because it was dominated by what he called the 'Anglo-Indian autocracy', in whose interests it was to let the British remain in India.[9] He also funded the early studies in London of Vinayak Damodar Savarkar, one of the most outspoken Hindu nationalist voices of the freedom struggle.[10] Krishnavarma advocated strategic aggression and 'disassociation' (clearly differentiated from Gandhi's 'non-cooperation') as fitting responses to the colonial presence, and he made no concessions to those he opposed, including Gandhi.

Krishnavarma's two most well-known criticisms of Gandhi were published in *The Indian Sociologist* in the first decades of the twentieth century. In 1908, he criticised Gandhi for siding with the British in the Boer War, suggesting that Gandhi was 'misguided' and 'weak-minded', for the Boers' defeat 'served them right' because they had trusted the British in the first place. The second criticism was a response to an editorial published in the *Indian Opinion* in 1914, in which Gandhi contrasted evolutionary ideas of the survival of the fittest unfavourably with the Christian creeds of turning the other cheek in the face of aggression and loving thy neighbour unconditionally. Krishnavarma thought the piece 'mischievous' and 'deluded'. He failed to see the logic in offering additional cheeks for an enemy to smite while calculating to thwart the same enemy.

Unlike the practical divergence of political philosophy suggested by the contrast between the terms 'non-cooperation' and 'disassociation', this second criticism of Gandhi reveals a more fundamental difference in thought on the nature of the self and its relationship with society. In Krishnavarma's view, the intellectual champion of the era was Herbert Spencer, a conservative sociologist known for his theories of social Darwinism. Krishnavarma read Spencer as an anti-imperialist who courageously pleaded the case of India, attributing to Spencer a condemnation of the use of native soldiers to extend subjugation, the salt monopoly and the merciless taxation of the peasantry. Spencer had shown that the British Empire operated on the basis of self-interest, calling the English a 'sociophagous' (society-eating) nation. Furthermore, Spencer seemed to support the idea that Indians should throw off the foreign yoke because their country would be in a better position without the British—and, importantly, Britain in a better position without India.[11]

Beyond the housing colony that memorialises Krishnavarma's controversial legacy is the ruin of the once prosperous trading post of Lakhpat. Only empty flatlands separate Lakhpat from the militarised border with Pakistan—lights from the neighbouring country can be seen on clear nights.

To take the road through Kutch to the border is to drive through the signs and ideas of Hindu nationalist India. Ever since the period of post-earthquake reconstruction, this grand road tour has been heavily marketed by the government throughout India as a once-in-a-lifetime adventure. The film star Amitabh Bachchan was signed up to encourage the mobile middle classes to 'breathe in a bit of Gujarat'. Festivals, spectaculars and Bollywood films set in the region, typically about heroism, war and nationalism, have boosted the tourist trade. The desert has bloomed with safari camps, fast food and 'traditional' cultural and musical evenings. Bright lights and technology have brought to life the personalities and ideas of the nation dramatically unfolding as the closed border approaches. Through these experiences runs the road; nationalism is consumed through the windscreen.

On the Road Through Sindh

In the late 1980s, the governments of Pakistan and the UK, along with private prospectors, conducted preliminary surveys of coal deposits in Sindh. Between 1985 and 1993/4, the United States Geological Survey (tagline: Science for a Changing World) assisted the Geological Survey of Pakistan in investigating coal resources in the country.[12] They called the collaboration COALREAP (Coal Resource Exploration and Assessment Program).[13] The deposits in Tharparkar District, also known as Thar District, in Sindh were mapped and test drilled between 1991 and 1993. Hydrological surveys estimated the field to be the sixth or seventh largest in the world.[14]

This was a major discovery, although not without logistical complexity. The seasoned US field workers of the time noted the deep poverty and absence of infrastructure in the marginal region. In India, similar coal deposits had been exploited for at least a century.[15] When extraction was stepped up there in the 1970s, roads and amenity infrastructure had had to come first, as the land was civilised with new names and political associations.

Plans were developed to exploit the coal in Thar for electricity by building power stations next to opencast mines. Given the scale and environmental impact of the project, the people who lived on the land would have to be moved. The World Bank initially supported the plan but later resisted because of the required population displacement and potential consequences for global climate targets. At the One Planet Summit in France in 2017, then president of the World Bank Jim Yong Kim announced that it 'would no longer fund upstream oil and gas after 2019', to the applause of President Macron and other global leaders. Instead, the bank encouraged an alternative focus on low-carbon energy alternatives.[16] Politicians in Pakistan took this to be a form of imperialism, intended to keep the country poor while America continued to burn dirty coal and shale oils.

However, from 2013, the bank in fact continued to provide technical assistance and attracted investment to the Thar coal field, without labelling these activities as concerning 'coal'.[17] Indeed, powerlines, capacity building and so forth are not strictly 'coal', even if these undertakings directly support coal mining and burning.[18] In the early days of the project, other international interests came and went, as difficulties over security and the carbon consequences of burning mountains of low-grade coal spoiled collaborative relationships. As the scheme progressed, the deposit was divided into thirteen blocks, each farmed to concessionaires.

Thar Coal Block II went to Engro (tagline: Enabling Growth) and its subsidiary Sindh Engro Coal Mining Company (tagline: 10 Million Tons Coal Unearthed). It was a joint venture with the government of Sindh, branded as part of CPEC in partnership with China Machinery Engineering Corporation (tagline: Create Ideas, Achieve Dreams), along with local partners Habib Bank and Liberty Mills. They constructed the mine and built the 'first-of-its-kind mine mouth power plant', inaugurated in 2019.

Thar I went to China Coal Technology and Engineering Group (tagline: Anytime, Anywhere) and Shanghai Electric (tagline: Empower Global Industry, Make Life Smarter); Thar III went to Asia Power Group (a group of experienced mines and metals men too hastily assembled to have developed a tagline); and Thar VI went to Oracle Power (a UK-registered company fronting Al Maktoum), China National Coal Development Company (tagline: Clean Energy Supplier) and Sheikh Ahmed Dalmook Al Maktoum (tagline: To Support Governments Through Investments, Strategic Partnerships, Collaborative Arrangements and Innovative Solutions to Create a Win-Win for Sustainable Development), a member of the ruling family of Dubai with a personal portfolio of energy investment.

The current rate of investment and construction is intense, almost wild. These coal projects are unsurprisingly controversial, not least because they highlight the complicity of banks and greenwashing investors in continuing the coal rush, despite climate change agreements.

At the Climate Ambition Summit in December 2020, Prime Minister Imran Khan appeared to announce that Pakistan 'will not have any more power based on coal'. Clearly stumbling to apply the right terms, Khan eventually settled on stating that coal would only be burned in liquid or gaseous form. Malik Amin Aslam, Pakistan's minister for climate change, qualified the prime minister's speech quickly, saying that coal plants under construction would not be cancelled because they have state guarantees that cannot be re-negotiated. Not one to miss a political trick, Aslam argued that the coal projects of the previous government, for which imported coal was shipped to Pakistan's prime agriculture belt, constituted a criminal act of ecocide.[19] Khan's slip was not completely without substance, because continuing US involvement in coal in Pakistan, the legacy of COALREAP, has promoted biomethanation of coal as a 'cleaner' energy source.[20]

I met Aslam at the 26th United Nations Climate Change Conference (COP26) in Glasgow in November 2021 and wanted to ask him about progress in Thar. He told me that although Pakistan was not part of the climate problem, it wanted to be part of the solution, and he was in Scotland to promote Pakistan's 'nature-based solutions' (tree planting and national parks).

The Engro segments of the project in Sindh provoked protest from the outset, but none of that was effective in preventing or slowing the development. At the start, people were enthralled by promises of wealth, employment and new horizons. There was insufficient experience in the region to understand the longer-term consequences of such a massive intervention. As work started, the local population began to feel the effects and opposed the contamination of groundwater, which pointed to more fundamental environmental degradation.

More recently, as the mine and its associated works have begun to bring great changes to the region's landscape and atmosphere, the Bheel Intellectual Forum, a Scheduled Caste organisation, protested in Karachi in 2019, drawing attention to the wholesale destruction of the climate and traditional economy, the lack of jobs for local people, and irregularities in land acquisition. In May 2020, the Centre for Research on Energy and Clean Air published a report stating that the Thar Engro power plant would have devastating and widespread health consequences.[21] The Alliance for Climate Justice and Clean Energy, a local Thar platform supported by some of Pakistan's leading metropolitan environmentalists, helped launch the report.[22]

The effervescence of civil society, now waking up to what was happening, came too late. Nawaz Sharif had revealed the plaque announcing the 'Open cast lignite mine' in January 2014. In 2015, contractors started work, backed by a sovereign guarantee from the government. Now the mine is over 70 metres deep, and the internet awash with positive images of successful rehabilitation—wizened pastoralist faces lit with the joy of prosperity, and choreographed machinery emptying the earth cleanly and efficiently.

***

There is much more that could be said about the coal, but our focus remains on the cultural and social multiplier effects of the roads developed to facilitate the mine. In southern Sindh, the landscape is flat; the sky's solid blue fades to white on the horizon. The 'coal road' here was constructed by upgrading old roads and building new ones, stretching around 360 km from Karachi via Badin to the village of Thariyo Halepota at the mouth of the mine. Sand-blown single-track roads have been expanded and reworked to carry heavy traffic and expensive engineers, consultants and technicians at high speed.

There is an airport to service the mine, first known as Islamkot International Airport, but it is not yet open for service. It was later renamed as Mai Bakhtawar Airport to engage with local sentiment and politics. Mai Bakhtawar, a farm worker, was born in this part of Sindh in 1880, her village part of a large estate whose owners employed her husband. In the late 1940s, the men from Mai Bakhtawar's village left to join a wider peasant farmers' movement to campaign for a better share of agricultural yields. The estate landlords decided to seize thousands of kilograms of flour from the village while the men were away. Bakhtawar confronted the party and was shot dead in the encounter. She is remembered for standing up to the Sindhi landlord, as a peasant heroine killed by the powerful.

The road between Karachi and the mine passes through Mithi, the capital of Tharparkar District. The town's central square is named after Kashmir, a reminder of Partition's painful divisions. The peak of Gadi Bhit hill is a popular picnic spot that offers the added thrill of imagining India over the horizon. Facing India on a row of concrete arches are large rusting letters spelling 'Pakistan Zindabad' (Victory to Pakistan).

Tharparkar District has Pakistan's largest Hindu population, as well as the lowest Human Development Index in Sindh. While the Partition of British India in 1947 equated religion and territory— Pakistan for Muslims, India for Hindus—the reality was, of course, never as simple as that: India today has one of the biggest Muslim populations of any country in the world, and there remains a sizable Hindu community in Pakistan. The new India–Pakistan border ruptured deep economic, political and kinship ties across the huge Thar Desert that encompasses parts of Rajasthan, Gujarat and Sindh, creating the 'borderlands' of Tharparkar and Kutch. People of both religions straddle this border, which does not cleanly divide Muslims and Hindus, and also separates Muslims from other Muslims and Hindus from other Hindus, all the while splitting communities with shared languages and cultural traditions.[23]

In the pre-colonial period, Thar was the site of vigorous networks of circulation whereby people and commodities travelled through arid lands. Sindh was eventually taken by the British in 1843, after decades of intrigue, political espionage and interest in routes used to transport opium from the Malwa Plateau in Central India to the port of Karachi. The first political agent, Stanley Napier Raikes, was struck by how Hindu Sodha Rajputs, Thar's local rulers, remained loyal to their Muslim overlords, the amirs of Sindh, while entering marital relations with the Jadeja rulers of Kutch. With the coming of the British, the Rajputs asked to be administered along with Kutch. Southern portions of Thar passed to Kutch in 1844, but after a rebellion by Sodha Rajputs in 1846, the British returned the region to Sindh.[24]

The British had built a strong presence in Kutch from around 1815 and had been influenced by what they had heard and seen there. In their residences in Bhuj, Kutch's capital, the courtesans and bards of the ruler's household impressed upon them the wildness and sadness of Sindh. Consequently, the British tended to think of Thar as part of the hereditary territories of Bhuj, and of Sindh as the final frontier. Maps produced at the time blurred the boundaries between districts of 'Thurr' and 'Parkur'. Raikes himself was of the view that Tharparkar ought to be integrated into Kutch or Marwar (in western Rajasthan), because the region shared the 'language, habits and feelings of the people'.[25]

The British arrival in Tharparkar disrupted established traditions of mobility and social and territorial loyalty. Thar included a number of small states built around desert forts, such as Umarkot in Sindh, and the authority of local rulers was based on the control of passage and pasture. Cattle stealing and breeding were important to pastoralist communities, and these earlier systems of tribute, patronage and clientelism were weakened by the British, though never entirely eradicated. The colonial government associated the population's mobility with criminality and increasingly sought to control and 'sedentarise' them, a policy goal that the post-colonial governments of both Pakistan and India would continue to pursue through various means.

In the decades after Partition, the Pakistan state gradually learned to assert sovereignty on its margins, particularly over the traditional networks of trade, kinship and banditry that transcended the new border. Stories from the archive of petty smuggling, banditry and organised trade in arms and narcotics highlight the flexible loyalties of the region's inhabitants, fuelled by the imaginative resource offered by the mysterious border.[26] Even as older cross-border networks began to rupture under state pressure, the perceived permeability and instability of the Partition line would generate different cartographic anxieties for the post-colonial governments.[27] Marginal areas such as borderlands are not necessarily peripheral to the central state's ideology, as they may be used to determine what is included in and excluded from national projects.[28] While many middle-class Karachiites regard Tharparkar as a romantic place of nomads, handicrafts and folk music, it is also a liminal space, a place of fear and projection, where 'we' end and 'they' begin.

Leaving Mithi, we see along the road the signs and slogans of another political project that challenges the state's ideology: Sindhi regionalism. Pakistani nation-building has been dominated by the Punjab, its most populous and wealthy province, but the 'newness' of Pakistan has left space for competing identity politics. The effect of Partition on these allegiances was twofold: a consolidation of Sindhi ethnic identity on the one hand, and a demand from central government to redirect local and regional loyalties towards the nation on the other.

During Partition, Sindh saw an exodus of wealthy, upper-caste Hindus to India and the arrival from Northern India of thousands of Muslims from poor families. The following years brought more mass migration; almost a quarter of a million refugees arrived in Sindh, largely through Tharparkar, in the mid-1950s as India suffered from recurrent religious violence. The result has been the growth of a 'sense of deprivation' within the Sindhi population along 'cultural, educational, economic and political' lines.[29] In response, a broad base of Sindhi regionalism emerged. While there is an anti-India strand to this regionalism, the cultural dynamics of difference and groupism have a strong local flavour.

The reaction of the Pakistan state to growing Sindhi regionalism was to promote national identity politics that opposed Hindu India. However, this idea of an Islamic polity was devoid of the syncretism that has characterised religious life in Sindh for much of its history. The state thus had difficulty accommodating Sindhi aspirations, which broke out into periodic acts of violence throughout the 1980s. Tensions were particularly acute during General Zia's Islamisation campaign, which placed an emphasis on orthodoxy. Thar generally remained quiet, which was seen as a betrayal by many Sindhi regionalists, an example of 'Hindu cowardice' from people regularly described as 'not quite Sindhi'.

***

Immediately after Partition, both India and Pakistan took strategic decisions not to build roads in the borderlands, a policy dubbed the 'political economy of non-road making'.[30] Inevitably, however, the region was progressively militarised. Tharparkar became an arena of action in the 1965 and 1971 Indo–Pakistani wars, which left further scars of suspicion and deeply influenced the direction of subsequent state policy. For the government, however, maintaining empty zones of transition on the border increasingly seemed like wasting a resource. The first motor road in Tharparkar was built in 1987. Arif Hasan, a well-known architect and planning consultant in Karachi, writes that new roads in Thar were intended to 'open up' local administrative centres to transport and to improve the functioning of government departments.[31] Tharparkar, rather like Kutch in Gujarat, was gradually reimagined, particularly from Karachi, as a resource-rich 'wasteland' that needed to be targeted for large-scale development, extractive activity and road building.

On both sides of the road out of Mithi, buildings have been broken in anticipation of further road-widening. The ADB and the Works and Services Department of the government are implementing the Sindh Provincial Road Improvement Project, intended to 'enhance connectivity' between urban centres and rural communities, providing 'much-needed access to education and health facilities' in addition to creating new employment opportunities.[32] These schemes fall under the Pakistan Vision 2025 national development strategy, in which regional road improvements are intended to promote national integration.

NGOs started to appear in Tharparkar in the 1970s, and their presence, alongside UNICEF, increased following a drought in 1987. In the 2000s, the neo-liberal embrace of the Musharraf military government, coupled with investment following 9/11, boosted the reach and confidence of NGOs and other civil society organisations. With the mines came funds for corporate social responsibility and the creation of forms of civil society run by company men.

The Thar Foundation (tagline: A Desert Blooms, Hope Awakens) is Engro's main corporate social responsibility arm and now one of the prominent NGOs in the region. The foundation claims to work to resettle and improve the lives of those affected and displaced by the Engro mine and power plant. Alongside scholarships for education and workshops for artisanal development, the organisation also trains women in how to drive dump-trucks so they can be employed in the mine and runs football competitions for girls, taking them to

Karachi for tournaments. The idea of girls in shorts running around a football field does not always sit comfortably with the realities of contemporary Pakistan.

Closer to the mine, the checkpoints are more robust, police more diligent, and the atmosphere tense. The landscape is littered with road-building machines; the land around the mine is fenced and guarded. According to businessman–politician Asad Umar, here is the 'seventh biggest coal reserve in the world, 175 billion tonnes of lignite, the energy content of 50 billion tonnes of oil, more than the combined oil reserves of Saudi Arabia and Iran, sixty-eight times bigger than the gas reserves of Pakistan'.[33] The entrance gate is strictly policed, the interface between coal and population.

The road and the coal mine have contributed to the creation of one of the most securitised regions in Pakistan, its checkpoints, military camps and the perceptible influence of security agencies reflecting an astigmatic view of government. The road passes through lands and histories of marginality, strategic neglect and mistrust of a 'suspect' Hindu minority. In the process, through vastly reduced travel times and competitive bus services, the road has opened the way for migrants from Thar to wage labour in Karachi. Conversely, miners and civil society organisations travel from the city to the province, bringing metropolitan ideas about the rural good life in their suitcases.

A consultancy firm's environmental assessment report for Thar Coal Block VI puts this scenario in different terms:

> [T]here will be many nonlocal workers coming into the area. The expected influx may bring about significant cultural changes, an increased risk of disease, insecurity and overburdening of existing yet limited social services. A worker code of conduct will be developed for non-local workers to adhere to and will raise awareness of cultural norms and customs of the local community.[34]

In the opposite direction, as the 'coal road' takes people from Thar to Karachi for work, football and education, they look away from the border to the bright lights of the big city, kept burning by the destruction of pastures and villages. The old ways are going.

***

When comparing India and Pakistan—especially through the borderlands—it is difficult to escape the jingoism and language of international rivalry. Partition, fragmented kin relations, religion and the artifice of new borders over older lands tend to become the primary focus. However, seven decades have passed since the countries were separated and, in the meantime, both have developed distinct identities and concerns, as indicated in the projects of Sharif and Gadkari.

India started to dig massive holes in the ground to remove lignite a few decades before Pakistan had the wherewithal to do so. The infrastructure that came to Kutch in the 1970s and 1980s to house the personnel to run the mines and power plants was a largely, although not exclusively, domestic affair. The cultural projects that followed were those of national integration and border pacification, as the wilderness proved to be a receptive canvas for the spectacle and theatre of road-led tourism. What happened in India will not be replicated in Sindh, because there the influx is international, temporary and interested in extraction rather than colonisation, although behind the scenes the government may have other ideas.

In both locations, however, roads work their effects, signalling a fundamental transformation of ways of life: the market, the decline of customary relations and the insertion of petro-mobility into most welfare and logistical problems. The city folk come to look and to develop and improve things through civil society organisations. In the process, the wilderness moves a step closer to Karachi, Ahmedabad and Mumbai as space and time are collapsed, again. The shared grazing lands and nomadic routes decline as people are drawn to new forms of labour and enterprise. They remind us that with the coming of the road, many things depart or are lost, often forever—not least the idea of loss itself, obscured by the clear promise of a future. The remote folk are at once embarrassed by their rustic ways and encouraged to play their instruments and sing their songs in tourist camps at night. They embody their own inferiority in the face of the modernity project, regardless of how many jokes they may share among themselves about incomers and their strange ways.

HIGHWAYS TO THE END OF THE WORLD

It took 100 years to put the first billion vehicles on the world's roads, and we are now more than halfway through the decade in which this figure looks set to double.[1] The 2021 total was 1.4 billion. In North America, there are 710 vehicles per thousand people. In Asia, there are 140 per thousand people. Transport produces carbon through the fuel it burns, but also because of the methods and materials of vehicle and road production, and, most significantly, because of the kind of 'system' being perpetuated. Particulate emissions and smog have resulted in public health concerns. Chronic congestion and safety questions over ever-lowering costs have done little to dampen general enthusiasm for automobility in many parts of the world. As I discussed at the start of this book, the energy and time that go into purchasing and maintaining petro-mobile machines are efforts of blind and expensive devotion when held up against rational choice and cost–benefit analysis.

As we have seen, roadmen routinely describe the benefits of their work in the teleological terms of economic growth: better access to markets and services, and, as a general principle, opening up previously inaccessible spaces (usually land and resources) to market forces and extractive industries.[2] However, from the perspective of critical social scientists, mobility and energy have become consumables rather than fundamental public goods and, by extension, forms of alienation rather than freedom.[3] They see, not unlike Gandhi, that the road and its machines enslave people, not only by exploiting their labour but also by binding them to particular forms of consumption.

To my mind, the $50-billion PMGSY scheme shows how deeply rooted the common sense of road building has become as a development reflex for rural and national reconstruction. It is telling that a project of such enormous size could be undertaken based on political imperatives and historical inertia rather than published evidence. Although roadmen generally claim to be evidence-oriented in their professional and intellectual lives, they saw no need for evidence in the foundations of their primary purpose—that was beyond question.

Throughout the world, it appears that collective decisions have been splintered into a disparate and confusing array of choices. In the process, the response to the climate crisis has been privatised and presented by influential actors as the 'low-carbon' or 'green' industrial revolution, heralding a new era of market-led economic growth.[4] At a global level, the UN Sustainable Development Goals of 2015 and the Paris Agreement of the following year have done much to sediment and promote the language of sustainable and inclusive growth. The problem of climate change has been framed as 'a deficiency of investment demand', the solution being to create frameworks for new investment. As part of this strategy, 'government-induced policy risk' must be reduced; thus, development banks help to emolliate the threats of nationalisation, dysfunctional and corrupt courts and so forth.

Good and sustainable infrastructure in 'emerging markets' is presented as essential for the future. Given a conservative annual growth rate of 3 per cent, the intensity of infrastructure 'required' (the word used by the roadman telling me this) in South Asia will need to more than double in the next twenty years, as increasing numbers of people can afford to buy cars and take holidays. Similarly, the clear message from the World Bank and other institutions is that sustainable and inclusive infrastructure must mean more investment and the creation of further markets and mechanisms.

Imagine the relief in road and transport communities when they heard the message that what they had been doing all along was actually the solution to the climate crisis—albeit with an impossible change needed in fuel. Consequently, global road trade shows remain full of talk about tremendous opportunities offered by technologies to combat climate change, particularly electrification. Think tanks and corporate spin-offs lobby and advertise to ensure that the narrative that supports their product or approach is the one that becomes embedded. The sector is booming.

Roadmen will claim that transport produces around a quarter of global carbon emissions; for some, this is a sign of the importance of their industry rather than an indication that things have gone wrong.[5] Road transport accounts for between 10 and 20 per cent of the total. The figures vary so much that there are obvious non-specialist questions to be asked about the reliability of such numbers in the first place. Most roadmen tend not to connect their work to the generalised condition called 'climate change', seeing their task as fundamental to national progress, with the traffic produced by new roads pointing to the role of tarmac in catalysing economic growth. They might acknowledge that storms and floods demand 'sustainable', 'resilient' and 'better' roads, but not fewer roads. There is open scepticism about the urgency of climate change solutions, considered at most to be a low priority when held up against the pressing concerns of national development and even more immediate career goals to win construction contracts.

At the same time, international calls for the reduction of global carbon emissions with a focus on Net Zero 2050 have grown increasingly urgent. The response of roadmen is to turn to new technology: 'It is not the roads or the cars, but the fuel that is the problem,' said one very senior Washington-based policy advisor to the American government in an interview. Experiments to reduce the carbon cost of building roads—i.e. the carbon used to transport materials and run road-building machinery—are in their infancy but booming as cottage industries. Carbon capture, burial and transformation are well-known technologies that many countries and organisations are reliant on to reach 2050 targets—but they do not yet exist. At the COP26 climate summit and elsewhere, I have listened to discussions about 'green hydrogen' and heard Saudi Arabia's plan to monopolise its distribution globally. India has taken the greenwashing one step further and now claims to be burning 'green coal'. Electrification is furthest advanced, but the global capacity for battery and energy production falls short of powering the world in most projections.[6] Even so, many roadmen seem confident that there will be leaps in technology and that electric or hydrogen-powered vehicles will allow us all to carry on motoring.

The problem with this approach is encapsulated in the oft-used quote: 'Trying to cure traffic congestion by adding more capacity is like trying to cure obesity by loosening your belt.'[7] The idea at stake is older, I was told, and was expressed in 1865 by the economist William Stanley Jevons, who observed that technology that improved the efficiency of coal use led to the increased consumption of coal. Contrary to common sense, technological advancement will not automatically reduce fuel consumption.[8]

I was fortunate to have been introduced quite early in the course of this project to a retired roadman who liked nothing better, it seemed, than talking me through the theories of road and transport planning that he had spent his life researching, writing and building. He had constructed hundreds of roads over a fifty-year career all over the world and had in later life gone into training and consultancy. For a while, we met in a restaurant without any natural light close to Victoria train station in London. He liked the place but would grumble about the price, although I always paid.

Over lunch, he patiently told me about 'induced demand' (the notion that after a supply increases, more of a good is consumed) and 'Braess's paradox' (building more roads within a network can slow overall traffic flow).[9] Similar paradoxes reliant on more recent data had been named after other researchers, 'Downs–Thomson' and 'Pigou–Knight–Downs', whose ideas appear in recent form as 'the Lewis–Mogridge position', which observes that new roads will fill with new traffic.[10]

Given this power of new roads to produce new traffic, it is salutary to learn that 25 million km of new roads are anticipated in the world by 2050.[11] For roadmen, the juggernaut, so to speak, had already gained momentum, and their task is to plan for its picking up speed, not to try and stop it or to question the direction of travel. This single path of human development was inevitable.

Many of these attitudes towards cars and mobility echo the claims that sociologist John Urry, whom we met at the end of Chapter 2, aimed to reveal as features of an ideology of fetishised consumption and growth. Seeking to understand the 'system' that produced these assumptions, Urry and his colleagues illuminated the economic, political and moral connections between the global mobility turn, carbon politics and ultimately climate change.[12]

If we take the 'system' argument seriously (although the word makes it sound more ordered that it is), then roads and the vehicles that move along them are only one part of a much broader energy-intensive way of organising society and the economy. In this structure, consumption and mobility are the primary goals—they are in many ways forms of each other. The issue is not simply that engines generate force and turn oil into movement but that the car is part of a system of never-ending production and consumption geared towards a happiness found in growth. This ongoing cycle is where the more substantial carbon consequences of road building will be located, although no one yet forecasts the industry's emissions with this broader view in mind.

***

The World Bank's 2017 'Global Mobility Report' aimed to develop mechanisms for decision-making in transport to promote 'universal sustainable mobility' and 'generate' investment.[13] The report was significant for me because it indicated an acknowledgement by elites (though their realisation was earlier) of the deeply ambiguous global situation: roads having been built as if there were no tomorrow for the last few decades, tomorrow is now under threat. This view was articulated from the comfort of senior positions within wealthy organisations, where 'game-changing' or 'paradigm-shifting' approaches are currently solicited in the hope that someone somewhere will have something sensible to say about the mess. In what could be read as a 'Great Oops!', the authors pointed out that actions that have already been taken and decisions that have already been made mean that mobility would only increase in the coming decades. In the same way that the emerging failure of PPPs in Central India led roadmen to return their trust to the state, the report presented equivocal observations and recommendations to limit the damage.

The report was produced by the Sustainable Mobility for All (SuM4All) initiative.[14] This is an international umbrella group of organisations that operates with the following mission: 'As members of the international community, we have a shared responsibility to shape the transport agenda. The overall aim is to achieve universal sustainable mobility. This will require greater coherence within the transport sector, to support global decision-making and influence investment.'[15]

Hosted by the World Bank, SuM4All includes such members as the United Nations, the International Transport Forum (tagline: Global Dialogue for Better Transport) and the International Energy Agency (tagline: Shaping a Secure and Sustainable Energy Future). These organisations bring a language and set of parameters to the table that often exclude other key players in global mobility thinking, notably those from the Global South. Nitin Gadkari and Nawaz Sharif, for example, were not asked for their views, despite their demonstrable influence on the future of roads.

I imagine myself in conversation with the essence of the report, which has been updated online to include some nuance and flexibility since its launch in 2017.

Report (the combined voice of fifty institutions): Putting the brakes on now is not possible; regardless of the environmental cost, more people, goods and ideas are going to be transported around than ever before. The creation of new markets for vehicles, falling costs of production and the continued expansion of existing markets will also contribute to an increasing number of vehicles. By 2030, annual passenger traffic will exceed 80 trillion passenger-kilometres—a 50 per cent increase compared to the distance travelled in 2015.[16]

Me: That is a large number! It reminds me of something your colleagues have pointed out to me: the number of vehicles in the world is also rapidly expanding and will soon be at 2 billion. Despite these forecasts, and although many people think that mobility is already overcooking the planet as it is, your report makes no suggestion that mobility itself is the problem; instead, the challenge is how to 'meet' the 'growing aspirations for mobility'. Might it not be better to reduce mobility?

Report: Meeting growing aspirations for mobility has the potential to improve the lives and livelihoods of billions of people—their health, their environment and their quality of life—and to help minimise the effects of climate change. But the future of mobility can also go in another direction: it can engender gross inequalities in economic and social advancement, promote fossil fuel use, degrade the environment and add to the number of deaths from transport-related accidents and air pollution.[17]

Me: It is not clear to me how mobility could achieve such salubrious goals. Neither do I understand why you claim there are two distinct pathways. What will adding a billion new exhaust pipes or batteries contribute to the bonfire of our vanities? Where will the resources come from to sustain mobility in forms that improve the quality of life? How can you suggest that the environmental costs of increasing mobility are inevitable and then also argue for mobility making a better world?

Report: Looking to the future, we have quiet cities and clean air; people ping and zip here and there using a variety of existing but 'improved' transport technologies; border crossings are efficient; and the world is punctual. There is minimal environmental impact and no reduction of opportunities for future generations.

Me: This is an old utopian vision that has been the hope for the future for a long time: we go on doing our business as usual—more of it even—saved by clean energy sources and the development of 'integrated' and 'efficient' thinking that translates clearly into the way we achieve consensus, attain political power and plan and construct our built environment. But roadmen on the ground have told me how they build roads for many reasons other than efficiency—and often on political whims that have nothing to do with plans for integration. Moreover, there are good reasons to believe that the commercially driven vision of a safe future run by global electric transportation is also technologically flawed and impossible to power.

Me to you, the reader, from now on: In the wings of a 2017 conference, a Delhi roadman told me disdainfully that the report was a 'science-fiction vision of transport', not only due to its technological assumptions but also because of its geopolitical vision of international cooperation.

Given the report's multiple authorship, there is an uneasy and inconsistent description of the relationship between mobility and market mechanisms. It is noted that the market does not distribute transport, infrastructure and services equitably, and elsewhere that vulnerable groups are not likely to be well served by the free market.[18] Those listed as vulnerable include women, children, those with disabilities and older persons—in other words, around two-thirds of the population. Given such numbers, might it not be better to see these vulnerabilities as produced by the market, rather than exclusions from it? Those who benefit from the operation of such markets (adult, able-bodied men) are likely to over-use their private automobiles to the detriment of public transport systems, resulting in congestion, excessive fossil fuel use and air pollution.[19]

At the heart of the vision of *Homo hodologicus* is the rational decision-maker, who 'naturally' wishes to 'satisfy private needs, without taking into consideration collective present and future needs'. Generally speaking, anthropologists are averse to regarding any form of human behaviour as simply 'natural', including fundamentals such as birth, death and incest—all of which, according to anthropologists, are culturally mediated and understood. The idea that it is 'natural' to serve private needs before those of the collective is pure politics. Furthermore, such 'natural' action is exemplified by high levels of car usage and the continued development of an automobile-focused transport system—as if this were really down to selfish individuals, rather than corporations, history and governments promoting automobility.

Nitin Gadkari was a couple of hours late to address the International Road Federation (tagline: A World of Safe, Sustainable, and Efficient Roads and Road Networks) in Delhi in November 2017 (conference tagline: Cross/Roads\: Linking Mobility Solutions).[20] With a twinkle in his eye, he blamed traffic. Gadkari told the audience that his country was now building 35 km of four-lane highways per day—an incredible rate, though still short of his audacious target. Banners around the massive hall of the India Expo Centre declared: 'Build roads not carbon footprints.'

When the 'Global Mobility Report' was released at the same conference the following day, one of the worst periods of air pollution in India's history was coming to an end. Traffic-jam-bound Delhiites blamed farmers in Punjab for burning stubble. The panellists congratulated José Luis Irigoyen from the World Bank for his excellent report, before turning to electric vehicles and smart technologies. Mr Irigoyen had previously led the Bank's Global Expert Team on PPPs. It was striking that there were no Indian or Chinese faces on stage as part of the global discussion—Gadkari had left the venue shortly after concluding his speech the previous day.

Many of the firms and institutions building roads in South Asia have offices around the world and believe themselves to be trading in universal values, such as UN Sustainable Development Goals, empowerment and transparency. Spending time at road conferences, in banks and on field trips with consultants taught me that this view is widely shared among those who recognise themselves as part of that global vision, who have a share in its resources and the cultural capital it affords. There are many in India who actively play these roles—those who bridge the World Bank and local road research institutions, for example—but there are many other people who work with roads in South Asia for whom such language and agendas are quite alien.

The conference's plenary discussions featured bright lights, massive LED screens and flamboyant TED-talk-style presentations led by North American think-tanks and global car manufacturers on sustainable mobility and the electric transition. The parallel sessions saw Indian road engineers presenting over-worded PowerPoint slides about culvert and junction design and pavement performance. Although they were at the same conference, these worlds did not strongly intermingle. This observation is not incidental: great gaps often appear between the claims of global stakeholders in mobility and local realities on the ground. While the international set practised the language of inclusivity, safety and sustainability through a technology-led vision of the future, Gadkari was building roads with a tremendous carbon combustion 'lock-in' for decades to come, and the Indian road builders continued the long conversation about road surfaces.

Since the report was launched in 2017, much additional work has been undertaken on 'sustainable transport'. SuM4All's website now presents the evolution of a coherent vision, as well as a series of papers that qualify and extend analysis in the original report in a framework called the Global Roadmap of Action toward Sustainable Mobility (GRA). However, assumptions and claims that are difficult for me remain: 'Mobility defines the human race'; transport has 'improved', making us go 'faster and farther everyday'; 'the mobility choices of today will either lock us in congestion and pollution or they will open the way for new possibilities'; 'sustainable transport for all is not a dream but it requires a revolution'.[21]

In the last few years, there has been an explosion in the number of organisations working in coalition to shape the future of clean and zero-emission mobility, frequently with a focus on cities, notably C40 Cities (tagline: Green and Healthy Streets). Numerous transport campaigns, often in partnership with vehicle manufacturers, have sprung up to advocate electrification, including RouteZero (tagline: Accelerating the Shift to Zero Emission Vehicles on the Road to COP26); the Drive Electric Campaign (tagline: 100% Electric Road Transport for the World); the Electrification Coalition (tagline: Electrifying the Way We Move Forward); and Calstart (tagline: Changing Transportation for Good). In India, Gadkari launched the Go Electric Campaign in February 2021. The revolution seems to involve replacing oil with electricity. What could go wrong?

***

Roads are one example of how particular ideas of progress and growth have been naturalised to the point that they overwrite climate concern. Even this relatively modest focus quickly entered contentious terrain during my fieldwork, raising provocative questions about colonial exploitation and the differentiated wealth of nations, and how gross inequality can be squared with common responsibility for the future. It also raised questions about knowledge politics and power: Who has the confidence to believe, assert and suggest that one way of knowing is 'better' in the longer term than others?

Throughout this book, I have attempted to place analysis before my own knee-jerk reactions to the things people have told me, but as we near the end, I will add a cathartic note. During interviews and research encounters, I was frequently belittled and patronised for not understanding local realities—twenty years of research in India were routinely dismissed, along with social science's methods and aims. I learned to nod along, but frankly, after years of being told the same story about roads bringing development and the primacy of economic growth, I began to grow weary, if not a bit depressed. However, though frustrating at times, the contrast in our assumptions, beliefs and ideas made visible the important differences between me and the roadmen in our underlying approaches and methods for understanding and knowing the world.

The most memorable conversation I had that revealed this polarity was with two roadmen in Delhi.

'Who are you to write about climate and development in India?' asked Roadman 1. 'We are a poor country; you took from us and have everything. It is now our turn to have wealth.'

'Yes,' said the second roadman, amplifying his friend's critical tone. 'Who are you to say we should not build roads? Do you want us to remain underdeveloped?'

'I am not saying roads should not be built in India,' I replied. 'I am asking you if you have thought about why you are building them and what the consequences might be.'

Roadman 2 dismissed the question out of hand: 'We cannot think like that. Our priority is to build roads.'

Colleagues in various parts of the world have read this blunt exchange differently. Some saw my questions as arrogant and revelatory of the Western biases of my social science. Some immediately thought of colonialism: the British Empire restricted roads, as we know, and now that the countries of South Asia are masters of their own destinies, they no longer need British anthropologists to develop critical narratives about their work. Others saw the conversation as a reflection of the idea that those from powerful countries do not want Pakistan and India to 'develop'.

Others yet drew a continuity between the roadmen's arguments and India's attitude throughout the 1990s that climate change negotiations constituted a form of neo-colonialism, the claim having persisted that India was a poor country and climate change mitigation was the responsibility of wealthier countries.[22]

While it would be lumpish to dismiss these interpretations wholesale, I will stress, as a counterweight, that the research process brought together different ways of viewing development, roads and climate futures to see what would happen. Some of this was orchestrated at roundtable events while other encounters took place in the wild, so to speak, such as the above exchange. If one maps this collision in terms of the geography of privilege, then the result is a confusion of moral and political standpoints in which hierarchy, history and colonialism are the important building blocks of the story. But can this be our main conclusion?

Social scientists writing on climate change have recently begun to think through the knowledge politics behind public and individual opinion.[23] Anthropologists and others have studied communication about climate change in specific locations, many focusing on small islands.[24] Others have addressed why climate change has provoked befuddlement and faltering action. Naomi Klein, for example, suggests that deniers and sceptics are so caught up in carbon that to acknowledge climate change would spell an end to their ways of doing things.[25] Anthony Giddens argues that because the dangers of global warming are intangible in everyday life, many will sit on their hands and do nothing.[26] According to him, such inaction is accentuated by 'future discounting', a condition in which people find it hard to give the same level of reality to the future as they do to the present.

For others, the dynamics of accumulation inherent in capitalist society have combined with the competitiveness of the global nation-state system to produce a form of development that is sustained by unequal mobility infrastructures such as roads.[27] In this view, methods of production have inertia and momentum of their own that cannot simply change or be stopped because too much is dependent on their continuation. When so many of our actions might have negative effects, we find ourselves in a condition of intellectual and practical paralysis. Considering harmful consequences becomes impossible; in the words of Roadman 2, 'We cannot think like that' when the priority is building roads or national development or paying the loan on the car.

I have found very useful, empirically and methodologically, Kari Marie Norgaard's work on how the socially organised denial of climate change in Norway connects to norms of emotion, conversation and attention.[28] Everyday interaction keeps the climate issue out of everyday life—the problem is just too big to be there. Norgaard's 'deniers' are not corporations or systems of production but ordinary people who have difficulty articulating and responding to the idea of a changing climate. She shows how it is best to approach the subject as an expression of sociality rooted in culture, identity politics and belonging, rather than as a matter of scientific communication or information. Indeed, it is striking to learn that giving people more 'science' or 'facts' has been shown not to alter behaviour.[29]

The arguments about force, value and historical inertia presented throughout this book constitute a way of understanding the 'knowledge problem' and show how context strongly influences the parameters of debate. Following Norgaard, then, these debates are not about 'science' or 'facts' in any simple sense but about power, history and politics as they manifest in the social life of roadmen. In fact, as I hope to have shown, the contours of thought about roads and the climate often have little to do with evidence or science at all. They have a shape, history and, as lines of guff, they follow roads into the endless future.

Frustrated, I wondered whether roadmen were in fact a bit stupid. Why did many of them sound like parrots? Not only pieces of eight, but 'opening up, opening up'. It bothers me that I thought this; perhaps indeed the limitation is my own, because the intention had always been to earnestly engage with their logic. In less formal circumstances, and when not a guest in someone's office, house or car, I have argued as a research methodology. After a heated debate with roadmen in a bar in Oxford about whether road building now would have climate change implications for our grandchildren, a country-level minister for roads took me outside into the early evening.

On the street, people walked and cycled along, the highly restricted traffic access to Oxford having brought quiet to many of the streets around the university. In the autumn air, he smiled warmly, and put his arm affectionately over my shoulders. He turned towards me to confide that he had seen for himself the joy on people's faces when a road comes to the village. 'You have to understand that,' he said. I took his words to heart, and into writing this book, by trying to understand just that: the joy and the passion people have for roads, and where the historical and moral force of this enthusiasm has come from.

On reading the earlier exchange with the two roadmen, some colleagues thought I was presenting Roadman 2 as rather unimaginative. I, on the other hand, understood him as saying something profound and important. Some of my analysis has been shaped in conscious response to his comments, which highlight just how and why reducing global carbon emissions is such a difficult task. The conversation had taken place at a friendly and relaxed meeting in the highly securitised offices of an international development bank in Delhi. I had known both men for a few years and spent time with them in a variety of locations, including Oxford, London and Madhya Pradesh. They are both deeply committed to road building, as careerists and as architects of PPPs in Central and Eastern India.

I ask you to consider again why Roadman 2 said that he cannot think like me, 'like that'. My view, which may or may not convince you, is simply this: he is a roadman; I am an anthropologist. I stress this difference to emphasise that this book has not been an exercise in common sense; rather, roadmen and anthropologists both have highly refined knowledge politics and priorities, which range from the gross and philosophical to the minutiae of our immediate aims for the day ahead. We both write far too many emails and have friends and interests in common, but we live and breathe different materials, ideas and modes of making connections between ideas and actions. He has had two decades of professional training and experience in building roads, while I have had a similar-length exposure to social research and analysis.

Our knowledges and frames of thought have different language and parameters. I teach at university, using boldly worded literature on climate change in which 'societal collapse', 'deep adaptation', 'degrowth' or 'the third Gaian revolution' are just around the corner.[30] This context introduces students to the intellectual frames of Timothy Mitchell's *Carbon Democracy* (2011) and Andreas Malm's *Fossil Capital* (2016), which show how inequality and exploitation are built into the world energy system in favour of the Global North.[31] Other scholars on our reading lists explain how the disciplines of geology and climate science build on colonial practices to form racist and discriminatory forms of knowledge in the contemporary period.[32] These ideas about climate politics are a long way from everyday life in the infrastructure division of a development bank like the one where I talked to the two roadmen. Indeed, I can imagine the profound incomprehension around the filing cabinets at the mention of some of the above terms.

For good or bad, intellectual fashions in higher education in the social sciences over the last couple of decades have taught me that nationalism is a politically constructed form of low-minded populism. The recent invention of the Anthropocene, in contrast, has encouraged me, perhaps along with relative prosperity and good fortune, to think about planetary and global rather than national futures. Although I am not zealous about these positions, they clash with ideas current among many roadmen, who are often nationalistic or at least institutional in their thought, particularly in South Asia, where roads are couched in heroic, masculine and parochial terms.

Roadmen tend to describe their work in terms of 'product', 'process' or 'sequence' (i.e. roads), rather than 'context', that is, why are roads built, and what are their effects? For Roadman 2, thinking 'like that' (like an anthropologist) means taking seriously the consequences of the road building. If your priority is to build roads, you cannot also think of the climatic implications too deeply or you would not continue. In this, roadmen are hardly exceptional, and it must be the same for many professions: cattle farmers, supermarket managers and jet-setting academics. Such thought would be maverick and outside the epistemological and linguistic frameworks of your daily activities, questioning as it does the foundation of a moral and epistemic community with the momentum and support of capitalist history on its side. That, as we have seen for people

231

like John Whitelegg, would be regarded as heretical and lead to excommunication—no more work as a roadman. Furthermore, and perhaps most influentially, roadmen tend to see their work not as contributing to a destructive system of endless consumption, but rather as building a better world, the immanence and self-evidence of which override the possibility of doubt.

I take pains to remind you that there are differences of opinion among roadmen, among whom can be found pioneers seeking to revolutionise techniques and practice while not undermining the fundamental ideas that sustain the industry. Over the course of this project, I regularly met a civil engineer who had constructed roads in many parts of the world. Now in a senior management position in the civil service of the British government, he was working hard to change the mindset of teams of engineers under him about roads and what he called a '*truly* sustainable transport future'—as distinct from the 'sustainable transport future' his colleagues talked about that he thought was a lie.

This man saw the practices, language and path dependency of his colleagues as barriers to change. He tried different ways of 'transforming', 'dislodging' and 'resetting' their culture. His minister, at the time, was a progressive Conservative who had experienced circumstances in other parts of the world. The engineer organised workshops, brought new faces into government and invited academics and disruptive thinkers from green finance and edgy think tanks to Whitehall to shake things up. In the end, however, his fellow roadmen kept on building roads—so he took early retirement to tend his garden in the home counties. In the same spirit as the engineer's former colleagues, Highways England ran a public consultation during COP26 in Glasgow for one of the largest road-building projects in the North of England in recent memory—seemingly without irony.[33]

It is clear that the world of roadmen, in general, is not set up to contemplate its own end. Roadman 2, for example, manages road projects that may take five years to negotiate and clear the ground for before the 25-year concession agreements are signed. That period, although future-oriented, is presented as one of surety and stability; it must be for the contracts to work, and creating certainty is part of the skillset of the roadman. The drawn-out timelines of roadmen, as well as the models of growth and ever-increasing traffic flow that all road institutions promote and rely on to attract investment and hype, are not self-reflexive tropes.

There is another more difficult story here in which climate change is a 'mental illness of Europeans', as one road engineer in India put it. Or, in the words of a joint secretary in government in Islamabad, when asked how Pakistan would meet its commitment to carbon reduction: 'What is Paris 2?' His sarcasm was biting, given that he clearly knew a lot about the international treaty to keep the global temperature rise below 2 degrees. In the offices of these men, the idea of carbon reduction is an abstraction, sometimes given lip service, while the tropes and clichés of economic development and poverty reduction are more readily articulated. However, generally, the priorities for them, as in most deeply institutionalised contexts, are to meet internal deadlines, to work well and with aspiration within office hierarchies, and to ensure that paperwork reflects what appears to have happened on the ground.

We can see that many ideas and interests intermingle to complicate the agenda of road building. Infrastructural expansion and economic growth have, for example, become nationalist political projects. In India, there is a race to regain lost glories, the early road network tarnished by colonial neglect, and to undo the legacy of the Congress party, which dominated India for much of the twentieth century and for whom the planned economy was the ideal. In Pakistan, roads similarly form part of a nation-building project and currently speak of an uneasy geopolitical relationship with China. In both countries, there is also a strong sense of pride and national service among road builders, who see themselves, quite literally, as building a country. To ask people to think differently would be to ask them to give up what they hold dear.

Nitin Gadkari, with his insatiable desire for more roads, is often called upon to represent the Indian government at climate change conferences. Gadkari owns factories in Maharashtra capable of producing ethanol, so his campaigns for alternative 'biofuels' might be dismissed as self-interested. He has, however, also pioneered electric buses in urban and inter-city contexts. More importantly, his hyperbolic language about the road promises a smooth future, in which technology might offer salvation, but on the whole we can go on building roads without consequence. Paradoxically, it is this quality that also makes Gadkari a good speaker on climate change. For him, I think it important to understand, sustainable energy sources have tended to be additional forms of energy (i.e. more energy) rather than replacements for fossil fuels.

Roads cannot easily be separated from ideas of development and progress because they are part of a 'system', in Urry's language. The analysis extended throughout this book shows how roads are also intertwined with history, political struggle, heroism, sacrifice and nationalism. Roads are equally at home in the drawing rooms of metropolitan sociologists as on the coal frontiers of India and Pakistan, or in the words of villagers acknowledging their own sub-humanity to camera. Roads are part of culture and the imaginative frameworks that people routinely use to imagine time and space. You can drive Gandhi's Salt March, travel to the big city in search of work, and consume the nation's imagery along borderland roads constructed by advertising agencies.

***

My final riff from Roadman 2 is to explain that I believe—as an anthropologist—that good social science research allows for understanding the logic of other people's views and, consequently, offers the opportunity for self-reflection on one's own starting points and assumptions by comparison. The next step in such an intellectual project is to bring these forms of knowledge into conversation where possible. This method of 'reflexive sociology' and 'understanding' has animated my approach throughout this book.[34]

To social scientists, this is simply a well-known, common-sense methodological approach. Non-practitioners, however, might view it as arrogant and wonder why the anthropologist is blessed with such capacity to understand. Others will find it bizarre; I learned from trying it out on roadmen that its goal orientation is seen by them as a curious and exotic form of project management (their own 'lessons learned' meetings are about as close as engineering consultancy firms get to 'self-reflexivity', but these tend to excavate mistakes that cost money).

The practices of roadmen do not fit well into my world of anthropology—and I do not want anthropologist readers simply to interpret this material in their own way to make them happy and untroubled. Roadmen have laughed out loud when I have described to them how some of my colleagues have turned roads into anthropological objects. These anthropologists might argue, for example, that a road is never complete, always-in-the-making, and that maintenance, disrepair and ruin are part of the ongoing social lives of infrastructural objects. Roadmen see these characterisations as ignorant of process, the division of labour and responsibility, and the ways contracts and materials are pegged to time. Oddly, in this type of literature, anthropologists seem to invest more agency and continuity in the road than they do in understanding the different social groups that provide that continuity.[35]

It is possible to gain an understanding of what roadmen believe about the world through the conceptual and epistemological tools of contemporary anthropology—participation, observation, talking and listening—but more difficult to know what to do with this understanding. Through this research, I have learned to articulate better what anthropologists aim to do and why. In the process, I have realised that practitioners of our discipline largely trade in esoterica. I have also developed scepticism of anthropologists who claim to be purveyors of a value-neutral form of meta-knowledge. Anthropological concepts and ethos tend to be liberal and left-leaning, favouring the downtrodden, and by default laced with scepticism of the state and of corporate and Bretton Woods-led development narratives. Take roadmen seriously, and my 'assumptions' begin to appear as political positions more than methods.

Yet, differing fundamentally from the holistic approach to the world at the core of contemporary anthropology, roadmen's own ideas are utopian and rooted in deeply held beliefs. Roadmen believe strongly in markets, with greater or lesser regulation—often with a similar righteous passion to the social scientists who have diligently recycled criticisms of development and market-led economic growth for at least fifty years. I use the word 'believe' deliberately

235

and explicitly because much of what the road builders said with confidence is not easily tested. The evidence base for PMGSY, for example, is fragmented and weak. As I hope to have shown, belief in roads is not singular, but roads are seen as proselytising for liberal market forces. In other words, roads are agents of a way of life in which mobility is the key ingredient and commodity. When seen like this, road building is an extension of underlying ideological convictions and is as much politics as method—not timeless or unchanging, of course, but quite clear in the present South Asian context—and quite possibly the practice itself reinforces the beliefs.

As an ingredient, mobility is a form and catalyst of economic growth that increases access to goods and services and as such could be seen as market welfarism—although, as we have seen, the 'exclusions' from the market are significant. As a commodity, people pay for fuel and machines to overpower the force of friction; in doing so, they may expect returns on their investment in cash or time. In this way of thinking, the political promise of the road is perennial, since we can always move faster: walking, bullock cart, bicycle, motorbike, car, bigger roads, hybrid vehicles, electric vehicles and so on: infinite growth, mobile futures without limits, highways to the end of the world, *na*?

How should I end this book? I have wavered. Social science publishing gives me some formulas. A manifesto intended to generate a critical mass? But that will fail to convert those selling road dreams to a different way of thinking about the future. My bookshelves already creak. A polemic on how the world should take social science more seriously? My own view is that social scientists need to take the world and its multiple disciplines more seriously before this can successfully happen. A corrective reflection on the state of geopolitics in South Asia, which, as we will see next, leads not to China but America? The material is there, but my impressionistic qualitative approach leaves more questions than answers.

Instead, I will follow through the rhetorical '*na*' from one of the first stories in the book by letting research undertaken on the road demonstrate how the world works. Remember my opening question as we go: Why are so many roads being built in South Asia in an era of human-induced climate change? We change gear, knowing what we now know about the history, institutions and the engineered creep of mobility into South Asia. We have heard the standard narratives, passed through extractive landscapes, and seen how the frenzy is whipped up by the kings of the road.

At the start of this book, I outlined Latour's view of the impossible squeeze of modernisation on the limited resources and capacity of the planet. The material has progressively shown what the modernisation project looked like in South Asia and how its torch has been carried and transformed by the Hindu nationalist BJP in the twenty-first century. Latour argues that the common world, supported by a common culture, has been abandoned by the elite. Those left in the common lands argue about trivialities such as party politics, the rights and wrongs of climate justice and, we might also add, disciplines and epistemologies. Global elites, meanwhile, have gone offshore—as we will find out in the next chapter. In the end, I learned that what I could see and what roadmen told me to see was not all there was, because the visible was supported by invisible frameworks.

I believe the conclusion we reach is normal, almost banal, and surrounds us all each and every day—but it is usually unseeable. I hope therefore that my long journey through roads provides others with a model to work through intractable knowledge problems and to see how the world works. Shouting at stressed roadmen or chaining yourself to overly insured diggers will not prevent roads from being constructed.

ON THE ROAD AGAIN
FOLLOWING THE MONEY FROM TOLL ISLAND

Back in Madhya Pradesh in Central India, we continue our journey on SH31, which travels from Jaora in the north to Lebad in the south. Leaving behind the feasting birds and wild poppies of Ratlam, we come across an overturned truck in a field a few kilometres south of the reservoirs. Sacks of flour have broken the ropes to give the land a white dusting. The driver was badly injured as the outer frame of the cab gave way on hard ground.

When a man died in traffic here in 2017, angry people gathered to demand compensation for the loss of their friend and relative. Local news channels broadcast images of a shrouded body on a stretcher being bumped hastily down the highway towards the toll booth by those calling for recompense. In interviews, they emphasised anger about poor road safety rather than their desire for compensation.

Road safety has become big business, and the mourners were not alone in picking up on a narrative pedalled heavily by the United Nations through national road associations. At trade shows, I had often heard the line from vehicle manufacturers that the solution to the dangers of the road was to get people off motorbikes ('two-wheelers') and into cars.

In 2015, India signed the 'Brasilia Declaration', the conclusion to a conference on road safety sponsored by the World Health Organization. Numerous advertising campaigns followed: '[E]mbrace life wear seatbelt', 'no mobile when mobile', 'speed thrills but it kills' and, fantastically, from a tyre company, the words 'I'm meant to be in the bar, not in your car' over an image of a driver holding a bottle of beer at the wheel.

Seventeen people die on India's roads every hour, often in horrific and heart-wrenching circumstances. That is 150,000 deaths annually, a figure that many commentators have noticed is equivalent to the population of a small town in India or a large town in other parts of the world. The mass deaths of wedding parties, school outings and cricket and football teams are especially popular with headline writers.

The origins of the country's dangerous roads are systemic rather than traceable to a single issue: many people have fake or no driving licences; the costs of maintaining vehicles and roads are high; the technology of the car has outpaced the design standards of most roads. To put these technical explanations given by roadmen another way: India is travelling at different speeds, in literal and metaphorical senses. On gated and 'controlled access expressways', it is possible to keep the fastest and slowest Indians apart; on the more accessible state highway, India of the speeding car collides with the slower pace of the countryside. All along the SH31, it is possible to see people running for their lives, as they realise the oncoming juggernaut is closing in on them faster than they had imagined. The kind of anticipatory apparatus required for crossing the road is not honed by village life.

In 2018, Renault played a prominent role in promoting National Road Safety Week by holding events at its dealerships across India. Renault manufactures the Kwid (tagline: India's Favourite Car), an 'entry-level crossover' with 'unprecedented features for its segment'. The car costs £3,000 and is available on credit for low monthly payments. Unlike many of the other vehicles in India with a similar price tag, the Kwid still looks like a car. When launched in 2015, it came with billowing clouds of puff in the motoring press that it was an engineering and production miracle. However, in the absence of a 'fail' rating, the Kwid was initially awarded a round '0' in safety tests conducted by the Global New Car Assessment Programme (tagline: For Safer Cars), while a much-improved model achieved only a single star (out of 5) in 2017. Other cars produced for the Indian market do not excel in such tests, but the Renault is particularly poor.[1] The managing director of Renault India could, however, honestly say: '[W]e are meeting all the safety requirements of current regulations in India.'[2]

Since then, an Indian version of the tests has been developed, with slower impact speeds than the global standards. A greater awareness of car safety has also been promoted. The 'price point' of automobility in India, however, is so low when compared to other national markets that the industry produces specialist cars with attractive veneers, coupled with low safety standards and relatively high emissions. If personal automobility is a sensible measure, then India is getting richer, but many of the signs of this wealth are low-cost versions of cars produced elsewhere—the price difference being paid in a yearly death toll equivalent to the population of a whole town.

On SH31, the ghosts of those who die prematurely in road accidents menace those who live nearby. At some crash sites, people gather annually to commemorate and soothe the restless. Many of these points are marked with stones to honour the dead; there are shrines in the dusty verges and on the central reservation amid the beautiful bougainvillea. Telling a different story of the road to the one narrated by its kilometre stones, these monuments mark the distance between losses in a global tale of resource and development inequality, a story of carnage.

The upturned truck in the verge had left the road at Prakash Nagar, an infamous crash site that locals claimed had taken more than 500 lives over the years. Despite its longstanding reputation as an accident black spot, the bend was not improved when the road was widened. The recurrence of death on the curve is upsetting to those who live nearby; they reason that death follows death. Of course, they understood that cost-cutting on the construction and maintenance of the road was the primary cause of the accidents, but another idea also prevailed about the bend being haunted. Referring to a tragic incident in which an entire family perished, a friend said that a ghost had plucked the car off the road and cast it off the side. According to him, the crash inspector found no skid marks, nor any possible 'scientific explanation'.

***

A shopkeeper in the village of Dharad tells us that the road has 'torn Dharad's soul'. The community had been divided, business is down, and school children straddle the road's central barriers to run with giggling fear through gaps in traffic. Everyone dreads the rumoured widening of the road to six lanes; four was hard enough. Nearby, a policeman tells us in enthusiastic tones that SH31 is the 'lifeline of Malwa'. We leave with contradictory messages.

Our toll-free journey ends as we leave opium country. The road ahead is barred by two sets of gates in close order. The northernmost toll plaza, 'Toll Booth 2' in the company literature, lies 15 km south of Ratlam and is known locally as 'Chikaliya'. The approach is well signed as the road surface widens, two lanes becoming four. Gantries remind us where we are, and a large green sign lists those who are exempt from tolls, president down. Speed-breakers bump the traffic to a crawl. Concrete and steel structures splattered with dried red spit and road filth funnel travellers towards the booth, from which there is no escape without payment. A clutter of rusting and scarred signs, CCTV cameras and iron-barred windows surround the closed barrier amid a cloud of dust, engine noise and diesel fumes. The signs of surveillance—its authority and intimidation—are unmistakable; we must now pay for our mobility. A hand reaches through the booth's bars to take our money, face obscured by dirty glass. The toll booth is a masterpiece of panoptic and behavioural architecture—it seems so sensible, almost logical.

Most people experience the toll as a simple interruption— slowing, queuing, payment, and acceleration away. As such, the toll booth is a 'non-place' for the forward-facing. But if one stops, gets out of the car and spends a few months hanging out as ethnographers do, then the men behind bars become people, with working patterns and anxieties. Tommaso Sbriccoli spent some months in and around the toll plazas of the SH31 in 2017. In time, he learned to see them as places of sociality in a huddle of painted shipping containers converted to offices at the side of the road. A land dispute drags in court, leaving the toll collectors to squat the verge. Given that those who farm the road, if not the road itself, are loathed—called 'worse than dogs'—by those in the hinterlands, we see the toll booth come to look like an island, a CCTV fortress surrounded by hostile country. This animosity, coupled with the extractive nature of the work, means daily life on toll island is violent and hard. Muscular behaviour orders the day ('non-veg', they call it in the local idiom). As the barriers rise and fall, mobility is converted into cash, and such mercurial transformation must generate heat.

Revenue collection is organised by three 8-hour shifts: A, B and C, with the last being the hardest because of aggressive drunks. Since 2018, biometric equipment has alerted the management of who is present at the start-of-shift roll call, replacing photographs sent by WhatsApp of the workers standing in line. A contractor provides the frontline staff: assistants, collectors, shift in-charge and safety officers. The company also provides cleaners, guards, drivers and a 'dog man', a Dalit, who clears carcasses. In theory, there is a 'medical aid post' and a private ambulance service; however, those manning the ambulances have little training; other workers mockingly call them 'doctors'. Another contractor supplies the back-office staff: cashiers, who reconcile collected tolls against expected revenue; validators, who cross-reference data provided by collectors with CCTV and registration records; and systems engineers. A thin layer of management overseeing the contractors is employed directly by Essel. All workers, however, identify strongly with 'the company' and as 'being under' Essel.

Subhash Chandra, chairman of Essel, believes red tape, a bloated state and burdensome regulation have slowed India's development, while private enterprise, entrepreneurship and recalibrated national ambition are the way forward. He sees himself as the 'self-made man' of the future, having started his career manufacturing tubes for toothpaste and going on to build the Zee media empire. A public figure and elected MP, he has been vocal about the regressive nature of the Indian government: 'I was so tired of the strange and restrictive regulations that I wanted to operate in places where I would be free of them.'[3] He continues: 'Apart from investing in the economic infrastructure, I also want to invest in social infrastructure in India. I am keen to inspire thousands of self-reliant people who can contribute to nation-building … I envision an India that is self-reliant, not dependent on government or on subsidies.'[4]

The profitability of media in decline, in 2006, Chandra was introduced by his friend Nitin Gadkari to infrastructure man Arun Lakhani, who was building highways in Maharashtra. Chandra invested in the business and in his own company's infrastructure arm, Essel Infraprojects (tagline: Building Modern and Sustainable Infrastructure for Progressive India). In 2008, Essel was awarded four public–private highway projects, including SH31, on the back of a competitive bidding process.

Several subsidiary companies and a few tiers of management down, for those overseeing the workers in the toll booths, Chandra's vision becomes about encouraging self-discipline and corporate compliance, with morale reinforced through upbeat posters about road safety, reducing environmental impact and participation 'in the growth story of our nation'. The promotion of company values requires careful attention; while the managers are far away from home and live alone, the booth workers are locals, entangled with all sorts of people and loyalties that constantly undermine the managerial vision of professional efficiency. To make their mark, the managers enforce commensality, or eating together, at the toll plaza to cut across hierarchy and caste. All workers bring home-cooked food and eat from collective plates, a practice unthinkable in their villages. At least at the toll plaza lunch table there are no untouchables and no caste bar, as men relate to one another as fellow employees and as 'equals' with common goals in the interests of the company.

In corporate training workshops, some of the toll booth managers elevated the ethos of the company to the level of philosophy and morality. One described the staff as 'raw matter' and asked open questions about encouraging productivity: How do you make other people work? How do you bring out the 'best' in employees? He was frustrated by the lack of education and 'capacity to improve' among the staff and tried to inspire them using league tables for revenue collection, prizes for the highest takes, and motivational speeches.

For him, management provided an opportunity to make new kinds of people, for whom punctuality, precision and motivation were key characteristics.

Another manager extolled the virtues of paying tolls, speaking to us with passionate conviction as he sketched a diagram of his logic on the whiteboard in the toll plaza offices. He conjured a world where people wanted to pay because they saw the higher purpose of financing national development, where order and discipline would invigorate personal rectitude and national strength. For him, the toll would make India great; it was the moral responsibility of citizens to contribute. The toll booth became a pedagogical device, reforming the expectations that road users had of themselves and their duties to the nation.

Neither of the men had swallowed the management manual fully; they were also aware of the exploitative nature of Essel and described figuratively the firm as 'raping' its employees. The company offered no pension, even to managers. It promised a path upwards through a corporate hierarchy, which in practice was always out of reach. As such, the managers were in a double bind, because as strangers in SH31 land, the intimacy of the local was also always beyond them. One of them explained that even when he thought he had understood the power dynamics and reputations of the local big men, a new connection would always take him by surprise. For example, after he sacked a collector for being rude to a customer, the other staff had gone on strike. The sacked man returned the next day with a group of friends from the Rajput Karni Sena, a right-wing, caste-based association with links to the ruling BJP. The men beat the manager with a chair, and the collector was subsequently reinstated. Following this incident, the group were able to pass along the road without paying, a concession that meant others in the permitted 6 per cent of exemptions now had to be squeezed for a toll. The manager felt alone on toll island, wondering who was running the show.

***

From inside the toll booth, the world looks grimy through a cloud of stuffy fumes. A screen shows the approaching vehicles, one after the other, after the other. Barrier down, check the plates, make notes, request money, distribute change and receipt, barrier up. Only 6 in 100 vehicles can pass without paying. The barrier falls, and in the booth you feel the pressure, the stress. Before the window rolls down, there is no way of telling who will be inside the vehicle, what they'll say, what their attitude will be. A camera above records the collector noting the details of the vehicle. Outside, the assistant picks up dropped money, bridging the gap between the hand of the driver and the hand of the collector if the approach has been poorly judged. The windows of the booth are barred for protection, but the back door is wide open to disperse the heat in the air.

Tolls rates are clearly displayed. Regular users get monthly discounts, and tractors, motorbikes, government and police vehicles, ambulances and hearses are exempt. All others pay; the heavier the vehicle, the higher the fee, with the main revenues being collected from trucks. In the early years, revenue was lost thanks to overloaded vehicles, and so in 2014 or 2015, weighbridges were installed and operated by yet another subcontractor as a way of countering the problem. Truck drivers resented the private policing. Claiming that the fees disproportionately penalised them, a truck drivers' association in a village near Ratlam, together with local politicians, led a protest at the toll plaza, during which seven people were arrested following violent altercations.

Despite published rules, collectors and road users are in constant, often heated and sometimes violent conflict over fees. Drivers are in a bind, since there is no sensible alternative route; that the toll road was built over an older non-toll highway adds further layers of exasperation. All manner of identity cards—with fake IDs being widely available—are flashed at the toll booth as 'proof' of exemption. Most of the liveliest negotiations take place with car drivers, the vehicle being a marker of class and affluence, as well as perhaps of a particular kind of argumentative or rights-aware citizen. Collectors must correctly judge the social stature, or lack thereof, of drivers refusing to pay tolls—a well-connected driver who is made to pay might then complain to the police or company.

Decision-making is also influenced by the revenue targets of the company and whether they are on course to be met, meaning that the ratio of collections to exemptions changes throughout the month.

The more exemptions, the easier the shift in the booth, while fewer exemptions give rise to an increase in tension and to phone calls from politicians, police and locals, angry that they or their followers have suddenly been charged. Villagers living close to the toll plaza frequently request exemption, arguing that they have been using the road since time immemorial; others point to the rule on national highways entitling those living within 20 km of a toll booth to free use. Although this rule does not apply to state-level highways, Essel has had a tacit agreement with some villages that they would not be subject to tolls on SH31. However, not all villages are included in these informal arrangements, and there is no written record authorising the exemptions, meaning that the understandings can be dropped as soon as there is pressure to increase monthly revenue, or when other more violent or influential people became exempt.

These informal understandings reflect the moving line that booth workers must tread between a corporate set of expectations and local webs of connections, privileges and sometimes their own kin relations. In one quite typical example, a visitor to the manager's office claimed to be a resident of a nearby village and thus had not been asked to pay for three months. Suddenly, however, tolls were being levied, leaving him confused. Like many others who came into the office, he shouted: 'Was there indeed a rule which exempted locals from paying?' The manager replied in measured tone: 'No, in fact, everyone does have to pay, but we have been letting you pass as a courtesy. Now, however, the company is enforcing the rules more strictly and you will have to pay.' The driver suddenly changed tack, perhaps having forgotten the purpose of his journey. He smiled: 'Okay, but I was taking my wife to give birth in Ratlam. Could you let me through?' The manager laughed and let him pass without payment, saying tolls would be levied on him from the next day.

The collectors were also on the lookout for ways to fleece drivers for their own personal gain. There was much joking among the booth workers about pulling tricks invisible to CCTV, the ubiquity of which is one of the reasons for the abundance of footage online of toll booth violence in India. Networked to control rooms of Essel and the MPRDC, cameras in SH31's toll booths record both the traffic and the staff at work: each vehicle passing through the barriers is recorded, with collectors manually inputting the numberplate, type of vehicle and any exemptions into a database. At the end of the shift, the collector reconciles bundles of cash with the theoretical total produced by the computer system. Essel absorbs excess, while shortfalls are deducted from wages. Amounts owed by each employee are displayed on prominent noticeboards. Quite often, however, workers steal money to cover their expenses in advance of payday. Road users can also be short-changed or overcharged. Truck drivers from South India were reckoned to be easy targets because they were far away from home and lacked local language skills and were therefore reluctant to make a fuss. With 400 or 500 vehicles passing through each shift, a gain of a few rupees per transaction could produce a tidy bonus.

As a contractual obligation, the toll booths held customer complaint books in the interests of transparency and accountability. Standard procedure was to dissuade road users from making complaints; indeed, in an entry from September 2015, one driver complained about how hard it was to make a complaint. There were also complaints that staff were rude, short-changed customers or passed on ripped bank notes. More than one complainant noted that the Lebad–Jaora highway was the only toll road in the entire country not to operate a cashless system. Most entries took issue with the state of the road, with many asking where their toll money was going when the road was in disrepair: Singh Chauhan observed a 'very poor road … they are taking toll for what when u cannot maintain road'; meanwhile Gauar Jaile assures, 'We are willing to pay but, pls do the patchup work regularly. Do not waste our money.' One comment from July 2015 claimed there were potholes 2 feet and 6 inches deep.

In the summer of 2018, the Ministry of Road Transport and Highways claimed that ten people died per day in pothole-related accidents, many more than the 800 or so per year killed by terrorism of any form. As Mumbai flooded with monsoon rain in 2017, the city's streets became pocked with holes. Opposition politicians counted potholes; those in power retaliated with specious claims that there had been more potholes under previous governments. In July, anti-corruption advocate Anjali Damania posted a popular tweet to the following effect: 'What dissolves fastest in water? Sugar? Salt? Wrong! The tar on Mumbai's roads.' The media discovered various men around the country who worked selflessly to fill holes following the deaths of loved ones in pothole accidents. Artists in Mumbai and Bangalore were inspired to work with the potholes, their street art featuring mermaids, dolphins and crocodiles. Headline writers, too, caught the bug: 'Modi's Great Road Trip Hits a Debt Pothole.'[5]

That responsibility for road maintenance is shared between the government and private companies means that both sides can shift blame—a political asset for all involved. In the Essel toll booths on SH31, employees shrugged that the state was in charge of road repairs, while the BJP pointed to Essel and claimed that they were failing to carry out routine maintenance. In turn, the opposition party claimed that problems on the road were caused by the government eating the profits. They also sought political capital by drawing attention to the close relationship between Essel and the BJP. The poor condition of SH31 even became a national concern when in the spring of 2019, Nitin Gadkari kept Subhash Chandra waiting outside his ministerial office in Delhi for over an hour as a sign of his displeasure at how Essel was running roads in Madhya Pradesh.[6]

***

At the booth, we pay the Rs 40 required for a car to pass—the 'toll tax', as locals call it. The barrier rises with a clunk and we accelerate away, four lanes narrowing to two. As we gather speed, we see that the road has dragged life out of the countryside towards its flanks. Passing through less fertile lands, the highway is confident and wide with a broad central reservation. When the soils again turn rich, the road narrows.

Within the verges, new enterprise flourishes; older truck stops and rest houses lie abandoned from a time before the new road was built at a higher elevation. The price of land near the highway rose dramatically after the four-laning, largely with the speculative promise of new property development. Many farmers cashed in and moved their efforts 'inland' away from the road, where pastures were cheaper and greener.

Along the side of the road, we see nomads walking with flocks of sheep, goats and camels. Belonging to a community known as Raikas, these pastoralists journey across state borders following routes that only sometimes overlap with the road network. For them, the spaces created at the side of SH31 opened new avenues for direct and faster travel. Fallow land left from excess land acquisition and the embankments and cuttings of the road provide food for their animals. Sbriccoli had previously also worked among Raikas in Rajasthan. Being familiar with Raika ways and greetings, he was able to take us straight past the ferocious guard dogs and into spaces of tea, hospitality and the aroma of opium.

The Raikas move between sedentary and nomadic ways of life, between the civilisation of the town and the wilds of the jungle. They are famous for their knowledge of the territory through the stories, practices and understandings that come with their traditions of pastoralism. As we squatted on the ground drinking tea amid the bleats and gas of animals, they told us with pride that kings used to call upon them to plot the best routes for new roads, an earlier form, perhaps, of road consultancy. We sat still with our nomadic hosts watching cargo thunder along the highway, contemplating the great movement along the road that enables modern sedentary living.

***

Back on the road, spell broken, dream-space gone, we quickly approach Essel's 'Toll Booth 1'. Security guards carry clumsy-looking rifles better suited for clubbing than shooting. They emerge from the shadows to meet the armoured van that has arrived to transport toll takings to a bank in Ratlam. The money smells of past transactions, a dank and heavy odour that lingers on the paper. Large bundles of notes are boxed and loaded. SH31 produces a great deal of cash, as one of the few profitable highways in Madhya Pradesh; most others have been bailed out by the state, as the public–private 'moment' or 'movement' turns out to have been an over-hyped bubble.

As we have seen, profits from SH31 are extended by trimming maintenance expenditure and running the entire operation on a cash-only basis, which undoubtedly aids cash flow forecasting. The road is managed by Western MP Infrastructure & Toll Roads

Private Limited (WMP), a special purpose vehicle (SPV) of Essel Infraprojects. SPVs are a type of subsidiary company used, among other reasons, to isolate parent companies from risk: if the SPV goes belly-up, the originating company (in this case Essel) has some measure of protection. In 2019, Essel was in the headlines for having used SPVs to hide debt and over-inflate value. The share price slumped by 30 per cent when it was revealed that the firm's longer-term assets were funded by expensive short-term borrowing, often from its own SPVs. Chandra admitted that 'aggressive bets on infra' were partly to blame.[7]

The widely applauded Infrastructure Leasing & Financial Services Limited (IL&FS), often referred to as the 'king' of PPPs, was also in trouble. Essel's collapse was a result. IL&FS was India's leading infrastructure finance company; when it defaulted on debt in 2018, the government took control and appointed a new board. Among the major international shareholders were car manufacturer Mitsubishi (via Orix; tagline: Creating New Value) and Abu Dhabi Investment Authority (tagline: A Legacy in Motion (among others)). The Serious Fraud Investigation Office spent nine months trying to untie the knots. The morticians uncovered a complex set of arrangements of subsidiaries, joint ventures and associates lending to each other and buying, selling and governing each other's interests—124 entities were registered overseas.[8]

The road arm subsidiary IL&FS Transportation Networks Ltd (ITNL; tagline: Better Roads for a Smoother Ride (one of many)) was the biggest BOT operator of roads in India at the time, specialising in revenue collection through toll booths. Today, the company's website (flagged by my browser as 'not secure') scrolls 'default intimation' messages: 'The Company is unable to service its obligations in respect of the interest on Non-Convertible Debentures due on …' Former chairman of IL&FS, Ravi Parthasarathy, was arrested by the Economic Offences Wing of the Tamil Nadu state police in 2021.[9] At least fourteen SPVs created through ITNL were used to hide deliberate cost overruns on road projects in a maze of shell and dummy companies to make them eventually untenable. Cases were also brought under the Prevention of Money Laundering Act against foreign nationals.[10] Laundered funds were used to either 'evergreen' loans or for the acquisition of personal assets (which could then be resold to regularise the money).

When Essel's website was up and running, it claimed: 'When legends come together, success follows.' For a while, one of these legends was a company called India Infrastructure Plc (IIP). With headquarters on the Isle of Man, IIP was listed on the London Stock Exchange in 2008. The company had roots in the former executive board of UK infrastructure investor firm John Laing (tagline: Making Infrastructure Happen) and was set up with a clear India focus. By the time of the listing, the board of directors comprised a British peer, a chartered accountant and two other men, one of whom was Indian.[11]

In 2008, IIP invested £11.3 million in SH31 through a Mauritian subsidiary, Roads Infrastructure India.[12] The investment gave a 26 per cent stake in what was then a road-building site as 'four-laning' was underway. IIP had a clear appetite for risk, buying into a hydropower project in Madhya Pradesh that required the displacement of 10,000 people.[13] On the road, there were delays caused by the construction of railway bridges and further payments were required. The public messages remained upbeat with the investment yielding significant returns according to IIP valuation methodology: as of March 2010, £22.2 million compared to the initial investment of £11.3 million.[14] It appeared to be boom time on Indian roads.

According to a widely read report from analytics firm CRISIL (tagline: Making Markets Function Better), road projects awarded before 2009 were expected to earn equity returns of around 22 per cent due to high traffic growth and reasonable practices adopted by bidders.[15] The years 2012 and 2013 saw the largest percentages of private investment in roads in the country to date.[16]

In 2010, IIP was demoted from the London Stock Exchange's Main Market to its Alternative Investment Market (AIM; tagline: Powering the Companies of Tomorrow).[17] The Laing executives resigned from their roles as advisors, and the board faced and survived a call for resignation as questions were asked about the high overheads of IIP and the wisdom of the SH31 investment.[18]

AIM does not spend much money on advertising and is little known among the public in the UK or elsewhere. According to one of the nominated advisors (known as 'Nomads') who regulate companies listed on AIM, 'it is a place where you have to know people—it is all about who you know'. A private investment banker said, 'it is the sort of place that if someone has just moved jobs, they are running away from something'. There was a further difficulty behind the scenes with IIP and the listing was again removed. It was readmitted a few months later when the American Guggenheim Global Infrastructure Company (GGIC) exchanged assets, notably hydropower in Madhya Pradesh and a logistics operation in Maharashtra, for shares in IIP (in addition to port facilities and wind turbines in South India).[19] These moves constituted a 'reverse takeover' or 'backdoor listing', the acquisition of a public company by a private company and a listing on the London Stock Exchange without going through the formal listing process.[20] The manoeuvre gave GGIC a 46 per cent stake in IIP, with assets converging in the heart of India.

GGIC is owned jointly by its American directors and Guggenheim Partners (tagline: Innovative Solutions, Enduring Values), a small group that represents the corporate legacy of the mining family and controls assets roughly equivalent to the GDP of Finland. A subsidiary of GGIC, Guggenheim Franklin Park Management LLC (GFPM; tagline: Providing Vital Infrastructure Services Worldwide), became IIP's asset manager. In 2011, the board of IIP said goodbye to the British peer and hello to the Americans from GGIC and GFPM.[21] With them came a sharper strategic investment policy that hinted at the problems caused to IIP by 'over-bidding' rather than negotiating infrastructure transactions—and the desire to move from AIM back to the Official List.[22]

The leaked Paradise Papers of 2017 included the names of two directors of GGIC–IIP, relating them to other infrastructure companies, one specialising in 'green' energy finance, the other in asphalt from recycled rubber—and both to the Cayman Islands.[23] The Linkurious and Neo4j visualisation tools used by the leak database also associate the pair with the same addresses in Arlington, Virginia. The publicity generated by the leaks often meant that criminal wrongdoing of those named was assumed rather than demonstrated. In fact, many people had simply been caught playing a game that was legitimate, if not exactly moral, if legal and financial representatives were up to speed with the complexity of moving names and money between jurisdictions.

The repeated financial leaks made the secretive Nomads even less willing to talk to outsiders. While I now know that AIM Rule 26 requires listed companies to identify their advisory firm and provide biographies of their directors, at the time, we tried to identify these people through trial and error. We found statutory reports of directors' share transactions, but these simply reproduced press releases from public relations firms written to conform to minimum reporting standards. Profiles on corporate websites were bland. To learn more, we turned to social media, but none of them had left much of an online trace.

We broadened the search, out of curiosity as much as anything else, and found more information on other people's profiles— memorably, there were videos recorded by phone of presentations at fundraising events and speeches at a tipsy wedding party. However, it was the old boy (and one home counties girl) networks that revealed the most, as universities and schools proudly publicised the gifts and goodwill they had received from alumni.

As we traced more links and associations, we learned more about the people who managed the funds and transactions that were placed through AIM and IIP into infrastructural assets in India. Global networks and diverse experiences of funding infrastructure and energy projects suggested a highly specialised world. The Americans had known each other for years, first meeting perhaps through their work at AES Tietê, the Brazilian arm of the AES Corporation (tagline: The Power of Being Global), a Fortune 500 power company headquartered in Arlington, Virginia, whose rapid expansion in Latin America has become legendary in American management circles. The new IIP chairman had left AES in 2000 to start his own infrastructure investment company, also featured in the Paradise Papers.

A second director was born in Chennai in South India and studied economics in America before becoming a financial analyst for a global investment bank. Another Indian was also appointed to the board—the director of a logistics firm, a portion of which GGIC had exchanged for shares in IIP. He was joined by a well-connected veteran and private-sector advocate from Indian Oil (tagline: The

Energy of India), who had witnessed the liberalisation of the Indian economy and the transformation of public utilities into state-owned companies. Soon after these boardroom changes, four-laning was completed on SH31 and both toll plazas were open by June 2011. In the language of IIP, SH31 had moved from 'construction' to a two-year 'ramp-up' phase, and they valued the asset at £29.4 million.[24]

***

IIP refinanced existing higher price debt (from Corporation, Canara and Axis banks) through the government of India's Takeout scheme run by the SPV India Infrastructure Finance Company Limited (tagline: Funding Foundation of the Future), noting 'higher than expected traffic growth rates'.[25] The IIP board now turned to new investments. They raised loans from GGIC at high interest rates of 12–15 per cent for hydropower and infrastructure in Nagpur. These loans marked the beginning of a long and complex series of subscription agreements, financial transactions and other arrangements between IIP, GGIC and various affiliated companies. The money raised mostly serviced financial, debt and management structures of IIP and Guggenheim affiliates. The directors commanded fees for their services on the boards of IIP and GGIC, as well as for raising money to pay the interest on IIP's loan from GGIC for taking over the latter's assets upon entering AIM.

The directors also continued to buy large quantities of shares in IIP, whose share price declined to practically nothing. Up to this point, all loan agreements had been made with entities directed by the Americans, who used SPVs to bewildering effect. Then, however, the Nomads announced that IIP had entered a subscription agreement with Barnet Holdings Ltd (no tagline) for 172,739,590 of a total 680,267,041 ordinary shares, giving Barnet Holdings a quarter of IIP and a stake in SH31.[26] The Nomad advising IIP on AIM was clinical, to say the least, in his refusal to talk me through these transactions.

My false friend the internet, however, told me that Barnet Holdings was owned by Conservative-controlled Barnet Council in North London as a subsidiary company through which the council subcontracts services. Such privatisation from within is called 'gutting', as councils have developed 'alternative delivery models' for the services traditionally provided by the state.[27] There was controversy around some of the council leaders, including allegations of financial and planning irregularities. A group of colourful campaigners, known as the 'Famous Five'—Mr Mustard, Mr Reasonable, Mrs Angry, Barnet Eye and VickiM57—were vocal and audacious in their attempts to understand the council's secretive restructuring. The story drew me in: frankly, the idea that a struggling London local authority could be investing in a toll road in Central India was exciting.

As the SH31 toll barrier continued to rise and fall, my fieldwork moved closer to home. I talked to people in Barnet about the council, privatisation, bureaucracy and activism. Along the way, while building up a picture of the financial management and structure of Barnet, I learned about the corruption and sometimes cosy arrangements that were rotting councils across England. I eventually learned enough to wonder why Barnet Holdings did not produce annual accounts for the UK's Companies House register. I asked a corporate accountant, who told me that this was because it was a subsidiary of a local authority; the accounts could thus appear as an unelaborate single-line entry in the council's general accounts. He then directed me to Barnet's pension funds. The annual report for 2015 listed investments in 'emerging markets', including infrastructural assets; however, the names given were fund managers not assets.

I took further advice from an old hand in the City of London, a neighbour, who told me that he thought it unlikely Barnet would put money through AIM. 'It is,' he said, 'the Wild West. The risks are so high that there are concessions on inheritance tax and stamp duty on long-term investments in the market.' I was surprised to learn there was an investment market in London on which the government offered personal tax relief, and not for the first time on this journey I felt naïve. I could see his point about risk and accountability, but my desire to see the story through overwhelmed sage advice.

In May 2017, I sent a freedom of information (FOI) request to Barnet Council. I had asked for help from the administrator at my university whose role was to answer the FOI requests we received, which were usually about staff salaries. He relished the boot being on the other foot and helped me draft something deft. The reply came:

> The council holds the information requested and the answers to your questions are below. There is no direct holding by LB Barnet Pension Fund in Infrastructure India Plc (also known as IIP), Guggenheim Global Infrastructure Company (GGIC), Franklin Park Management LLC (FPM), and Franklin Park Holdings, LLC (FPH). London Borough of Barnet [does] not [have] investments in any of the above named funds.

The phrase 'no direct holding' did not rule out 'indirect'— nonetheless, these connections were not those described by IIP as direct investments. After two years of being convinced that a London borough was tolling SH31, I saw I had built a fantasy from fragments—perfectly plausible, but perfectly incorrect.

Yet the question of what happened to the toll money would not leave me alone. As Essel's public autopsy revealed in 2019, many of their assets were covers for debt. Building a road, extracting a toll, paying 7 per cent to the state government for the privilege, honouring maintenance and concession agreements, and calling what was left profit seemed a very long way from what was happening in Madhya Pradesh, where debt restructuring and tying knots in corporate finance and tax laws seemed to be the actual business concern. Providing roads for India's national progress and pro-poor development did not really seem to be part of the picture.

Municipal finance had led me into an impenetrable and confusing place, where people speak and think in an argot incomprehensible to most of us—something that the activists in Barnet had also repeatedly said about the council. Those who manage money are locked into an exclusive world that has offshored not only the cash but also the knowledge about organising the cash. I was disappointed, of course, to reach a dead end, but in truth I had been stuck in this cul-de-sac for a long time, and so it was something of a relief to be given a way out.

***

Some time later, I re-examined IIP's company reports. I noticed that within the corporate language of the subscription agreement,

Barnet Holdings Ltd was described as 'an affiliate of IIP's indirect shareholder GGIC Ltd'.[28] If it was an affiliate, then it would seem probable, if not certain, that it was linked to the Americans—rather than a London borough. I decided to look again at what we already knew: the Paradise Papers connected them to the Cayman Islands. I found mention in the Bahama Leaks of a company with which Barnet Holdings had intermediary relations, but it was struck off back in 2002. The signs began to point away from North London and towards the Caribbean.

Then, unexpectedly, a luxury yacht came up for sale that was managed and owned by Barnet Holdings Limited operating from an address on Tortola in the British Virgin Islands (BVI). *Clifford II* was a 2008 creation of the American firm Palmer Johnson Yachts—asking price: $17.5 million. The brokers Moran Yacht & Ship (tagline: A Proactive Approach) were instructed to proceed to sale in 2015. The vessel's home port was listed as George Town in the Cayman Islands, a city in which Barnet Holdings had another registered address. The GPS tracker confirmed that *Clifford II* was regularly chartered from the south of France into the Mediterranean. In this world, luxury yachts are symptoms rather than failsafe symbols of wealth because of the tax concessions that come with ownership and registration. Yachts also act as figurative money boxes. *Clifford II* was sold in 2017.

A request for information from BVI Financial Services Commission (tagline: Vigilance, Integrity, Accountability) said that Barnet Holdings Limited had been incorporated on the island of Tortola in 2008 and reincorporated in 2011.[29] IIP had also been formed in 2008, and the reverse takeover took place in 2011. The information received stated that Barnet Holdings had paid annual fees until 2017, but shortly thereafter, and along with the yacht, had pulled down the shutters, closed shop and disappeared. Fantastically, the registered office in Tortola had been on the third floor of the Yamraj Building, Yamraj being the Hindu deity of death.[30]

A year earlier, in 2016, IIP sold their stake in SH31—the only profit-making asset in the portfolio—valued at £25.4 million. The company settled for £21.4 million from an affiliate of troubled Essel, who took on the whole asset. The board announced that it was 'pleased with the terms of the sale of IIP's minority interest in WMP, which have been achieved amidst difficult market conditions in the Indian road sector'.[31] The chief engineer of the state told me in clear terms that the SH31 was a profitable concession. Whatever the reason for the sudden and under-priced sale, the difference between the advertised purchase and sale prices was nearly $10 million.

***

At Toll Booth 1, 'my driver' pays the Rs 40 'toll tax' (as he calls it) again to see the barrier fall in the rear-view mirror of our Toyota as we drive away, four lanes narrowing back to two. As the road curves gently southwards, a dystopic cement factory looms behind a half-open gate. Smoke billows from a rotten-looking and cracked chimney. A thick layer of dust coats everything, including the rusted corrugated iron walls of the factory and tangled metal of old car crashes heaped in the yard. Further along the road are disused plants for bottling water and mixing motor oil: gates padlocked shut, entrances overgrown. Images of ruination are sharpened by the closed shutters and peeling paintwork of abandoned truck stops.

These dilapidations are from the last boom on SH31, when the road was widened to two lanes and the government gave land to industry. Times have changed: special economic zones to the south, towards Nagpur, brought new subsidy to industry. Important, too, has been the speeding up of traffic, as journeys that took many hours can now be completed in only a few. Speed has curtailed the cosmopolitan mingling of locals with truckers and tourists, as fewer stops for food, refreshment and rest have led to the dwindling of passing trade, the death of roadside businesses and the appearance of new services for those in the hinterlands. As we arrive at the steel plant junction at Lebad, the SH31 'concession' ends, and we join another PPP road run by different interests.

We are left with blurred impressions of nomads in a fast-moving world—the seasonal transhumance of goats and camels, the button-lipped Nomad in the City of London, the stoned long-distance truck driver, and the unmoored yacht on the bay of Saint-Tropez. Below and above the economy of Latour's commoners, one sits on the side of the road with an opium pipe, the other on the deck of a superyacht, the rest of the world desperately mobile within a system designed and promoted to generate expanding revenue streams.

Investment in the expansion of roads is necessary—this has become an unquestioned truth. The government cannot leverage sufficient funds or expertise to match the demand, because the government has been shown-and-told that it is inefficient and cumbersome—this is becoming an established truth. Lightly regulated private enterprise can better capitalise state wealth and influence. Private investment and efficiencies bring the benefits of roads to the people and profits to the investor. Win-win! Lock-in. This is how the world works in the age of BOT, a footnote in the early history of the Anthropocene.

The SH31 moves India at speed, but old India keeps making 'incursions', as the roadmen say. Locals remove fences and curbs so they can better access the highway; cuts are made clean through the central reservation at night, as the older routes and accessways refuse to succumb to linear four-lane logic. Off the tarmac, India slows right down in the fields and villages, and from the sluggish pace of the hinterlands, hawkers, stray dogs, halting buses and markets are pulled towards the highway like iron filings to a magnet. These impede the free flow of traffic, hindering the smooth operation of the toll. They cannot help themselves: the road draws them as if by magic out of their farms and ways of subsistence living, away from lush fields and caste inequalities, towards the promise of wealth and development, towards paying the toll—a South Asian version, perhaps, of the paradoxes discussed in the previous chapter in which new roads produce new traffic. Moving at different paces, India collides on the highway, and the result is the death of the population equivalent of a small Indian town every year.

In South Asia, China's involvement in Pakistan through CPEC has received a great deal of attention, the role of the United States in India or Pakistan less. On SH31, British consultancy firms sold governmental reform through overseas development aid, and the Dutch flogged the state government the highway's CCTV system. Yet America has appeared most frequently influential along the highway, not as a coordinated interest but as victor in the Cold War, as dramatical voice against drug trafficking, as conglomerate producing sticky and reflective materials, and as home to offshoring investors. The state of Indian roads must play a part in the quote from John F. Kennedy on Gadkari's Delhi office wall: 'American roads are good not because America is rich, but America is rich because American roads are good.' I will leave the exact wordcraft to you.

I have not found the original source for the quote. Kennedy might have said, 'It is not our wealth that built our roads, but it is our roads that built our wealth'—but it, too, is widely circulated as an 'unsourced quote'.

The organised availability of opium and sex to get people on to the road, the historic and orchestrated flow of pilgrims bound by faith en route to Jaora, and the farmer moving onions to market in Indore—all helped with the upkeep of a superyacht and the beautiful gardens behind the metal gates of a GGIC director's residence in Pasadena, California. His neighbourhood is one where many of Latour's commoners would wish to live in a fantasy world. When I visited, there was a glamour photoshoot on the road outside his house.

The economy of the road intermingles with sustained Hindu nationalist messages and the amorphous but tangible influence of Central India, the recurrent appearance of Nagpur, and the electoral politics of Subhash Chandra and Nitin Gadkari, for whom the future of India is in private enterprise and infrastructure, welcoming American-managed capital into the cracks and on to the signboards of SH31.

The connection of used bank notes of the toll tax to island tax havens, luxury yachts and ultimately to California and Virginia is the story of SH31 until 2016, when the scene began to change. Nitin Gadkari launched a new era of road finance (Hybrid Annuity Model) with a different pegging of private and state responsibility. The older story unfolded in this book is the everyday tale of how mundane transactions, such as paying a toll, become island-hopping funds. This relationship of transformation is everywhere but usually invisible, at least for those paying. The story of SH31 did, however, cast a different light on the long-term ambassadorial and policy work of the World Bank just over the river from Arlington. The heroic and proud tales of South Asian roadmen building nations and lifting people out of poverty suddenly seemed too far down the food chain to have much real explanatory power. Gadkari and Sharif appear as tricksters engaged in distracting magic.

Imagine what the world would look like if you could map the passage of money from the 372 toll booths currently operational in India. Or, better still, extend the analysis to the global flows of profits from mass mobility.

POSTSCRIPT
OTHER ROAD DREAMS

In Central India, those bound to provincial economies feed the lives of an elite unmoored from the geography of the twenty-first century. This was not the story road builders had told me about their work; nor was it the story politicians told their citizens. I found the layers of the story difficult to reconcile. None of it was surprising in isolation, but when put together the world began to appear as a giddy game played by a few with a supporting cast of billions. I took some time to use the research techniques developed over the last few years to explore roads in other parts of the world. I did so confident that the South Asia story was common to elsewhere and the bind of development and politics was far from unique to the region.

***

The 120-km expressway between Lagos and Ibadan in Nigeria was opened in 1978 at the peak of the oil boom as a toll road, a period now remembered as 'paradise on wheels'.[1] Due to increased population and traffic levels and poor maintenance, the road became known as 'Highway of Death' (a name also given to other roads in Nigeria). In 1984, toll collections were abolished. The road now carries around 250,000 vehicles per day. Journey times have slowed from seventy-five minutes, when the road was first opened, to at least three hours a few years ago. Death on the road was a near-daily event, and accidents involving the demise of ten or more people occurred at least twice a year.

After delays, corruption allegations and the dismissal of the original contractors in controversial circumstances, President Goodluck Jonathan arrived by helicopter at the 'Old Toll Booth' to inaugurate the rehabilitation and improvement of the road in July of 2013. The project was then scheduled to last for four years, with partial closures and diversions anticipated (and later confirmed) to generate chaos. Reconstruction finance was arranged by The Infrastructure Bank (of Nigeria; tagline: Beyond Finance) in partnership with six other banks and the Federal Government. The revenue was to be recuperated through the reintroduction of tolls. Local newspapers campaigned for twelve lanes in each direction. The road that is currently still being built is less grand, but a significant expanse of paved surface, nonetheless.

Works on a major section were undertaken by Julius Berger Plc (tagline: Unmatched Excellence in Construction), one of Nigeria's main infrastructure contractors, and Reynolds Construction Company (tagline: Since 1969 Building the Future). The latter is a subsidiary of SBI International Holdings, which is based in Switzerland (tagline: Connects Border to Border). SBI Switzerland is in turn a division of Shikun & Binui (tagline: Our Environment, Our Future), Israel's leading infrastructure and real estate group, which in turn was owned by Arison (tagline: Doing Good Is Good Business), a strategic investment company also based in Tel Aviv owned by Shari Arison.[2] At an earlier point in the research, Arison was described as the richest woman in the Middle East—but is now listed by *Forbes* as the richest woman in Israel. She is the author of the self-help book, launched in partnership with ABC News in New York, *Activate Your Goodness: Transforming the World through Doing Good* (2013).[3]

***

In November 2021, the UK hosted COP26, the global conference of parties to negotiate crucial climate change targets. Delegates crowding into the secure spaces of the Scottish Event Campus in Glasgow had to wait until the second week for a discussion of transport. The playful tagline for the day: Driving the Global

Transition to Zero Emission Transport. The UK billed the event as 'the COP that will kick start the mass market for zero emission vehicles'.[4] The ZEV (Zero Emissions Vehicles) agenda was led by Trudy Harrison of the Department for Transport, UK, keen to drive forward growth of 'non-polluting vehicles'.

Bill Van Amburg from CALSTART opened the discussion with a metaphor for the connoisseur:

> We often talk about being at a threshold or a crossroads, but we are right now beyond the crossroads—sometimes you get blocked at crossroads, they hold you back. We are moving forward on a new path with clarity, err, an ambitious and achievable goal to reach clean air, decarbonisation and net zero for transport.[5]

When Trudy Harrison returned to the mike, she said:

> For so long, the motorcar has been emblematic of the rise in carbon emissions and the damage that human activity inflicts upon our planet. Now we have the opportunity to transform that image of zero emission cars to become *symbolic* of our awakening to climate change, of our duty to reverse rising global temperatures as a matter of supreme urgency.[6]

Meanwhile, Trudy's colleagues in Highways England were running a public consultation for one of the largest road-building projects in the North of England for a generation. The dualling of the trans-Pennine A66, a long-running and controversial strategic route connecting east and west, mainland Europe and Northern Ireland, and an alternative route to the M1–M6 between London and Scotland. The route was presented as part of the UK government's 'levelling up' agenda, a strategy to reduce regional disparities and 'strengthen the Union'.

According to UK government figures, transport is the single highest emitting sector, accounting for 28 per cent in 2019.[7] Ninety per cent of these come from road transport.[8] The A66 is a major government project, the only road upgrade described in the National Infrastructure Strategy (tagline: Fairer, Faster, Greener).[9] All of the documentation for the project stresses the need for the electrification of transport and Net Zero 2050. Abstract claims on Net Zero mean that gross increases in traffic emissions can be separated from the road-building calculus. However, the new road, which is expected to carry an increased volume of traffic, does not have land set aside for vehicle charging stations or any special electrical charging infrastructure at all.

***

I moved out of the 'reality-based community' some time ago, realising that solutions to problems and the impetus for just social change do not emerge from reasoned empirical research or argument. The politician will stand up and say with clarity 'the data/science shows', and meanwhile behind his or her back the scientists are arguing about what the data means and why it shows what it does as they attempt to outdo one another in the competition to be nominated for the next award for service to the country. The political appeal to reality is to justify an approach or to create an electoral bond, rather more than it is to change everyday behaviour or minds. Some of the strongest earlier climate change literature reviewed in Chapter 9 also demonstrated that facts and logic have little to do with changing attitudes towards climate change. The explanations for this disconnect were multiple—future discounting, business as usual, sublime magnitude.

Using research-based arguments to change people's minds is not the way the world works today, if indeed it ever was. A leftist persuading a rightist to defect, a secularist turning religious nationalist? It does happen, but seldom because of a reasoned argument or piling fact on fact. Such 'change' is more usually entwined with personal life trials, trajectories and traumas. In the early twenty-first century, realities are for the making rather than to be discovered. Change can be orchestrated, but the A to B model has been overtaken by a scattergun of claims, sometimes contradictory and anarchic, that come together to create hybrid and contingent forms of change and new realities. There are very few instances where a single argument defines a new reality.

If a roadman tells me that roads 'open-up' the countryside and draw people into new forms of economy, I know enough now and can use empathy to see what he means—even if the evidence from actual research undertaken by actual academic colleagues suggests piecemeal and unequal effects. However, using ideals I value, such as community, environment and localism, then the aim of introducing mass mobility to fuel a provincial economy to sustain a global elite seems retrograde and undesirable from the outset. What would the roadman have to do to convince me that their vision is positive and contributes to the long-term betterment of the world? Having had the story explained to me hundreds of times, I have not been moved; if anything, my resistance to the narrative has grown stronger.

Then the most frightening thought occurred to me: What if my unusual questions have retrenched, even in a small way, the conviction of road builders—at least to the extent that they know there are dissenting voices other than those whose living rooms are threatened? It is not an impossible outcome, given my own recoil from ideas I found uncomfortable. That is not the result I wanted. If you have read this far, what would you have done differently?

ACKNOWLEDGEMENTS

I learned a distinct version of mature politics from the late Hasmukh Shah. Dilip Vaidya encouraged me to marvel and fear roads in Gujarat. The late Peter Gow mocked me for being interested in something as low-minded as transport. I would like to think we got there in the end. Earth First! opened my mind in the early 1990s to good and bad. I thank Jo Hill for sharing time on Twyford Down. Matthew Paterson influentially said that early experiences of transport tend to haunt later life. When not on my bike, much of my road time in India has been spent on my way to or from visiting Aditya Dogra in Diu (before he moved to Goa). I met all manner of people around his hearth, and the ecumenical approach to an evening out still warms me. I am indebted to Indira Varma for running around in circles in north London while insisting that there must be a point—again.

This book emerges from a team effort and an evolving agenda that I did not generate alone. The idea was seeded by Kanchana Ruwanpura, who brought Andrea Nightingale and Laura Jeffery to SOAS for discussion in 2012 and 2013. Ben Fine, Laura Hammond, Richard Black and Seamus Casey helped with the presentation that went to the European Research Council in Brussels in 2014. Ben, a heterodox economist, provoked me (as I remember it) in a mock interview: 'In what way do you think your little anthropology questions will get to the heart of global capitalism?' I took my initial inability to answer as a personal failing—and have worked on a response ever since.

I was fortunate enough to work with Marloes Janson on the first roundtable in 2013. Participants in the first event included: Clive Bell, Penny Harvey, Rob Petts, John Urry, J.-B. Gewald, Frank Schipper, Dimitris Dalakoglou, Nitin Sinha, Alessandro Rippa and Peter Merriman. The second roundtable benefited from the contributions of D.P. Gupta, Scott Bradford, Rajesh Bhushan, Nandini Sundar, Shilpa Aggarwal, Ravi Sundaram, Ashok Kumar, Deepak Thapa, Partha Mukhopadhyay, Tulasi Sitaula, Durba Chattaraj, Nitin Sethi, Swargajyoti Gohain, Radhika Mongia and Sugandha Srivastav.

This project was funded by a European Research Council (tagline: Supporting Top Researchers from Anywhere in the World) Consolidator Grant (no. 616393) awarded to Edward Simpson and hosted by SOAS University of London. Institutional Partners were University of Edinburgh and CAMP, Mumbai. For coordination and support, I am grateful to Urvi Makwana, Rob Whiteing, Ada Amadi, Silke Blohm, Ilona Bowyer, Carolyn Charlton, Maureen Green, Alex Lewis, Nicole Roughton and Ying Chen. The project was advised by an excellent academic board comprising Ben Campbell, Penny Harvey, Laura Jeffrey, Lucia Michelutti and Rob Petts.

The staff of many institutions were generous with access and time, including: the ADB, New Delhi; The British Library; CRRI, New Delhi; National Transport Research Centre, Islamabad; The Chartered Institution of Highways & Transportation (CIHT), London; DFID, London; IMC Worldwide; MPRDC, Bhopal; Royal Geographic Society, London; World Bank, Pakistan and Washington; IRC; Traffex; International Road Federation and World Road Congress.

At various moments, I have received influential academic advice from Adrian Mayer, Danny Miller, Surinder Jodhka, Carla Bellamy, Galen Murton, Katherine Rankin, Chris Fuller, Noman Baig, Johnny Parry, Tania Li, Nauman Naqvi, Akhil Gupta, Andrew Barry, Thomas Blom Hansen, Aasim Sajjad, Patricia Uberoi, Penny Harvey and the late David Graeber. I thank my past and present SOAS colleagues, Andrea Cornwall, Steve Hopgood, Steve Tsang, Ben Bowles, Rachel Dwyer, Mike Hutt, Navtej Purewal, Avinash Paliwal, Sunil Pun, Jim Mallinson, Richard Fardon, Fabio Gygi, Marloes Janson and David Mosse. I am also grateful to Barnet Council and to 'Derek', 'Dave', 'Rob' and 'another Rob' who talked me through finance, accounting and investment markets in their homes, city bars and on the sidelines of football pitches.

I would particularly like to thank Colin Gourley for taking me on as an anthropologist with little track record in the road world, for introducing me to the stalwarts of the scene, and for the opportunity to explore ideas with other 'roadmen'. At what was DFID, I would also like to thank Mark Harvey and Magda Leisten Johansson. In and around the work of IMC Worldwide (tagline: We Connect People and Societies), I have benefited from speaking to Bruce Thompson, Robert Petts, John Hine, Gary Haq and Bernard Obika. I am also indebted to the late John Urry for his inspirational work and for helping us to get the research off the ground.

With such a long project, there have been many meetings, conversations and differences of opinion. Ideas have been tried out and shot down; others have changed hands and been handed back; still others have been ridiculed, only later to return in enlarged and elaborated form. The project held workshops in London, Delhi, Mumbai, Kathmandu and Cumbria in the North of England. Deepak Thapa, Julia Brodacki, Michele Serafini, Sanderien Verstappen took part in the discussions in Nepal where the groundwork for what was to come later was completed. Niamh Collard, Luke Heslop, Laura Jeffery and Debbie Menezes participated in one of the more influential Cumbria gatherings.

Mustafa Khan was a doctoral student on the project. He came to anthropology late in life having held down a respectable career. He wrote a thesis on roads and development in Sindh in Pakistan.[1] I draw on his material in the second part of Chapter 8 as we journey through the borderlands. It has been a pleasure to work with and learn from him.

Khalid Chauhan worked on the Hazara part of the story and used his influence and charm to secure the time of senior roadmen in Pakistan. I have used some of Khalid's interview transcripts in the Pakistan section of Chapter 7 and, although he may doubt my analysis, I found his initial observations on the context and situation of the roadmen to be invaluable.

Srinivas Chokkakula followed PMGSY through the government of India and into the fields of Andhra Pradesh. Sections of the PMGSY

271

material in Chapter 4 draw from his observations. I am also grateful to him for facilitating and participating in a stint of the research in Madhya Pradesh. Through his good offices, we held a roundtable at the Centre for Policy Research in Delhi with government officials, academics and activists on rural roads in India that feeds Chapter 4.

Tommaso Sbriccoli, Niamh Collard and Sanjukta Ghosh worked on the SH31 materials. Tommaso walked the length of the road, conducting interviews in the hedgerows and ethnographic research in the toll booths. He is responsible for the excellent material on the toll booths and the organisation of the road. We are grateful to the Indian Institute of Management at Indore, particularly to Swapnil Garg and Surbhi Dayal. We also acknowledge the generosity of MPRDC, Mr Bourasi and the many private 'company men'.

Tommaso's ethnographic work was complemented by archival research in The British Library and elsewhere by Sanjukta Ghosh and Niamh Collard. Sanjukta traced the SH31 through the archives—a journey worthy of another book. Niamh also supported research for other sections, notably those on Gandhi, Nehru, Gadkari and Sharif. Jon Galton provided early editorial assistance. Farhaana Arefin came later with a deft eye for deletion and re-arrangement. At Hurst I am grateful to Lara Weisweiller-Wu for pandemic patience and encouragement at the end.

I shared material with seminar audiences at the following universities: Ahmedabad, Amsterdam, Berkeley, Calcutta, Cologne, Colombia, Colorado, Copenhagen, Geneva, Habib, Jadavpur, Los Angeles, Manchester, Presidency, Santa Barbara, Sister Nivedita, Stanford, TISS (Mumbai), Toronto, Vidya Sagar and Visva-Bharati. I have also presented some of the work at the conference of the British Association for South Asian Studies, the Royal Anthropological Institute, what was the DFID, British Academy, London School of Economics, SOAS and The Asiatic Society in Calcutta.

For a decade, I have collaborated with CAMP in Mumbai. Ashok Sukumaran and Shaina Anand have been friends and generous travelling companions. We worked together with the team, fieldwork and developing arguments. We made a film on a pharaonic road off the coast of Réunion Island. Sadly, friends and professional reviewers consistently felt the geographical leap was also a conceptual stretch and the material was cut from this book. In 2019, we took a road trip, influential for Chapter 8, through Gujarat to the border with Pakistan. The trip coincided with the announcement of the Supreme Court judgment on the Babri Mosque. The judges held that the demolition of the mosque by Hindu nationalists in the wake of Advani's *yatra* in 1992 was an illegal act; however, the court also awarded the land to a trust for construction of a temple in the name of Lord Ram.

This book evolved with CAMP's visual practice and understanding of the research locations. Long storyboarding sessions at CAMP studios and in the UK led to two products, a book and film *A Passage through Passages*. At CAMP, I am also grateful to Zi Ambapardiwala, Faiza Ahmad Khan, Simpreet Singh and Zulekha Sayyad.

The project culminated in an exhibition and premier of a five-screen 85-minute film at the Brunei Gallery in London. For work on the exhibition, I am grateful to Ali Rizvi, Spectrum, Gibson Frames, Love Print Group, DG3, Liz Hingley, Daniela Neri, Edwin Wingard and John Hollingworth. The exhibition closed its doors prematurely in March 2020, when COVID-19 was recognised as posing a threat in the UK. Nonetheless, the labour that went into the exhibition and film production stayed with me through lockdowns and all that— good and bad—came with those.

As my family knows, I have been interested in roads for a very long time. They have been patient and let me travel. Thanks to Bill and Margaret for starting the journey off. Isabella, Jack, Henry and Albert have continued the journey with me. Over the last few years, they have patiently engaged with endless hours of road talk, road guests and road movies. I apologise now if roads return to unwelcomingly haunt my children in later life. I would not have been able to complete this project without the generosity and care of my wife Isabella.

Most of all, I am indebted to those who informed this research but who are not named because if I name them, unless they are public figures or have expressly given their consent, then you will know who they are, and this is not permitted in the current social science regime. Errors, oversights and omissions are mine.

NOTES

INTRODUCTION

1. On the grand history of roads see Gregory (1931), and for a masterful display of what the contemporary historian can do Guldi (2012).
2. Virilio (1986).
3. Here I have in mind the combination of a social theory view of acceleration as given by Hartmut Rosa (2013) and the intensifying use of environmental resources in the twentieth century as described by McNeill and Engelke (2014).
4. Drawn from Latour's brilliant *Down to Earth* (2018) on politics in the new climactic regime. Latour has also taken up his own interpretation of Gaia (2017, 2019; Latour and Lenton 2019) as a critical way into discussing and animating climate debate. Leah Aronowsky (2021) subtly illustrates how the early research on Gaia was funded by oil companies and forms a frame that underplays human culpability in climate damage.
5. Latour (2018: 16). Italics in the original.
6. Latour (2018: 62).

CHAPTER 1. ON THE ROAD

1. Anthropologist Carla Bellamy (2011: 43–8 and Appendices A and B) recounts conflicting origin stories for the pilgrimage site.
2. 'Manual for Specifications and Standards for Four Laning of Highways through Public–Private Partnership', 1st revision, New Delhi: IRC SP 084-2014.
3. MPRDC was incorporated as a 'wholly government owned company' under the Companies Act 1956.

4. MPRDC, 'Profile', 2017.

5. The crop is mentioned in the *Ain-i-Akbari*, a Persian-language administrative report commissioned by Akbar (Markovits 2009: 90), while Garcia da Orta, an early sixteenth-century Portuguese botanist, argued that much of the opium exported from Cambay (present-day Gujarat) was obtained from Malwa (Farooqui 2006: 21n16), suggesting longstanding networks of local dealers (see also Farooqui 1995: 488).

6. Historian Amar Farooqui argues that Bombay's 'indigenous capitalist class' emerged from the 'participation of Indian business groups in the opium enterprise and the profits they earned from it' (2006: xiv).

7. Farooqui (1995: 450; 2006: 8) calls for 'a little circumspection' regarding popular claims that raw cotton, rather than opium, was the principal commodity exchanged for Chinese tea.

8. Farooqui (1995: 449–51; 2006: 24).

9. Markovits (2009: 108).

10. Kate Boehme has explained how the East India Company's concerns over an 'immense illicit [opium] trade flowing out of Karachi' impacted its setting of tariffs and duties before eventually 'contributing heavily to the annexation of Sind[h]' (2015: 702).

11. Markovits (2009: 93); Farooqui (1995: 451). Many of these merchants, such as Jamsetjee Jejeebhoy and Mohammed Ali Rogay, are chiefly remembered today as philanthropists, their involvement in the opium trade downplayed or ignored.

12. Farooqui (1995: 254; 2006: 24–5).

13. See data catalogued by the Central Bureau of Narcotics of the Government of India, http://cbn.nic.in/html/opiumhistory1.htm

14. File No. 127, Ratlam, Central India Agency Records, Old Files, nos. 121 to 140, Calcutta, 1919. Letter from the joint superintendent, Sellana, to the chief of Rutlam, dated 15 January 1852.

15. Detail extracted from 'Part 1, Major Routes, Route no. III, from Burhanpur to Sisada, Length Being 656m 7f and Comprises of 60 Marches; Compiler and Date: HQ Mhow District, 1928', pp. 1–27. Thanks to Sanjukta Ghosh for painstaking cross-referencing of sources in The British Library to map this route through time. Like many sentences in this book, days of work were involved.

16. Royal Commission on Opium, 'Minutes of Evidence Taken before the Royal Commission on Opium from 29th January to 22nd February 1894 with Appendices', vol. IV, London: Eyre and Spottiswood, 1894, p. 89.

17. Ibid., p. 154.

18. Ibid.
19. Ibid., p. 156.
20. Farooqui (2006: 38–9); Markovits (2009: 96).
21. K. Marx, 'Free Trade and Monopoly', *New York Daily Tribune*, 25 September 1858.
22. As with other former Criminal Tribes, they are now officially referred to as a 'Denotified Tribe'.
23. See, for example, 'Communal Riot near Khandwa: Over 20 Injured', *Times of India*, 9 October 1937; 'Communal Clash in Ratlam: Over Thirty Persons Injured', *Times of India*, 31 March 1956; 'Muslims in Alot Not Tyrannized', *Times of India*, 22 March 1967; 'Ratlam Riots: Probe Demanded', *Times of India*, 2 October 1989; 'Riots Erupt in Ratlam; Curfew On', *Times of India*, 2 October 1989. On student conflict, see 'Student Stir Rocks More Towns in M.P.', *Times of India*, 21 September 1966; '"Communists" Work in Ratlam: Mr K.M. Munshi's Report', *Times of India*, 27 September 1966.
24. 'Curfew in Ratlam: Shop Looted, 28 Injured', *Times of India*, 29 September 1967; 'Curfew Continues in Ratlam', *Times of India*, 24 March 1979.
25. On starvation: 'Bhils on the Verge of Starvation: Many Suicides', *Times of India*, 20 June 1933; 'Spectre of Starvation over MP Villages', *Times of India*, 3 January 1988; 'Adivasis & Bhils Affected Most by Scarcity', *Times of India*, 24 December 1952.
26. Political scientist Christophe Jaffrelot notes that Kushabhau Thakre, one of the leading lights of the right-wing BJP in Madhya Pradesh, cut his teeth as an RSS volunteer in Ratlam, Chittor and Mandsaur districts in the 1940s (1998: 269).
27. Jaffrelot (1996: 357).
28. 'Alleged Smuggling of Opium: Man with Five Aliases', *Times of India*, 15 June 1938.
29. Deshpande (1998: 53).
30. 'Cold Wave Hits Opium Crop', *Times of India*, 6 May 1984.
31. B. Pal, '… Gone to Opium Everyone', *Times of India*, 21 July 1991; C. Panchal, 'Severe Curbs on Poppy Cultivation', *Times of India*, 10 February 1987.
32. Deshpande (2009: 139).
33. N. Thacker, 'Where Smuggling Is King', *Times of India*, 18 August 1974.
34. 'Opium Pedlars Held', *Times of India*, 19 February 1976.
35. N. Mishra, 'Sister Morphine Comes to Opium Country', *Outlook India*, 8 March 1999.

36. Ibid.
37. R. Parihar, 'Political Patronage, Corrupt Officials Help Opium Become Booming Industry in Rajasthan', *Outlook*, 19 December 2005.
38. Mishra, 'Sister Morphine Comes to Opium Country', *Outlook*, 8 March 1999.
39. A. Kallmee, '50% of Drug Peddlers Are Women', *Times of India*, 18 March 1997.
40. L. Kumar Mishra, 'MP Police Get Tough on Opium Trade', *Times of India*, 29 March 1997.
41. UNODC, 'Bi-Annual Seizure Report 2002/01: Summary of Individual Significant Seizures of Narcotic Drugs and Psychotropic Substances as Reported by Government; Covering the Period 1 January–30 June 2002', Vienna: UNODC, 2002. I also draw on the same report for 2002 and 2003.

CHAPTER 2. READING ROADS

1. I am influenced by the work of Martha Lampland and Susan Leigh Star (2009) on 'standards', which discusses how quantifying and classificatory practices shape everyday life.
2. The traditional and single location of anthropological research was unsettled by the liberating and seemingly revolutionary idea of conducting fieldwork in more than one place: 'multi-sited ethnography' (Marcus 1995). Research here is influenced by multiple sites of engagement with roads, particularly a state highway in Central India and offices and conferences in South Asia, Europe and North America; however, much of the material is unmoored from geography and goes with the flows of transnational road builders. In this respect, the research was a methodological response to maturing globalisation and the old traps of regional studies paradigms.
3. *The Open Road: 1951 Highway Construction*, voiceover, Bethlehem Steel Company: Princeton Film Center, 1951.
4. Niira Radia talking to N.K. Singh, IAS and MoP, Rajya Sabha, Friday, 29 May 2009, p. 94 of CAMP Studio transcript. The quote is from Niira Radia.
5. For an account of those times, see Simpson (2013).
6. Deneault (2018).
7. Building on the sociology of Pierre Bourdieu (1977), Timothy Jenkins (1994) convincingly demonstrates that what people say they do is not what they actually do. What they say they do is the 'standard account', often refined in relation to the expectations the speaker has for the

listener and through repetition and rehearsal. What people actually do usually involves unsaid and embodied knowledge, inter-subjectivity, power and history.

8. See acknowledgements for a detailed description of the division of labour and key contributions.

9. Taglines in the text date from 2019 to 2022. I have not gone back in time to look at changing language.

10. A.B.C. Whipple, 'Superhighway—Superhoax', *New York Times*, 17 May 1970.

11. Schneider (1971: 191).

12. Illich (1974: 18–19).

13. Christian Wolmar (2016) is excellent on this question in the UK context. It is also the case that socialist governments have embarked on road-building programmes and centralised car production as part of national planning but without the same enduring effects. China might be a counterpoint, but the literature is not there.

14. John Whitelegg (2016) has also written about his personal frustrations.

15. There have been anti-road movements in the UK, but these tend to have been oriented around particular locations rather than wholesale affairs. Anti-road protest in the 1990s, for example, focused on Twyford Down in the south of England led by the direct action group Earth First! (Wall 1999).

16. Star (1999): 377.

17. Star (1999): 377; Stephen Graham and Nigel Thrift surface the invisible maintenance and repair work that they suggest are 'the main means by which the constant decay of the world is held off' (2007: 1). Sarah Green (2017) argues that infrastructural failure can be the lens through which to examine broad political crises.

18. Larkin (2013); also Anand, Gupta and Appel (2018).

19. Ash Amin (2014) sees in infrastructure the 'political intermediary of considerable significance' that shapes both the rights of the poor in relation to the city and the individual ability to exercise those rights.

20. For Augé (1995), a 'non-place' is a site of transience and anonymity, such as an airport or supermarket, devoid of symbolic associations unlike more conventional 'anthropological places', which he defines as 'relational, or historical, or concerned with identity'.

21. Till Mostowlansky (2011) studied the Soviet Pamir Highway, which prompted large-scale labour migration and gave rise to regional ethnic and religious diversity. Sharon Roseman (1996) explores the gap(s) between 'official' and local community understandings of the implications of such road-building projects.

22. Dimitris Dalakoglou (2017) illuminates the political economy of the Balkans in the aftermath of the Cold War through the analysis of a road as a text from which stories of nationalism, securitisation and pyramid schemes can be read.

23. Adeline Masquelier (2002) draws on individual stories to place roads in Niger in a 'complex economy of violence, power, and blood'. The road, she argues, is not an uncomplicated symbol of modernity but rather a 'hybrid space' in which diverse religious, economic and technological strands of history are condensed alongside the 'perils and possibilities of modern life'.

24. A 'mobility turn' in the social sciences focused on the 'social aspects of movement' (Vannini 2010); also John Urry's (2007) 'new mobilities paradigm' was to render opaque social phenomena—such as oil wars, airport expansion and social networking—comprehensible through the identification and description of the underpinning mobility system; also Cresswell and Merriman (2011). There is an excellent literature on cars and automobile politics, which shares much in common with writing on roads. However, throughout this book I focus on the road, not least because the car story in South Asia, as I discuss briefly in Chapters 5 and 6, is quite distinct and is not readily approached through the categories of the Euro-American literature. On cars in ways that support the Urry–Latour line taken in this book, see Paterson (2007), Sheller (2004), Ross (1996) and Weston (2012). Wolfgang Sachs (1992) is outstanding in 'looking back into the history of our desires'—and environmental blindness pre-climate change. For global literature from the 1980s, see Bardou et al. (1982); on ecology, see Freund and Martin (1993); on globalisation, Friedman (2000); and imperialism Jaffe (2005)—among many others.

25. Caroline Melly (2013) describes a road-building programme in Senegal that was accompanied by a discourse that 'rationalized, emphasized, and even celebrated' the inconveniences and hardships endured for the sake of 'future-focused' development.

26. Some have focused on the impact of the One Belt, One Road initiative on specific countries or regions, such as Bhavna Dave (2018) on Kazakhstan, Yang Yue and Li Fujian (2019) on the ASEAN region, and Anoushiravan Ehteshami and Niv Horesh (2018) on the Middle East. Others, like Bruno Maçães (2018), take a global approach, envisaging a new world order and a completely redrawn map of Eurasia (nevertheless, even in such a wide-ranging analysis, Maçães places special emphasis on China's infrastructural interventions in Pakistan and India's resulting anxieties over its capacity to exert influence in

Central Asia). For a social activist perspective on resource extraction in Africa, see Wengraf (2018).

27. Stefano Bellucci and Massimo Zaccaria (2014) explain how the Italian colonial regime in Eritrea pursued a mix of capital investments in construction and transport in the late nineteenth and early twentieth centuries, significantly boosting regional levels of free wage labour. Jo Guldi (2012) argues that a century earlier in Britain a nation was constructed through roads on libertarian principles, transforming social relationships in the process as road travellers became increasingly isolated from each other.

28. Thomas Zeller (2007) assesses Third Reich propaganda that claims Hitler's *autobahn* reconciled technology with nature.

29. Frank Schipper (2008) explores the archived debates and planning decisions behind the European road network. Schipper and Johan Schot (2011) trace the history of 'infrastructural Europeanism'.

30. Jan-Bart Gewald, Sabine Luning and Klaas van Walraven (2009) argue that whether a means for colonial domination or for economic growth and environmental damage in post-colonial nations, motor vehicles and roads have transformed the continent.

31. Anthropologists have increasingly taken to the road in recent decades. Prior to Penny Harvey and Hannah Knox's (2015) studies in Peru (see also Harvey and Knox 2012 and Harvey 2010), Fiona Wilson (2004) examined the practices of rural mobility in indigenous societies of the Peruvian Andes and the detrimental effects of the neo-liberal state's road-building projects. Jeremy Campbell (2012) takes the 'gap' between the 'muddy track as manipulated by migrants and the would-be road of planners' maps' in Amazonian Brazil as a starting point for an ethnographic enquiry into the infrastructures of colonial occupation and state-making; also see Melly (2013), Masquelier (1992, 2002), Saunders (2008), Klaeger (2009, 2013) and Chilson (1999) on African contexts; for Nepal, Katharine Rankin et al. (2017) envisage roads as 'stretched out spaces of social'. Ben Campbell (2010) examines the rhetoric of 'connectivity' and 'livelihoods' used by road builders to see their product. Galen Murton (2017, 2019) takes the Nepal–China border as site of production of social identity and geographical imagination; on Mongolia, Pedersen and Bunkenborg (2012); Pakistan, Rippa (2018); and in the Xinjiang Uyghur Autonomous Region, Joniak-Lüthi (2015).

32. Masquelier (2002).

33. Masquelier recounts being shown a photograph of an *iskoki*, a bloodthirsty spirit that terrorised Niger's Route 1—a 'smiling, blue-

eyed, fair-skinned woman that had been, in a prior incarnation, promoting tires for Dunlop' (2002: 831).

34. Hyde (2008).

35. In previous work on post-earthquake reconstruction in Western India, I have explored how people are remade along with plans (Simpson 2013).

36. Phelan (1950: 18).

37. NITI Aayog, 'Transforming India's Mobility: A Perspective', MOVE Global Mobilities Summit, 7–8 September 2018, p. 6.

38. Planning Commission, 'Pakistan Vision 2025: One Vision, One Nation', Islamabad: Government of Pakistan, 2014, p. 86.

39. Kynnersley (1945: 15).

40. This was true to a greater extent at the start of the research, particularly in India, than it is now because some private arrangements have been exposed as vehicles for hiding debt rather than building roads.

41. An example is Sir Henry Maine, historian and comparative jurist, who spent seven years as a legal member of council in India. He described the country as an 'assemblage' of 'fragments of ancient society', arguing—for example—that contemporary Indian methods of cultivating and holding land are 'in all essential particulars identical' to ancient European systems (1881: 13 and 108).

42. The concept of 'infrastructure deficit' or 'infrastructure gap' is promoted by the World Bank. For example, L. Andrés, D. Biller and M. Herrera Dappe, 'Reducing Poverty by Closing South Asia's Infrastructure Gap', Washington, DC: World Bank and Australian Aid, 2013. There is a related concept, 'infrastructure financing deficit' (see S. Ra and Z. Li, 'Closing the Financing Gap in Asian Infrastructure', Manila: ADB, 2018). Another ADB document notes that South Asia's fast growth is not matched by infrastructural investment and concludes that 'South Asia needs to invest almost 9% of its gross domestic product on infrastructure development over 2016–2030' (see: S. Jha and R. Mia Arao, 'Infrastructure Financing in South Asia', Manila: ADB, 2018).

43. The over-used phrase 'invention of infrastructure as an asset class' originates in the financial world and is regularly reproduced in academic writing. Throughout this book, I resist the temptation to uncritically repeat corporate, project management and marketing ideas. Nicholas Hildyard is a strong critical voice against the public–private system of infrastructure finance, calling it 'licensed larceny' to question the logic of infrastructure development. He has also expressed reasoned doubt about the truth and integrity of labels such

as 'Green Finance' and 'alternative fuels', calling instead for new ways of organising social, political and economic life. For a condensation of such ideas, see Hildyard (2016).

CHAPTER 3. STANDARD GEOGRAPHY

1. Stewart (1996).
2. For context and the reasons China and Pakistan may have agreed to CPEC, see Wolf (2020), Maçães (2018) and Miller (2017).
3. New China TV, 'The Belt and Road Is How', 2017.
4. Lyric from song broadcast by state media China Global Television Network by Vilayphone Vongphachanh, a Laotian journalist based in China. State media also produced a useful guide to the song: 'Mutual benefits and win-win results', 'keeping close communication and better understanding each other' and 'enhancing connectivity across nations'.
5. There is a substantial literature from international relations on the topic dating back three decades. For an intelligently updated version that speaks to the CPEC context, see Small (2020).
6. On the KKH in historical and contemporary perspective, see Ispahani (1989: 145–213), who emphasises the 'borderland' aspect of road building and international relations.
7. This expression was used by an Indian government spokesperson in 1969 and crystallised Indian fears of Chinese territorial ambitions in Ladakh and the Pakistan-administered parts of Kashmir (Ispahani 1989: 202–3).
8. *The Karakoram Highway*, dirs G. Neuhaus and A. Scudeletti, Surrey, England: Journeyman Pictures, 2002.
9. The State Council of the People's Republic of China, 'Making New Progress in Growing China–Pakistan All-Weather Friendship', 2013.
10. W. Sharp, *Field Administration in the United Nations System: The Conduct of International Economic and Social Programs*, United Nations Studies 10, New York: Praeger, 1961, p. 305.
11. 'The Asian Highway: From Caravan Routes to Modern Roads', *United Nations Review*, 5 (10) (April 1959): 42–4.
12. 'Conference on the Organization and Administration of Social Services in Asia and the Far East', *United Nations Review*, 6 (7) (January 1960): 96.
13. 'The News in Review', *United Nations Review*, 8 (1) (January 1961): 5.
14. *Everyman's United Nations: The Structure, Functions and Work of the Organisation and Its Related Agencies during the Years 1945–1962 and*

United Nations Chronology for 1963, 7th edn, New York: UN Office of Public Information, 1964, p. 222.

15. 'The Work of ECAFE's Eighteenth Session', *United Nations Review*, 9 (4) (April 1962): 57.

16. 'The Economic Commission for Asia and the Far East: Twenty Years of Progress', *UN Monthly Report*, 4 (4) (April 1967): 80.

17. Ibid., p. 84.

18. U. Nyun, 'ECAFE's Twenty-Fifth Anniversary: National Progress through Regional Co-operation', *United Nations Review*, 9 (11) (February 1972): 50.

19. United Nations Economic and Social Commission for Asia and the Pacific, 'Review of Developments in Transport in Asia and the Pacific 2005', New York: United Nations, 2005, p. 149.

20. United Nations Economic and Social Council (file no. E/ESCAP/FAMT/SGO/2), United Nations Economic and Social Commission for Asia and the Pacific (UNESCAP), 'Major Issues in Transport: Transport Infrastructure', Forum of Asian Ministers of Transport: Meeting of Senior Government Officials, First Session, 14–16 December 2009, Bangkok. Bangkok: UNESCAP, 2009, p. 12.

21. UNESCAP, 'Review of Developments in Transport in Asia and the Pacific 2009', New York: United Nations, 2009, p. 138.

22. Historians and critical geographers are best on these relations. My impressionistic description of invisible lines (that are not always borders) in South Asia is a product of complex historical processes. See, for example, Guyot-Réchard (2020) and Saha (2016) on Myanmar. A rich and productive literature on borderlands, perhaps exemplified by van Schendel (2005), illustrates the cultural and political complexities that underpin the thrust of massive infrastructure investment.

23. Bajpaee (2017: 349).

24. Referring to Arunachal Pradesh as 'Zangnan' (Southern Tibet) has been common Chinese practice since 2005, according to Sumit Ganguly and Manjeet Pardesi (2012: 477). See also Khanna (2017: 61).

25. For a published version of this argument, see Uberoi (2014: 3).

26. 'India to Thailand on Wheels!', *Times of India*, 24 October 2017.

CHAPTER 4. STANDARD NARRATIVE

1. See Gupta (2005) and Jodhka and Simpson (2020) among many others for this long and complex story.

2. World Bank, 'International Development Association Project Appraisal Document on a Proposed Credit in the Amount of US$235 Million to the Republic of India for Bihar Rural Roads Project November 29, 2016', Transport and ICT Global Practice South Asia Region, Report no: PAD2150, 2016, p. 12.

3. 'All-weather road connectivity' was previously identified as a metalled water bound macadam.

4. When the act was finally passed, the cess was divided thus: 41.5 per cent for national highways; 33.5 per cent for rural roads; 10 per cent for state roads; 14 per cent for the always tricky road-rail crossings; and 1 per cent for border roads (CRF Act 2000, sections 7 and 10).

5. `Criss-crossing the Roads Network', *Financial Express*, 18 July 2005.

6. Government of India, Rural Road File no. P-17017/2/99-RR dated 6 January 2000.

7. Letter from Nitin Gadkari to Shri Sunderlal Patwa, then the minister of rural development, dated 2 May 2000.

8. World Bank, 'Implementation Status & Results Report PMGSY Rural Roads Project' (44000-P124639), 2017.

9. 'Online Management, Monitoring and Accounting System', Pradhan Mantri Gram Sadak Yojana, http://omms.nic.in

10. Shilpa Aggarwal, development economist, Second Roundtable, Delhi 2016.

11. Shilpa Aggarwal, development economist, Second Roundtable, Delhi 2016. For this argument in published form, see Aggarwal 2018: 376–7 and 387.

12. World Bank, 'International Development Association Project Appraisal Document on a Proposed Credit in the Amount of US$235 Million to the Republic of India for Bihar Rural Roads Project November 29, 2016', Transport and ICT Global Practice South Asia Region, Report no. PAD2150, 2016.

13. Fan, Hazell and Thorat (1999: 46).

14. Sen (1996).

15. Fan, Hazell and Thorat (1999: 46).

16. Riverson, Gaviria and Thriscutt (1994).

17. Fan, Zhang and Zhang (2000), quoted in Mohapatra and Chandrasekhar (2007: 109).

18. Fan, Hazell and Thorat (1999).

19. See also Kumar and Kumar (1999).

20. Kumar and Tillotson (1991).

21. Swaminathan, Lal and Kumar (1981).

22. In this and other quoted extracts from the roundtables, I have abbreviated the speaker's words in places.
23. 'Monitoring Division Consolidated Report', New Delhi: PMGSY, 2004.
24. Bell (2012a, 2012b); Bell and van Dillen (2012, 2015).
25. Aggarwal (2014); Asher and Novosad (2014); Panda (2015). There are also several technical papers on PMGSY that detail materials, durability, technologies of road construction and the bureaucratic process and techniques for the best delivery of roads.
26. Aggarwal (2018).
27. Many of these studies have focused on the experiences of specific states, including Gujarat (Shah 2010), Karnataka (Rajasekhar, Lakha and Manjula 2013) and more recently Odisha (Parida 2016). Martin Ravallion (2012), meanwhile, examines corruption within the programme but cautions against simplistic comparison between states. In some cases, of course, the critique may have been a politically motivated attempt to promote PMGSY further.
28. Aggarwal (2018: 377).
29. Aggarwal (2018: 378) lists the following datasets used: the Government of India Online Management and Monitoring System (OMMS); population censuses from 2001 and 2011; the Ministry of Agriculture's 5-yearly agricultural inputs survey; and the National Sample Survey (NSS), which provides household-level consumption data and individual-level information on education and labour-market participation.
30. See also Asher and Novosad (2014).
31. S. Asher and P. Novosad, 'Rural Roads and Local Economic Development', Policy Brief no. 30, Bonn: IZA Institute of Labour Economics, 2019.
32. Rural Economic and Demographic Survey (REDS).
33. Shamdasani (2016).
34. Bell and van Dillen (2012). For the original surveys, see van Dillen (2008).
35. Bell and van Dillen (2012). The paper also estimates that replacing 1 km of *kachcha* (unpaved) road by a PMGSY road yields an increase in the net price of paddy of Rs 7.95 per quintal.
36. Bell (2012a).
37. Bell (2012b: 22).
38. Panda (2015).
39. Banerjee and Sachdeva (2015).
40. Aggarwal (2018: 385).

41. Asher and Novosad (2014).

42. Blaikie, Cameron and Seddon (1980: 8). They observe that much road building in Nepal was motivated more by internal security concerns, or the interests of foreign donors, than by the aim of reducing poverty.

43. Blaikie, Cameron and Seddon (2000).

44. Bucheli, Bohara and Villa (2016: 2).

45. Bucheli, Bohara and Villa (2016: 24).

46. Hine et al. (2016: 64).

47. Ibid.

48. File no. P-17034/3/2015-RC (FMS No. 344707), 'Government of India: To: The Secretaries of Nodal Departments of 9 LWE States Dealing with Implementation of "Road Connectivity Project in LWE Affected Areas" [AP, BH, JH, CH, MH, MP, OD, TL, UP]'.

49. *India: The Bottom Line*, Spotlight Films for the World Bank, 2008.

50. Bourdieu (2008).

51. Gupta (2005).

52. Parry (2003).

53. For 'townizing', see Guldin (2001); for 'hermaphroditic', see Davis (2007); and for 'in-between city', see Sieverts (2003). 'Rurban', coined by the American sociologist Charles Galpin, dates back to 1915.

54. From Lipton (1968) onwards.

55. Maine (1881).

CHAPTER 5. GANDHI, NEHRU AND THE ROYAL ROAD THROUGH THE TWENTIETH CENTURY

1. 'Improvised Bullock-Cart Transport for Rural Roads in India', National Seminar Papers, Rourkela: Regional Engineering College, Department of Applied Mechanics and Hydraulics, 1979.

2. 'Bullock Professor Builds Kinder Cart', *New Scientist*, 110 (1509) (22 May 1986): 32; see also, Raghavan and Rao (1979a; 1979b).

3. Histories such as *Tracks of Change* (Prasad 2015) and *Engines of Change* (Kerr 2007) focus on the transformative impact on society and politics, with emphasis on nationalism and new forms of social proximity. Anthropologist Laura Bear (2007) explores how railway bureaucracy created new public spaces and social relationships. Aparajita Mukhopadhyay (2018) places a strong emphasis on passengers in determining the development trajectory of railways.

4. The *Imperial Gazetteer of India* (vol. 21) notes Thomason Engineering College (later Indian Institute of Technology Roorkee) 'has its origins

in a class started in 1845 to train local youth in engineering to assist in public works then beginning' (1907: 325). The college formally opened in 1847, as a response to the decision to construct a canal system between the Ganges and Yamuna Rivers, passing through Roorkee. For a fascinating history of the engineering profession in India, see Aparajith Ramnath (2017).

5. Motoring journalist Gautam Sen (2011) evokes the Indian princes' love affair with the automobile.

6. There is lack of scholarship on the history and culture of cars or automobility in India. Tom Barnes (2018) and Jatinder Singh (2019) cover the history while focusing on labour and the structure of trade and technology respectively.

7. The report contains accounts of roads in ancient and mediaeval kingdoms such as Mauryas and Mughals; statistics on contemporary road mileage, expenditure and conditions; comparisons with roads in Great Britain, France, the United States and China; and recommendations on the financing of roads in India. See: 'Report of the Indian Road Development Committee 1927–8', Calcutta: Government of India Central Publication Branch, 1928.

8. See: 'CTPC Paper No 187', New Delhi: Government of India, Planning Commission; British Library, Indian Office Archive, MSS Eur F 158/309, 1963.

9. *Proceedings of the Fifth Meeting of the Indian Roads Congress*, Calcutta: 14–18 February 1939.

10. 'The Nagpur Plan', IRC, 1943.

11. The 'Salt March' was the first decisive step towards India-wide civil disobedience. Gandhi maintained his schedule of spinning, praying, writing and speech-making throughout the march (Nanda 1981). Political scientist Denis Dalton emphasises the religious symbolism that many observers accorded the march, identifying Gandhi with Lord Ram or the Buddha, and notes Gandhi's own framing of the march as a *yatra* (1993: 108–16). Historian Kathryn Tidrick covers similar ground, bringing human detail to the fore: marchers demanding excess food from villagers before they 'hopped into cars and casually accepted delicacies from local people', leading Gandhi to appeal 'to them not to disgrace him' (2006: 229–30).

12. J. Nehru, *Selected Works of Jawaharlal Nehru* [*SWJN* hereafter], vol. 4, New Delhi: Orient Longman, 1973 [1930], p. 289. 'Inqilab Zindabad', in *Young India*.

13. 'Our cities are not India', Gandhi famously wrote in 1921. 'India lives in her seven and a half lakhs of villages, and the cities live upon the

villages' (M.K. Gandhi, *The Collected Works of Mahatma Gandhi* [*CWMG* hereafter], vol. 24, New Delhi: Publications Division, Ministry of Information and Broadcasting, Govt of India, 1999 [1921], p. 414. 'The Great Sentinel' in *Young India*). Dennis Dalton writes that Gandhi 'continually emphasized the necessity for identification with the villagers, who represented the masses of India' (1993: 59) and connects Gandhi's quest for *Sarvodaya* (literally social equality, but in a Gandhian context with strong connotations of village uplift) to his wide reading—Tolstoy and the Bible as well as Indian religious texts—and also to broader intellectual currents of the age.

Surinder S. Jodhka (2002) compares the thoughts of Gandhi, Nehru and Dalit social reformer Babasaheb Ambedkar on villages, noting that all three spent most of their lives in cities and made somewhat generalising assumptions about the uniformity of villages across India. However, unlike Nehru and Ambedkar, who saw the Indian village as a site of 'backwardness' and 'oppression' respectively, Gandhi viewed the village as a 'site of authenticity'. In a similar vein to my argument that Gandhi's thoughts and rhetoric on roads shifted at stages in his life, Jodhka suggests that Gandhi used the idea of the village in different ways: as evidence of the equivalence between Indian and European civilisations; as a critique of urban life and 'modern western culture and civilisation'; and as an actual location in need of reform.

14. Kuusisto (2009: 283).

15. Gandhi, *CWMG*, vol. 6, 1999 [1907], pp. 221–2. 'Ethical Religion II', in *Indian Opinion*.

16. Ibid., vol. 8, 1999 [1908], p. 459. 'Sarvodaya IX', in *Indian Opinion*.

17. Ibid., vol. 10, 1999 [1910], p. 159. 'Speech at Emerson Club', in *Indian Opinion*.

18. Ibid., vol. 6, p. 263. 'Ethical Religion V', in *Indian Opinion*.

19. Ibid., vol. 14, 1999 [1914], p. 176. 'Letter to Raojibhai Patel'.

20. Ibid., vol. 12, 1999 [1911], p. 4. 'India's Sorry Plight' in *Indian Opinion*.

21. Ibid., vol. 25, 1999 [1922], p. 397. 'Khilafat Conference', in *Navajivan*.

22. From Herodotus, *Histories*, Book 8, Chapter 98 (De Sélincourt 1972: 556). His further praise of the messengers is often now associated with the US postal service: 'Neither snow nor rain nor heat nor gloom of night stays these couriers from the swift completion of their appointed rounds', the words inscribed on what was the general post office in New York.

23. Gandhi, *CWMG*, vol. 34, 1999 [1926], p. 287. 'Letter to Antoinette Mirbel'.

24. Ibid., vol. 42, 1999 [1928], p. 247. 'Questions of a Graduate', in *Navajivan*.

25. Ibid., vol. 37, 1999 [1926], p. 24. 'Letter to Feroze'.

26. Ibid., vol. 81, 1999 [1941], p. 357. 'Constructive Programme: Its Meaning and Place'.

27. Ibid., vol. 5, 1999 [1906], p. 65. 'Black and White Men', in *Indian Opinion*.

28. The general point about the enduring influence of Saurashtra (a region within Gujarat) on Gandhi's political thought is well made by Howard Spodek (1971).

29. Gandhi, *CWMG*, vol. 130, 1999 [1925], p. 381. 'Talk to Inmates of Satyagraha Ashram Vykom', in *The Hindu*.

30. Ibid., vol. 64, 1999 [1934], p. 325. 'Letter to Annapurna'.

31. Ibid., vol. 31, 1999 [1925], p. 200. 'Roads in Gujarat', in *Navajivan*.

32. Shah (1991: 44).

33. Gandhi, *CWMG*, vol. 16, 1999 [1917], p. 158. 'Letter to J.L. Merriman'.

34. Misra (1995: 7–8).

35. Gandhi, *CWMG*, vol. 98, 1999 [1947], p. 20. 'Speech at Prayer Meeting' broadcast over All-India Radio.

36. Ibid., vol. 33, 1999 [1925], pp. 183–4. 'Reminiscences of Kutch: I', in *Navajivan*.

37. Ibid.

38. Ibid.

39. Ibid.

40. Ibid., p. 207. 'Interview to Press', in *The Hindu*.

41. Ibid., vol. 48, 1999 [1930], p. 307. 'Village Roads', in *Navajivan*.

42. Ibid.

43. Ibid.

44. Ibid., vol. 38, 1999 [1927], p. 64. 'Speech at Meeting, Gaya', in *The Searchlight*.

45. Ibid., vol. 42, p. 362. 'Speech at Bardoli', in *Young India*.

46. Ibid.

47. Ibid., vol. 53, 1999 [1931], p. 409. 'Interview to "John Bull"'.

48. Ibid., vol. 15, 1999 [1916], p. 277. 'Speech at Muir College Economic Society', in *The Leader*.

49. Ibid., vol. 21, 1999 [1920], p. 343. 'Speech to Students and Teachers, Surat', in *Navajivan*.

50. Ibid., vol. 54, 1999 [1931], p. 266. 'Answers to Questions: Lausanne'.

51. Ibid., vol. 84, 1999 [1944], p. 173. 'Letter to Horace G. Alexander'.

52. Ibid., vol. 32, 1999 [1925], p. 321. 'New Rituals', in *Navajivan*.

53. Ibid., vol. 62, 1999 [1934], p. 357. 'Speech at Public Meeting, Vizagapatam', in *Harijan*.

54. Ibid., vol. 71, 1999 [1937], pp. 408–9. 'A Plea for the Village Cart' (extract from correspondence with Ishverbhai S. Amin), in *Harijan*.

55. Ibid., vol. 65, 1999 [1934], pp. 19–20. 'Letter to Shantikumar Morarjee'.

56. Ibid., vol. 90, 1999 [1946], p. 286. 'Speech at Kasturba Balika Ashram', in *Harijan*.

57. 'National Highways Prog Second Plan Targets', *India News*, 13 April 1957, p. 72; 'Another Rs 95m for Road Development', *India News*, 16 August 1958, p. 64.

58. 'India's Road Development Plan 1961–81', *Far East Trade*, October 1959, p. 57.

59. 'New Road Plan Drawn Up of 675,000 Target', *India News*, 10 January 1959, p. 61.

60. CTPC report, pp. 24–5.

61. J. Nehru, *SWJN*, vol. 20, 2nd series, 1952, p. 140.

62. Ibid., vol. 26, 2nd series, 4 August 1954, p. 84.

63. Ibid., vol. 71, 2nd series, 1961, pp. 546–9.

64. Ibid., vol. 4, 1930, p. 246.

65. Ibid., vol. 3, 1928, p. 238.

66. For example, ibid., vol. 6, October 1933; vol. 8, 2nd series, 19 December 1948, p. 384.

67. Ibid., vol. 11, 27 August 1940, p. 170.

68. Ibid., vol. 8, 2nd series, 11 December 1948, pp. 5–6.

69. Ibid., vol. 15, part 2, 2nd series, 1951, p. 25.

70. Ibid., vol. 21, 2nd series, 21 February 1953, p. 129.

71. Ibid., vol. 3, 15 November 1928, p. 265; vol. 24, 2nd series, 14 December 1953, pp. 129–30.

72. Ibid., vol. 19, 2nd series, 16 July 1952, pp. 129–30.

73. Ibid.

74. Ibid., vol. 24, 2nd series, 14 December 1953, pp. 129–30.

75. Ibid., vol. 5, 13 October 1931, p. 141.

76. Ibid., vol. 8, pp. 41–2.

77. Ibid., 29 July 1937, p. 172.

78. Ibid., vol. 6, 24 January 1934, pp. 186–7.

79. Ibid., vol. 15, part 1, 2nd series, 9 September 1950, p. 168.

80. Ibid.

81. Ibid., vol. 29, 2nd series, 24 July 1955, pp. 163–4.

82. Ibid., vol. 43, 2nd series, pp. 235–6.

83. Ibid., vol. 65, 2nd series, pp. 315–16.

84. Ibid., 14 December 1960, p. 285.

CHAPTER 6. TOYOTA TO TESLA

1. Kynnersley (1945): 15.
2. Accounts of road development in South Asia typically list Aryans, Buddhists, Mauryans, Guptas and Moghuls as road builders before getting down to the business of the twentieth century. See: 'Report of the Indian Road Development Committee 1927–8', Calcutta: Government of India Central Publication Branch, 1928; and also: *History of Road Development in India (A Brief Account of the Genesis and Development of the Indian Road System)*, New Delhi: CRRI, 1963.
3. Pilgrimage is commonly thought of as a sacred journey. Anthropologists report how pilgrimage transforms individuals, facilitates and accompanies trade, and sustains religious and social networks. Pilgrimage can also be a public expression of loyalty, opposition or protest. In other words, pilgrimage can be inwardly meaningful but also an outward and visible sign of broader intent. See, for example, Surinder M. Bhardwaj (1973) on pilgrimage and hierarchical networks and Peter Van der Veer on the political economy of pilgrimage (1988; 1994).
4. Kakar (1996: 49).
5. Much has been written on Advani's antics. David Ludden (1996) has an excellent introduction. Sudheendra Kulkarni (2004) chronicles favourably; Amrita Basu (2015) and Kakar (1996), among many others, provide critical gloss.
6. Fourth Plan, p. 199.
7. Ibid., p. 301.
8. Fifth Plan.
9. Lucknow Plan.
10. Eighth Plan. Chaired by ex-Prime Minister Narasimha Rao; the deputy chair was ex-President Pranab Mukherjee.
11. Ibid., p. 39. Para. 2.8.11.
12. Ninth Plan, p. 1193. Para. 7.1.103.
13. Ibid., p. 1193. Para. 7.1.104.
14. Ibid. Chaired by A.B. Vajpayee and deputised by K.C. Pant.
15. Ibid. Note by Atal Behari Vajpayee, chairman Planning Commission, 5 April 1999.
16. Ibid., p. 1202. Para. 7.1.130.
17. Ibid., p. 119. Para. 2.151 (iii).
18. Ibid., p. 1204. Para. 7.1.136.

19. 'Prime Minister's Committee on Infrastructure: National Highways', in *India's Five-Year Plans: Mid-term Appraisal of the Tenth Five Year Plan (2002–2007)*, part 2, Sectoral and Other Issues, Planning Commission GOI, 28 June 2005, New Delhi: Academic Foundation, 2005.

20. Tenth Plan. Mid-term appraisal, p. 11.

21. Eleventh Plan, p. xi.

22. Ibid., p. 290, Para. 9.3.7.

23. Ibid., p. 12. Para. 1.76.

24. Ibid., p. 12. Para. 1.78.

25. Ibid., p. 223. Box 15.9.

26. Ibid., p. 217. Box 15.8.

27. Twelfth Plan, p. 76.

28. Population figures are from the national census; road figures are from 'Basic Road Statistics of India 2015–16', New Delhi: Government of India, 2017; and vehicle numbers are from the Government of India's Open Data Initiative.

29. H. Kaushik, 'Soon, Drive Down the Path Mahatma Gandhi Walked', *Times of India*, 19 July 2016.

30. Georgieva's father was a road builder in Bulgaria—a fact frequently recalled in interviews focused on her credentials and influence.

31. See Prabhu (2017) for a historical review of World Bank lending in India.

32. Campaign advertisement 'Connecting Places, People, and Profits in Pakistan', August 2019.

33. Ibid.

34. ADB, 'Pakistan Highway Promotes Growth and Connectivity', video, 25 October 2016.

35. 'West Pakistan: Second Highway Project (English)', Technical operations projects series; no. TO 651, Washington, DC: World Bank, 1968.

36. 'West Pakistan: Highway Project (English)', Technical operations projects series; no. TO 406, Washington, DC: World Bank, 1964.

37. 'Foreign Assistance Act of 1963: Hearings before the Committee of Foreign Affairs House of Representatives Eighty-Eighth Congress First Session on H.R. 5490', part 1, Washington, DC: US Government Printing Office, 1963, p. 265.

38. 'Transportation Survey of West Pakistan, 1962', vol. 1, Washington, DC: Department of the Army, Office of the Chief Engineers, 1962, p. 2.

39. 'Memorandum and Recommendation of the President of the International Bank for Reconstruction and Development to the

Executive Directors on a Proposed Loan of US$ 152 Million to the Islamic Republic of Pakistan for the Fourth Highway Project', World Bank, Report no. P-4419-PAK, 1987.

40. World Bank, Report no. P-4419-PAK, 1987.

41. World Bank Info Shop, 'Integrated Safeguards Data Sheet', Report no. AC 32, 2003.

42. David Engerman (2018) offers critical assessment of India's decision to take a path of non-alignment. In this view, the decision led to institutional decline and the subsequent distortion of the political economy as the country was caught between the incompatible aid agendas of the United States and the Soviet Union. Markus Daechsel (2015) offers an original account of Pakistan's experiences following the development of Islamabad by the urbanist Constantinos A. Doxiadis. Begüm Adalet (2018) describes the construction of post-Second World War modernisation attempts in Turkey, along with a discussion of roads and American interventions, including attempts at developing a network and training engineers.

43. J.L. Hine and A.S. Chilver, 'Pakistan Road Freight Industry: An Overview', Research Report 314, Crowthorne, Berkshire: Transport and Road Research Laboratory, 1991.

44. USAID video, 'Pathway to Prosperity', https://www.usaid.gov/news-information/videos/pathway-prosperity

45. IMF-led reforms and encouragement from the World Bank led to an institutional transition from state-led import substitution to deregulation and globalisation. See Mukherji (2014).

46. For a condensation of some of these ideas, see Hildyard (2016). Also see manuals such as Weber, Staub-Bisang and Alfen (2016) for an industry approach.

47. Recent forms of PPPs have had a brief but eventful history in South Asia. Universities provide expensive training courses for PPP managers. The development banks have produced guides on how to structure and govern such arrangements. For a critical overview of the consequences and liabilities of PPP forms of organisation, see Pratap and Rajesh (2019), Van Waeyenberge and Bayliss (2017).

48. Such arrangements include: concessions, usually lasting from 25 to 30 years, in which a private concessionaire takes responsibility for operation, maintenance of assets and financing and managing investment; BOT, typically used in greenfield new building projects where a public sector body grants a private company development rights over a project that would otherwise be managed by the public sector; and DBO (design-build-operate), a simpler model in which

the public sector owns and finances the construction of new assets carried out by the private sector. For further details, see: World Bank Group, Concessions, Build-Operate-Transfer (BOT) and Design-Build-Operate (DBO) Projects, Public–Private–Partnership Legal Resource Centre, 2018.

49. For example, the then DFID of the Government of the United Kingdom funded consultancy firms to develop mechanisms within state governments in India to administer PPPs. The development consultancy Adam Smith International (tagline: Think. Deliver. Transform) worked on behalf of the World Bank to introduce public–private funding mechanisms for road construction in Chhattisgarh and West Bengal.

CHAPTER 7. EMPERORS OF THE ROAD

1. V.K. Dethe, 'Sharif Permits Pvt Banks in Pakistan', *Times of India*, 4 December 1990.

2. 'P.M. Renames Motorway', *Pakistan Affairs*, XLV (4), 16 February 1992, p. 4.

3. 'Pakistan: Sharif's "Address-to-the-Nation" Reported', *The News*, 1 November 1997.

4. 'New Motorway Opens in Pakistan', *Gulf News*, 26 November 1997.

5. 'Nawaz Sharif Says Industrial States Would Be Built across Motorway', *Pakistan Press International*, 15 December 2014; N.A. Dhakku, 'PM Says His "Plan D" Is for Development', *Dawn*, 16 December 2014.

6. 'Pakistan Prime Minister Denies Contempt Charge', CNN, 17 November 1997.

7. H. Haqqian. 'Highways to Nowhere', *Friday Times*, 7–13 November 1997.

8. 'Pakistan: Nawaz on IPPs, Economy, Terrorism, Issues', *The Nation*, *Islamabad*, 7 April 1998.

9. 'Sharif Says Kashmir to Be Part of Pakistan "Soon"', *The Nation*, 27 July 1999.

10. 'Sharif: India to Accept Proposal for Kashmir Talks', *The Nation*, 31 July 1999.

11. 'Another Reference against Sharifs Sent to Accountability Bureau', *The News*, 9 October 2000.

12. 'MNS's Peshawar–Kabul Motorway Vision', *Pakistan Observer*, 9 May 2013.

13. 'Pak–China Trade Corridor: Prime Minister Approves Proposed Alignment', *Business Recorder, Karachi*, 17 August 2013.

14. 'Western Alignment of China–Pakistan Economic Corridor to Be Operational by December 2016: Prof Ahsan Iqbal; Press Note Issued by Press Information Department', *Pakistan Press International*, 1 July 2015.

15. 'PM: Uplift Project Will Usher in an Era of Prosperity', *Pakistan Observer*, 24 May 2014.

16. 'PM Orders to Start Work on Lahore–Karachi Motorway', *Pakistan Observer*, 17 August 2017.

17. 'PM Inaugurates Khanewal–Multan Motorway Section', *Pakistan Press International*, 21 November 2015.

18. 'Bhuran–Havelian Expressway: Project Facing Rs Three Billion Cost Escalation', *Business Recorder*, 29 November 2014.

19. 'Pakistan Launches Expressway as Part of ADB, DFID-Supported Economic Corridors Program', ADB, News from Country Offices, 27 December 2017.

20. 'Rs42bn Approved for Malir Motorway', *Pakistan Press International*, 11 July 2014.

21. 'Nawaz Sharif Lays Foundation Stone of M-9 Motorway', *Pakistan Press International*, 11 March 2015.

22. H.K. Ghori, 'First Phase of Karachi–Lahore Motorway Launched', *Dawn*, 12 March 2015.

23. 'Motorway Inauguration', *Business Recorder*, 24 August 2016.

24. A. Manan, 'We'll Keep Building Roads for You to Protest on, Nawaz Tells Imran', *The Express Tribune*, 20 May 2016.

25. 'PML-N Striving to Curb Load-Shedding: Nawaz', *The Nation*, 3 May 2017.

26. 'Children of Pakistan's Prime Minister', ICIJ Offshore Leaks Database, https://offshoreleaks.icij.org/stories/mariam-safdar-hasan-and-hussain-nawaz-sharif

27. H. Bhatti, 'Nawaz Sharif Steps Down as PM after SC's Disqualification Verdict', *Dawn*, 28 July 2017.

28. 'Deposed Pakistani PM Calls Ouster "Insult to Voters"', Radio Free Europe/Radio Liberty, 9 August 2017.

29. S. Ali, '"Homegoing Rally": 38-Foot Long Bomb-Proof Container Prepared for Nawaz Sharif', *Daily Pakistan*, 9 August 2017.

30. 'Metro Bus Service Makes Shehbaz Immortal', *Pakistan Observer*, 11 February 2013.

31. Survey by Pakistan Institute of Legislative Development and Transparency and reported as 'Nawaz Most Favourite Leader: Survey', *Dawn*, 20 October 2015.

32. M. Elahi and S. Haider, 'PML-N Remains Most Popular Party, Nawaz Most Favourite Leader: Survey', Geo TV, 24 November 2017.

33. 'Progress Won't Stop: PM', *Pakistan Observer*, 12 November 2016.

34. The name of the ministry has changed frequently as responsibilities are added and removed.

35. J. Chandra, 'Centre Targets to Build 45 km of Roads a Day in FY19: Gadkari', *The Hindu*, 17 April 2018.

36. P. Donthi, 'Son of the Sangh: Nitin Gadkari's Heritage as the RSS's Man in Reserve', *Caravan*, 1 April 2018.

37. 'Clean Water for Nagpur Assured', *Times of India*, 12 April 1989.

38. 'Rice: Corruption in Rice', *Times of India*, 16 June 1989; 'Coal: Vidarbha Coal Fraud to Be Probed', *Times of India*, 29 April 1989; 'Nagpur Improvement Trust: Probe Panel for Nagpur Trust', *Times of India*, 6 April 1990.

39. 'Council Walkout Over Sugar Sale Issue', *Times of India*, 6 August 1991.

40. 'Govt. Taken to Task Over Orange Plants', *Times of India*, 18 December 1991.

41. 'Times' Relief Fund List of Contributors', *Times of India*, 22 October 1993.

42. 'Letters to Ministers Not Replied: Opposition', *Times of India*, 28 July 1993.

43. 'Walk-Out Over "Vidarbha State"', *Times of India*, 15 December 1993.

44. 'Vidarbha Bandh Peaceful', *Times of India*, 21 December 1993.

45. 'Walk-Out Over Farmers' Relief', *Times of India*, 30 March 1994.

46. 'Opposition for Steps against Khushwant', *Times of India*, 18 July 1991. The demand for a separate Vidarbha was first heard in 1938 when the Central Provinces Legislature passed a resolution to create a separate state. Subsequently, the States Reorganisation Committee recommended a state be formed from the Marathi-speaking areas of Madhya Pradesh on the basis of 'a deep-rooted regional consciousness'.

47. 'Misleading Map Leads to Walk-Out', *Times of India*, 29 March 1994.

48. 'Central Aid Sought for Nagpur Road', *Times of India*, 20 July 1991.

49. 'Minor Reshuffle Announced in State Portfolios', *Times of India*, 29 May 1995.

50. D. Chaware, 'Offers on Pune Expressway Will Be Opened Today', *Times of India*, 20 January 1996.

51. Ibid.

52. S. Balakrishnanthe, 'Govt. to Expedite Work of Expressways', *Times of India*, 18 June 1995.

53. 'Environmentalists "Are Like Hindi Movie Villains"', *Times of India*, 11 January 1997.

54. Byung-Chul (2015); also see Barry (2013) on the complicated life of transparency practices in relation to infrastructure projects.

55. 'High-Power Panel Will Okay Pvt. Projects, Says Manohar Joshi', *Times of India*, 28 August 1996.

56. 'Survey on New Bombay–Goa Highway Begins', *Times of India*, 1 November 1995.

57. Sinha (2013: 5).

58. 'Centre Urged to Set Up Cargo Complex at Nagpur', *Times of India*, 24 September 1995.

59. D. Chaware, 'Congress–BJP Clash May Escalate', *Times of India*, 10 March 1996.

60. P. Joshi, 'Govt. Signs MoU on Nagpur Air Cargo Complex', *Times of India*, 18 March 1996.

61. V. Taksal, 'Centre Approves Nagpur Air Cargo Terminal Plan', *Times of India*, 15 November 1998.

62. 'Environmentalists "Are Like Hindi Movie Villains"', *Times of India*, 11 January 1997.

63. Sinha (2013: 51).

64. 'Few Takers for a Magnificent Obsession', *Times of India*, 21 July 1997.

65. P. Donthi, 'Son of the Sangh: Nitin Gadkari's Heritage as the RSS's Man in Reserve', *Caravan*, 1 April 2018.

66. Ibid.

67. 'Environmentalists "Are Like Hindi Movie Villains"', *Times of India*, 11 January 1997.

68. Sinha (2013: 59).

69. 'Minister's Proposal Fails to Enthuse Cong. Men', *Times of India*, 1 July 1997.

70. S. Phadke, 'Fancy Toll Plaza at Mankhurd', *Times of India*, 10 June 1997.

71. 'First BOT Scheme Implemented', *Times of India*, 22 June 1997.

72. 'Blatant Disregard for Norms', *Times of India*, 21 July 1997.

73. 'Gadkari Advocates Greater Use of CNG in Vehicles', *Times of India*, 2 October 1997.

74. A. Fernandes, 'Letters', *Times of India*, 22 May 1998.

75. 'Nitin Gadkari Excels', *Times of India*, 21 January 1999.

76. 'State Expressway Projects to Ease Traffic', *Times of India*, 5 March 1999; 'Sena–BJP Govt. Has Built More Flyovers', *Times of India*, 13 April 1999.

77. 'Advani Ignores Joshi's Plea on Alliance Govt', *Times of India*, 19 January 1999.

78. 'Ratan Tata Lauds Public Works Ministry', *Times of India*, 30 April 1999.

79. 'Pramod Mahajan Inaugurates Flyover at Mahim', *Times of India*, 7 May 1999.

80. '"We Did It without World Bank Aid" Says Mr Flyover', *Times of India*, 12 May 1999.

81. N. Gadkari, 'Why Such a Fuss about the Toll?', *Times of India*, 19 July 1999.

82. A. Singh, 'Roads Buckle under Pressure as Rains Wash Away Promises', *Times of India*, 24 July 1999.

83. 'Straight Answers', *Times of India*, 28 July 1999.

84. N. Yeshwantrao, 'Flyovers a Costly Bargain for Citizens', *Times of India*, 28 September 1999.

85. D. Chaware, 'Gadkari Asks CM Not to Paint a Grim Picture of State Economy', *Times of India*, 25 October 1999.

86. 'Gadkari Appointed Road Development Panel Chairman', *Times of India*, 10 January 2000.

87. D. Chaware, 'Centre Will Okay Ambitious Road Project Soon', *Times of India*, 1 February 2000.

88. 'BJP's *Rasta roko* against Hike in PDS Prices Hits Normal Life', *Times of India*, February 11, 2000.

89. 'Sena–BJP Team Will Meet Advani to Demand Delhi Rule', *Times of India*, 16 March 2000.

90. 'Probe into Construction of Cement Roads in Nagpur Demanded', *Times of India*, 7 April 2000.

91. 'New Road and Bridges May Go Unchristened', *Times of India*, 18 February 2000.

92. M. Ambarish, 'Gadkari Hopes to Create a Tehelka with Own Dotcom', *Times of India*, 30 March 2000.

93. 'State Govt. Dissolves Nagpur Civic Body', *Times of India*, 31 March 2001.

94. 'DF Govt. Is Ignoring Vidarbha: Gadkari', *Times of India*, 29 March 2001.

95. R. Bhagwat, 'Mass Arrest of Corporators Saves a Jolt to BJP in Nagpur', *Times of India*, 12 June 2001.

96. R. Bhagwat, 'DF Has Sabotaged Rural Roads Project: Gadkari', *Times of India*, 7 September 2001.

97. 'State Incurs HC Ire for Dissolving Civic Body', *Times of India*, 27 November 2001; S. Deshmukh, 'Straight Answers', *Times of India*, 4 December 2001.

98. R. Bhagwat, 'Mithai Boxes Create a Flutter in the House', *Times of India*, 5 December 2001.

99. 'Vilasrao Has a Dig at Gadkari', *Times of India*, 7 February 2002.

100. 'Gadkari Takes Over State BJP Reins', *Times of India*, 19 November 2004.

101. 'Gadkari Takes Up Cudgels for Farmers', *Times of India*, 29 October 2006; 'Gadkari Dares CM to a Debate on TV', *Times of India*, 7 November 2007.

102. 'Gadkari's PA Found Dead', *Times of India*, 29 March 2004.

103. *Times of India*, 31 March 2004, frontpage, no headline.

104. 'BJP Takes to the Streets for Power-Less Citizens', *Times of India*, 31 May 2005.

105. R. Bhagwat, 'What I-T Survey? Asks Gadkari', *Times of India*, 24 August 2006.

106. Ibid.

107. S.S. Bose, '7-Yr-Old Found Dead in State BJP Chief's Car', *Times of India*, 21 May 2009.

108. S.S. Bose, 'Nagpur Girl's Autopsy Hints at Sexual Abuse', *Times of India*, 24 May 2009.

109. S. Bose, 'Yogita's Death: 13 Days on, Cops File Murder Case', *Times of India*, 2 June 2009; 'Yogita Case: Mum, Sister Identify Car', *Times of India*, 5 June 2009.

110. N. Yogesh, 'I'm Ready for CID Probe: Gadkari', *Times of India*, 6 June 2009.

111. 'HC Again Pans Shoddy Probe in Yogita Case', *Times of India*, 19 June 2009.

112. 'MSRDC Looks for Gold under the Over', *Times of India*, 15 August 2007.

113. S. Balakrishnan, 'Gadkari Book Attacks DF on MSRDC', *Times of India*, 23 February 2005.

114. M. Chatterjee, 'Gadkari's Appointment Seems a Mere Formality', *Times of India*, 13 November 2009.

115. A. Mishra and R. Bhagwat, 'Decks Cleared for Gadkari's Election', *Times of India*, 19 November 2009.

116. S. Balakrishnan, 'Will Gadkari Become BJP's Mr Development?', *Times of India*, 20 December 2009.

117. R. Ashish, 'New to Delhi, Nat'l Politics: Gadkari', *Times of India*, 21 December 2009.

118. Sinha (2013: 6).

119. Sinha (2013: 7).

CHAPTER 8. THE BORDERLAND'S NEW ROADS

1. Simpson (2007, 2010, 2013).

2. In 2007, Sahib Singh Verma was killed in a car crash in Rajasthan, his Tata Safari (tagline: Redefine Success, Reclaim Your Life) hit a truck head-on.

3. Rambhau Mhalgi Prabodhini, 'Training', 2019, https://rmponweb. org/training

4. The philosophy is laid out in a book of the same name (Upadhyaya 1965) based on lectures delivered in Bombay in 1965.

5. Upadhyaya (1965: 16).

6. Ashapura Group of Companies, 'Vande Mataram Memorial', 2017, http://vmm.ashapura.com

7. *The Indian Sociologist*, IV (8), 1908, pp. 30, 32; IV (9), pp. 34, 36.

8. The university is called Krantiguru Shyamji Krishna Verma Kachchh University. The airport's name was not allowed to stick by the central government.

9. In Krishnavarma's creed, the 'Anglo-Indian' was complicit as either a supporter or beneficiary of British rule in India.

10. Savarkar was implicated in the assassination of Gandhi.

11. *The Indian Sociologist*, I (1), pp. 3–4.

12. J.R. SanFilipo, S.A. Khan and A.H. Chandio, 'Coal Resource Assessment of Jherruck Area Sona Coal Field, Sindh Province, Pakistan' (Open-file Report 93-523), Reston, VA: US Geological Survey, 1994.

13. For a summary of COALREAP, see 'Mission to Pakistan and Afghanistan: Project Assistance Completion Report, Energy Planning and Development (391-0478)', USAID, 1994.

14. J.R. SanFilipo et al., 'Potential for the Occurrence of Thick Lignite Deposits in the Thar Desert and Adjacent Lower Indus Plain, Sindh Province Pakistan' (Open-file Report 92-576), Reston, VA: US Geological Survey [also published as US Geological Survey Project Report (IR)PK-91], 1992.

15. Wynne and Fedden (1872).

16. For the initial outline of the project, its strengths and weaknesses, see: 'Project Information Document (PID): Appraisal Stage', no. AB4630, Washington, DC: World Bank, 2009.

17. The World Bank runs a programme called 'Just Transition for All' on phasing out coal mines and power—some might argue that the transition has been turned into a business.

18. Heike Mainhardt, 'World Bank Helps Develop Asia's Largest Coal Field: How the World Bank's Coal Road Map Leads Pakistan into a Debt Spiral and Undermines the Paris Climate Agreement', 2021, Urgeworld.org. Mainhardt also documents how guaranteed electricity pricing mechanisms were used to attract commercial banks to the project.

19. 'Pakistan Signals Coal Power Exit, in Potential Model for China's Belt and Road', Climate Home News, 16 December 2020, https://www.climatechangenews.com/2020/12/16/pakistan-signals-coal-power-exit-potential-model-chinas-belt-road

20. Aneela Younas Malik et al., 'Coal Biomethanation Potential of Various Ranks from Pakistan: A Possible Alternative Energy Source', *Journal of Cleaner Production*, 255 (8) (2020): 255.

21. Lauri Myllyvirta, 'Air Quality, Health and Toxics Impacts of the Proposed Coal Mining and Power Cluster in Thar, Pakistan', Centre for Research on Energy and Clean Air, 2020, https://energyandcleanair.org/publications-old/https-energyandcleanair-org-wp-wp-content-uploads-2020-05-thar-coal-cluster-case-study_pakistan-pdf

22. An umbrella for three organisations: Rural Development Policy Institute (RDPI), Pakistan Fisherfolk Forum (PFF) and Alternative Law Collective (ALC).

23. Ibrahim (2011).

24. Raikes (1977 [1856]).

25. Raikes (1977: 2).

26. Ibrahim (2017: 83); 1948 file no. 7(2)-PMS/48.

27. Sankaran Krishna (1994) uses 'cartographic anxiety' to describe the fear India's political leaders display over border territories being contested or annexed by neighbours.

28. Das and Poole (2004); Simpson (2006).

29. Rahman (2007: 115).

30. Demenge (2011).

31. Hasan (2010).

32. 'Project Development Manual: Islamic Republic of Pakistan; Sindh Provincial Road Improvement Project', ADB, 2015, p. 3.

33. TEDx talk by the politician to promote the pro-Thar project, https://www.youtube.com/watch?v=-4wnHtM-y7M

34. 'Thar Coalfields Block VI 2x330MW Coal-Fired Power Plant', Brighton: Mott MacDonald, 2017.

CHAPTER 9. HIGHWAYS TO THE END OF THE WORLD

1. 'Global Mobility Report', World Bank, 2017.
2. 'African Development Report', African Development Bank, 2013.
3. Particularly, Weston (2012), Ross (1996) and Urry (2004, 2007).
4. For example see Stern and Rydge (2012)—a theme continued in much of Stern's later published work following his very influential review (2007) of the economics of climate change, which focused on opportunities for 'growth and development'. Stern was chief economist at the World Bank between 2000 and 2003.
5. Also see these ideas formally expressed: 'Global Mobility Report', World Bank, 2017; UN Intergovernmental Panel on Climate Change (IPCC), 'Global Warming of 1.5 °C', 2018, states the urgent need for change to behaviour and policy.
6. This is contentious terrain, with lobbyists and counter-lobby groups working hard to spread information. A well-known example of which is the controversy over an open letter from IASTEC (The International Association of Sustainable Drivetrain and Vehicle Technology Research) to the EU in June 2021. The letter suggested that the reduction of CO_2 emissions from electric vehicles was less than was usually reported when the mode of electricity production was also accounted for. The authors were mostly academics calling for legislative frameworks to provide other transitional fuel pathways (ReFuel and hybrid vehicles). The letter produced a social media frenzy of expert positions and numbers, making it impossible to reach an informed opinion based on the material available—other than that the stakes are exceptionally high. See 'Position Paper: Technical, Regulatory and Social Challenges for Realising CO_2-Neutral Drive Technology for Cars and Commercial Vehicles during the Coming Decades', Karlsruhe: IASTEC, 2021.
7. Mumford (1956: 219).
8. Jevons (1866).
9. For discussion, see Steinberg and Zangwill (1983); and Braess, Nagurney and Wakolbinger (2005).
10. For discussion and modelling, see Lewis (1977); Mogridge et al. (1987); Mogridge (1990); Clément (1995); and Afimeimounga, Solomon and Ziedins (2005).
11. J. Dulac, 'Global Land Transport Infrastructure Requirements: Estimating Road and Railway Infrastructure Capacity and Costs to 2050', Paris: International Energy Agency, 2013, p. 6.
12. Featherstone, Thrift and Urry (2005); Dennis and Urry (2009); Urry (2011).

13. Sustainable Mobility for All, 'Global Mobility Report 2017: Tracking Sector Performance', Washington, DC, License: Creative Commons Attribution CC BY 3.0, 2017. I was able to talk to some of the authors and research assistants about how the report was put together. Around fifty people representing road-building organisations are attributed authorship.

14. The SuM4All Global Transport Stakeholder Mapping visualisation tool aims to clarify who is who and who does what in the sustainable mobility arena. SuM4All aims to bring all agencies together to 'speak with one voice'.

15. 'Global Mobility Report 2017', p. 5.

16. Ibid., p. 6.

17. Ibid.

18. Ibid., p. 38.

19. Ibid., p. 25.

20. Active since 1948, the International Road Federation (IRF) takes a fee from corporate and institutional 'players' from the road and mobility sectors. Its website states that '[t]he IRF promotes the development of roads and road networks that enable access and sustainable mobility for all'. The IRF hosting this conference is based in Geneva with a chapter in India; there is another International Road Federation based in Washington, DC, with a factional history.

21. 'It's Not a Dream, It's a Revolution', 2019, https://www.sum4all. org/resources/in-motion

22. See Dubash (2012) for an important discussion and analysis of the history and evolution of this position.

23. For example, Hoffman (2015).

24. Baer and Singer (2014), Crate (2011), Kelman (2010) and Rudiak-Gould (2013).

25. Klein (2015).

26. Giddens (2009).

27. Paterson (2007), Urry (2011).

28. Norgaard (2011) draws on the ideas of Stanley Cohen, Robert Lifton and Eviatar Zerubavel.

29. Hoffman (2015).

30. Bendell (2020), Hickel (2020) and Latour (2018) respectively. This literature strongly reminds me of the anti-roads and environmental arguments from the 1970s with which I opened this book. The arguments against economic growth seem to have gone full circle, from the oil crisis and the fear of the end of oil to frustration about apparent lack of climate action.

31. Mitchell (2013) and Malm (2016).
32. For example, Yusoff (2018) and Danowski and Viveiros de Castro (2017) respectively.
33. For the A66 between Scotch Corner and Penrith through Durham and Cumbria.
34. These ideas derive from the work of the French sociologist Pierre Bourdieu. My favoured path through his work is through France rather than the well-trodden route from Algeria (1977) to taste (1987). The two works that have had the greatest influence on me have been *The Bachelors' Ball* (2008) and *The Weight of the World* (1999).
35. Some anthropologists may call this the 'material turn', itself a response to a changing set of global governance priorities.

CHAPTER 10. ON THE ROAD AGAIN

1. Global New Car Assessment Programme, 'Results: #Safer Cars for India', 2019, http://www.globalncap.org/results
2. Y. Patel, '2018 Renault Kwid Crash Tested: Gets 0 Star Safety Rating', Rushlane-Daily Auto News, 11 July 2018. Available at: https://www.rushlane.com/2018-renault-kwid-crash-tested-12198216.html
3. Chandra and Sharma (2016: 120).
4. Chandra and Sharma (2016: 270–2).
5. A. Trivedi, 'Modi's Great Road Trip Hits a Debt', Bloomberg, 18 July 2018.
6. 'Don't Mess with Gadkari', *The Hindu Business Line*, 21 January 2019.
7. 'Zee Group Shares Crash, Subhash Chandra Blames "Negative Forces"; Apologises to Lenders', *Indian Express*, 25 January 2019.
8. 'Progress Report: Before the National Company Law Tribunal Bench at Mumbai, Company Petition no. 3638 of 2018 in the Matter of Petition under Sections 241 and 242 of the Companies Act, 2013', 2018. See Annex 2 of vol. 1 of 5. https://www.ilfsindia.com/media/163358/ilfs-ca-4127-of-2019-ca-1011-of-2020-in-cp-3638-of-2018-nclt-on-05102020-final.pdf
9. 'Special Court Denies Bail to ex-IL&FS Chairman Ravi Parthasarathy', *Economic Times*, 28 June 2021.
10. 'IL&FS Money-Laundering Case: Enforcement Directorate Attaches Assets Worth Rs 452 Crore of British National', *The Hindu Business Line*, 5 January 2021.
11. M. Goodman and I. Dey, 'Ex John Laing Bosses Support Infrastructure India Flotation', *The Times*, 29 June 2008.

12. 'Reports and Accounts 09', Infrastructure India Plc, 2009, https://www.iiplc.com/wp-content/themes/iiplc/downloads/InfraIndia_R&A_09_2.pdf

13. Shree Maheshwar Hydel Power Corporation Limited, a subsidiary of Mumbai-based Entegra Ltd.

14. 'Reports and Accounts 2010', Infrastructure India Plc, 2010, https://www.iiplc.com/wp-content/themes/iiplc/downloads/InfraIndia_R&A_10.pdf

15. 'Operational BOT Toll Road Projects Earn Impressive Returns', Mumbai: Crisil Limited, 2012.

16. 'Rekindling Private Investment in Roads and Highways', Mumbai and Delhi: CRISIL and FICCI, 2019.

17. 'Reports and Accounts 2010', Infrastructure India Plc, 2010.

18. S. Pallavi, 'Infrastructure India Arm Serves Notice to Investment Advisor', 16 April 2010, https://www.vccircle.com/infrastructure-india-arm-serves-notice-investment-adviser

19. 'Guggenheim Global Infrastructure Company Announces Sale of Indian Assets to Infrastructure India PLC', 18 February 2011, https://www.businesswire.com/news/home/20110218005122/en/Guggenheim-Global-Infrastructure-Company-Announces-Sale-of-Indian-Assets-to-Infrastructure-India-PLC; 'Reports and Accounts 2011', Infrastructure India Plc, 2011, https://www.iiplc.com/wp-content/themes/iiplc/downloads/InfraIndia_R&A_11.pdf

20. S. Pallavi, 'Guggenheim Partners Takes 46% in AIM-listed Infra India', 16 February 2010, https://www.vccircle.com/guggenheim-partners-takes-46-aim-listed-infra-india

21. 'Infrastructure India NAV Per Share Falls 16%', *Telegraph Investor*, 21 July 2011.

22. 'Reports and Accounts 2011', Infrastructure India Plc, 2011.

23. The leaked papers are held and managed by the International Consortium of Investigative Journalists and are available under a Creative Commons Attribution-ShareAlike licence.

24. 'Reports and Accounts 2011', Infrastructure India Plc, 2011.

25. 'Infrastructure India Plc Report & Accounts for the Year Ended 31 March 2012', Isle of Man: IIP, 2012.

26. 'Infrastructure India Plc Report & Accounts for the Year Ended 31 March 2014', Isle of Man: IIP, 2014.

27. A. Chakrabortty, 'Outsourced and Unaccountable: This Is the Future of Local Government?', *Guardian*, 15 December 2014.

28. 'Infrastructure India Plc Interim Results for the Six Months Ended Report', Isle of Man: IIP, 30 September 2014.

29. BVI Financial Services Commission, 'Register of Companies Search Report', 25 May 2017.

30. For South Asian immigrants from Guiana to the island, this is also a surname.

31. 'Asset Sale and DLI Operations Update' (RNS no. 5679U), 8 April 2016, Infrastructure India Plc.

POSTSCRIPT

1. Janson (2021).

2. Arison sold Shikun & Binui to the US–Israel Saidoff Group in 2018.

3. See Arison (2013).

4. COP26, 'Transport', 10 November 2021.

5. COP26, 'Presidency Event: Accelerating the ZEV Transition; A One Way Street', 10 November 2021.

6. Ibid. My emphasis.

7. 'Provisional UK Greenhouse Gas Emissions National Statistics', London: Department for Business, Energy & Industrial Strategy, 2019.

8. 'Transport Statistics Great Britain', London: Department for Transport, December 2019.

9. 'National Infrastructure Strategy: Fairer, Faster, Greener', London: H.M. Treasury, November 2020.

ACKNOWLEDGEMENTS

1. Khan (2020).

BIBLIOGRAPHY

Adalet, B. 2018. *Hotels and Highways: The Construction of Modernisation Theory in Cold War Turkey*. Stanford, CA: Stanford University Press.

Afimeimounga, H., W. Solomon and I. Ziedins. 2005. 'The Downs–Thomson Paradox: Existence, Uniqueness and Stability of User Equilibria'. *Queueing Systems: Theory and Applications* (archive), 49 (3–4): 321–34.

Aggarwal, S. 2014. 'Three Essays in Development Economics'. PhD Thesis, Santa Cruz: University of California.

Aggarwal, S. 2018. 'Do Rural Roads Create Pathways Out of Poverty? Evidence from India'. *Journal of Development Economics*, 133: 375–95.

Ahuja, R. 2004. 'Opening Up the Country? Patterns of Circulation and Politics of Communication in Early Colonial Orissa'. *Studies in History*, 20 (1): 73–130.

Amin, A. 2014. 'Lively Infrastructure'. *Theory, Culture & Society*, 31 (7/8): 137–61.

Anand, N., A. Gupta and H. Appel, 2018. *The Promise of Infrastructure*. London: Duke University Press.

Arison, S. 2013. *Activate Your Goodness: Transforming the World through Doing Good*. Carlsbad, CA: Hay House Inc.

Aronowsky, L. 2021. 'Gas Guzzling Gaia, or: A Prehistory of Climate Change Denialism'. *Critical Inquiry*, 47 (2): 306–26.

Asher, S. and P. Novosad. 2014. 'The Employment Effects of Road Construction in Rural India'. Unpublished.

Augé, M. 1995. *Non-Places: Introduction to an Anthropology of Supermodernity*. London: Verso.

Baer, H. and M. Singer. 2014. *The Anthropology of Climate Change*. London: Routledge.

Bajpaee, C. 2017. 'Dephasing India's Look East/Act East Policy'. *Contemporary Southeast Asia: A Journal of International and Strategic Affairs*, 39 (2): 348–72.

Banerjee, R. and A. Sachdeva. 2015. 'Pathways to Preventive Health. Evidence from India's Rural Road Program'. USC–INET Research Paper nos. 15–19.

Bardou, J-P., J-J. Chanaron, P. Fridenson and J.M. Laux. 1982. *The Automobile Revolution: The Impact of an Industry*. Chapel Hill, NC: University of North Carolina Press.

Barnes, T. 2018. *Making Cars in the New India: Industry, Precarity and Informality*. Cambridge: Cambridge University Press.

Barry, A. 2013. *Material Politics: Disputes along the Pipeline*. Oxford: John Wiley and Sons.

Basu, A. 2015. *Violent Conjunctures in Democratic India*. Cambridge: Cambridge University Press.

Bear, L. 2007. *Lines of the Nation: Indian Railway Workers, Bureaucracy, and the Intimate Historical Self*. New York: Columbia University Press.

Beck, U. 2016. *The Metamorphosis of the World*. Cambridge: Polity.

Beckmann, J. 2001. 'Automobility: A Social Problem and Theoretical Concept'. *Environment and Planning D: Society and Space*, 19: 593–607.

Behrends, A., S.P. Reyna and G. Schlee. 2011. *Crude Domination: An Anthropology of Oil*. London: Berghahn.

Bell, C. 2012a. 'Estimating the Social Profitability of India's Rural Roads Program: A Bumpy Ride'. Policy Research Working Paper 6168. World Bank (South Asia Region, Transport Unit).

Bell, C. 2012b. 'The Benefits of India's Rural Roads Program in the Spheres of Goods, Education and Health: Joint Estimation and Decomposition'. Policy Research Working Paper 6169. World Bank (South Asia Region, Transport Unit).

Bell, C. and S. van Dillen, 2012. 'How Does India's Rural Roads Program Affect the Grassroots? Findings from a Survey in Orissa'. Policy Research Working Paper 6167. World Bank (South Asia Region, Transport Unit).

Bellamy, C. 2011. *The Powerful Ephemeral: Everyday Healing in an Ambiguously Islamic Place*. Berkeley, CA: University of California Press.

Bellucci, S. and Zaccaria, M. 2014. 'Wage Labor and Mobility in Colonial Eritrea, 1880s to 1920s'. *International Labor and Working-Class History*, 86: 89–106.

Bendell, J. 2020. 'Deep Adaptation: A Map for Navigating Climate Tragedy'. Occasional Paper 2. Ambleside: IFLAS, University of Cumbria.

Bhardwaj, S.M. 1973. *Hindu Places of Pilgrimage in India: A Study in Cultural Geography*. Berkeley, CA: University of California Press.

Blaikie, P.M., J. Cameron and D. Seddon. 1980. *Nepal in Crisis: Growth and Stagnation at the Periphery*. Oxford: Oxford University Press.

Blaikie, P.M., J. Cameron and D. Seddon. 2000. *Nepal in Crisis: Growth and Stagnation at the Periphery* (republished with a new chapter). Delhi: Adroit Publishers.

Boehme, K. 2015. 'Smuggling India: Deconstructing Western India's Illicit Export Trade, 1818–1870'. *Journal of the Royal Asiatic Society*, 25 (4): 685–704

Bourdieu, P. 1972. *Esquisse d'une théorie de la pratique: précédé de 'Trois études d'ethnologie kabyle'*. Geneva: Librairie Droz.

Bourdieu, P. 1977. *Outline of a Theory of Practice*. Translated by R. Nice. Cambridge: Cambridge University Press.

Bourdieu, P. 1987. *Distinction: A Social Critique of the Judgement of Taste*. Translated by R. Nice. Cambridge, MA: Harvard University Press.

Bourdieu, P. 1999. *The Weight of the World: Social Suffering in Contemporary Society*. Stanford, CA: Stanford University Press.

Bourdieu, P. 2008. *The Bachelor's Ball: The Crisis of Society in Béarn*. Translated by R. Nice. Cambridge: Polity.

Braess, D., A. Nagurney and T. Wakolbinger. 2005. 'On a Paradox of Traffic Planning'. *Transportation Science*, 39 (4): 446–50.

Byung-Chul, H. 2015. *The Transparency Society*. Stanford: Stanford University Press.

Campbell, B. 2010. 'Rhetorical Routes for Development: A Road Project in Nepal'. *Contemporary South Asia*, 18 (3): 267–79.

Campbell, J. 2012. 'Between the Material and the Figural Road: The Incompleteness of Colonial Geographies in Amazonia'. *Mobilities*, 7 (4): 481–500.

Chandra, S. and P. Sharma. 2016. *The Z Factor: My Journey as the Wrong Man at the Right Time*. New Delhi: HarperCollins India.

Chilson, P. 1999. *Riding the Demon: On the Road in West Africa*. Athens, GA: University of Georgia Press.

Clément, L. 1995. 'La conjecture de MJH Mogridge: test sur l'agglomération de Lyon'. *Cahiers Scientifiques du Transport*, 30: 51.

Corbridge, S. 2007. 'The (Im)possibility of Development Studies'. *Economy and Society*, 36 (2): 179–211.

Crate, S.A. 2011. 'Climate and Culture: Anthropology in the Era of Contemporary Climate Change'. *Annual Review of Anthropology* 40: 175–94.

Cresswell, T. and P. Merriman (eds). 2011. *Geographies of Mobilities: Practices, Spaces, Subjects*. Farnham: Ashgate.

Daechsel, M. 2015. *Islamabad and the Politics of International Development in Pakistan*. Cambridge: Cambridge University Press.

Dalakoglou, D. 2017. *The Road: An Ethnography of (Im)Mobility, Space, and Cross-border Infrastructures in the Balkans*. Manchester: Manchester University Press.

Dalton, D. 1993. *Mahatma Gandhi: Nonviolent Power in Action*. New York: Columbia University Press.

Danowski, D. and E. Viveiros de Castro. 2017. *The Ends of the World*. Cambridge: Polity.

Das, V. and D. Poole. 2004. *Anthropology in the Margins of the State*. Santa Fe: School of American Research Press.

Dave, B. 2018. 'Silk Road Economic Belt: Effects of China's Soft Power Diplomacy in Kazakhstan'. In *China's Belt and Road Initiative and its Impact in Central Asia*, edited by M. Lauruelle. Washington, DC: George Washington University Central Asia Program, pp. 97–109.

Davis, M. 2007. *Planet of the Slums*. London: Verso.

De Sélincourt, A. (trans.) 1972. *Herodotus: The Histories*. London: Penguin Books.

Demenge, J. 2011. 'The Political Ecology of Road Construction'. PhD Thesis, University of Sussex.

Deneault, A. 2018. *Legalizing Theft: A Short Guide to Tax Havens*. Translated by C. Browne. Halifax, NS: Fernwood Publishing.

Dennis, K. and J. Urry. 2009. *After the Car*. Cambridge: Polity.

Deshpande, A. 1998. 'Transition from Traditional Opium Use to Heroin Use: India and Its Neighbourhood'. In 'South Asia Drug Demand Reduction Report'. New Delhi: UNDCP-ROSA.

Deshpande, A. 2009. 'An Historical Overview of Opium Cultivation and Changing State Attitudes towards the Crop in India, 1878–2000 AD'. *Studies in History*, 25 (1): 109–43.

Dillen, S. van. 2008. 'Income and its Variability in a Drought-prone Region: Seasonality, Location and Household Characteristics'. *European Journal of Development Research*, 20 (4): 579–96.

Dubash, N.K. 2012. 'The Politics of Climate Change in India: Narratives of Equity and Co-benefits'. Working Paper no. 2012/1. Delhi: Centre for Policy Research Climate Initiative.

Dulac, J. 2013. 'Global Land Transport Infrastructure Requirements: Estimating Road and Railway Infrastructure Capacity and Costs to 2050'. Paris: International Energy Agency.

Ehteshami, A. and N. Horesh. 2018. *China's Presence in the Middle East: The Implications of the One Belt, One Road Initiative*. London: Routledge.

Engerman, D.C. 2018. *The Price of Aid: The Economic Cold War in India*. Cambridge, MA: Harvard University Press.

Fairless, M. 1902. *The Roadmender*. London: Duckworth.

Fan, S., P. Hazell and S. Thorat. 1999. 'Linkages between Government Spending, Growth, and Poverty in Rural India'. Research Report 110. Washington, DC: International Food Policy Research Institute (IFPRI).

Fan, S., L. Zhang and X. Zhang. 2000. 'Growth, Inequality, and Poverty in Rural China: The Role of Public Investments'. Environment and Production Technology Division Discussion Paper no. 66.

Farooqui, A. 1995. 'Opium Enterprise and Colonial Intervention in Malwa and Western India, 1800–1824'. *The Indian Economic & Social History Review*, 32 (4): 447–73.

Farooqui, A. 2006. *Opium City: The Making of Early Victorian Bombay*. Gurgaon: Three Essays Collective.

Fassin, D. 2012. *Humanitarian Reason: A Moral History of the Present*. Berkeley, CA: University of California Press.

Featherstone, M., N.J. Thrift and J. Urry. 2005. *Automobilities*. London: Sage.

Ferguson, J. 1990. *Anti-politics Machine: Development, Depoliticization, and Bureaucratic Power in Lesotho*. Cambridge: Cambridge University Press.

Freund, P. and G.E. Martin. 1993. *The Ecology of the Automobile*. New York: Black Rose Books.

Friedman, T. 2000. *The Lexus and the Olive Tree*. London: HarperCollins.

Galpin, C. 1915. *The Social Anatomy of an Agricultural Community*. Research Bulletin 34, Madison: Agricultural Experiment Station of the University of Wisconsin.

Gan, E., A. Tsing, H. Swanson and N. Bubandt. 2017. 'Introduction: Haunted Landscapes of the Anthropocene'. In *Arts of Living on a Damaged Planet*, edited by A. Tsing, H. Swanson, E. Gan and N. Bubandt. Minneapolis, MI: University of Minnesota Press, pp. G1–G14.

Gandhi, M.K. 1869–1948. *The Collected Works of Mahatma Gandhi*. New Delhi: Publications Division, Ministry of Information and Broadcasting, Government of India.

Gandhi, M.K. 1922. *Hind Swaraj or Indian Home Rule*. Ahmedabad: Navajivan Publishing House.

Ganguly, S. and M. Pardesi. 2012. 'Can China and India Rise Peacefully?' *Orbis*, 56 (3): 470–85.

Gewald, J., S. Luning and K. van Walraven, 2009. *The Speed of Change: Motor Vehicles and People in Africa, 1890–2000*. Leiden: Brill.

Giddens, A. 2009. *The Politics of Climate Change*. Cambridge: Polity.

Graham, S. and N. Thrift. 2007. 'Out of Order: Understanding Repair and Maintenance'. *Theory, Culture & Society*, 24 (3): 1–25.

Green, S. 2017. 'When Infrastructures Fail: An Ethnographic Note in the Middle of an Aegean Crisis'. In *Infrastructures and Social Complexity: A Companion*, edited by P. Harvey, C.B. Jensen and A. Morita. London: Routledge, pp. 271–83.

Gregory, G.E. 1931. *The Story of the Road: From the Beginning Down to AD31*. London: Alexander Maclehose & Co.

Guldi, J. 2012. *Roads to Power: Britain Invents the Infrastructure State*. Cambridge, MA: Harvard University Press.

Guldin, G.E. 2001. *What's a Peasant to Do? Village Becoming Town in Southern China*. Boulder, CO: Westview Press.

Gupta, D. 2005. 'Whither the Indian Village: Culture and Agriculture in "Rural" India'. *Economic and Political Weekly*, 40 (8): 751–8.

Guyot-Réchard, B. 2020. 'Tangled Lands: Burma and India's Unfinished Separation, 1937–1948'. *Journal of Asian Studies*, 80 (2): 293–315.

Hart, S.I. and A.L. Spivak. 1993. *The Elephant in the Bedroom: Impacts on the Economy and Environment*. N.p.: Hope Publishing House.

Harvey, P. 2010. 'Cementing Relations: The Materiality of Roads and Public Spaces in Provincial Peru'. *Social Analysis*, 54 (2): 28–46.

Harvey, P. 2012. 'The Topological Quality of Infrastructural Relations: An Ethnographic Approach'. *Theory, Culture & Society*, 29 (4/5): 76–92.

Harvey, P. and H. Knox. 2012. 'The Enchantments of Infrastructure'. *Mobilities*, 7 (4): 1–16.

Harvey, P. and H. Knox. 2015. *Roads: An Anthropology of Infrastructure and Expertise*. Ithaca, NY: Cornell University Press.

Hasan, A. 2010. 'Migration, Small Towns and Social Transformations in Pakistan'. *Environment & Urbanization*, 22 (1): 33–50.

Hickel, J. 2020. *Less Is More: How Degrowth Will Save the World*. London: Penguin Random House.

Hildyard, N. 2016. *Licensed Larceny: Infrastructure, Financial Extraction and the Global South*. Manchester: Manchester University Press.

Hine, J., M. Abedin, R.J. Stevens, T. Airey and T. Anderson. 2016. 'Does the Extension of the Rural Road Network Have a Positive Impact on Poverty Reduction and Resilience for the Rural Areas Served? If So How, and if Not, Why Not? A Systematic Review'. London: EPPI-Centre, Social Science Research Unit, UCL Institute of Education, University College London.

Hoffman, A.J. 2015. *How Culture Shapes the Climate Change Debate*. Stanford, CA: Stanford University Press.

Holzwarth, S. 2014. 'A New Education for "Young India": Exploring *Nai talim* from the Perspective of a Connected History'. In *Connecting Histories of Education: Transnational and Cross-cultural Exchanges in (Post)*

Colonial Education, edited by B. Bagchi, E. Fuchs and K. Rousmaniere. New York: Berghahn Books, pp. 123–39.

Holzwarth, S. 2015. 'Gandhi and *Nai talim*: Rural Craft Education for a New Village-minded Social Order'. PhD Thesis, Humboldt University.

Hutchins, E. 1996. *Cognition in the Wild*. Cambridge, MA: MIT Press.

Hyde, L. 2008. *Trickster Makes This World: How Disruptive Imagination Creates Culture*. Edinburgh: Canongate.

Ibrahim, F. 2011. 'Re-making a Region: Ritual Inversions and Border Transgressions in Kutch'. *South Asia: Journal of South Asian Studies*, 34 (3): 439–59.

Ibrahim, F. 2017. 'Bureaucracy and Border Control Crime, Police Reform and National Security in Kutch, 1948–52'. *Economic and Political Weekly*, 52 (15): 79–86.

Illich, I. 1974. *Energy and Equity*. New York: Harper & Row.

IPCC. 2007. *'Small Islands': Climate Change 2007; Impacts, Adaptation and Vulnerability*. Cambridge: Cambridge University Press, pp. 687–716.

Ispahani, M.Z. 1989. *Roads and Rivals: The Political Uses of Access in the Borderlands of Asia*. Ithaca, NY: Cornell University Press.

Jaffe, H. 2005. *Automobile: pétrole et impérialisme*. Paris: Paragon.

Jaffrelot, C. 1996. *The Hindu Nationalist Movement and Indian Politics, 1925 to the 1990s: Strategies of Identity-building, Implantation and Mobilisation (with Special Reference to Central India)*. London: Hurst.

Jaffrelot, C. 1998. 'BJP and the Challenge of Factionalism in Madhya Pradesh'. In *The BJP and the Compulsions of Politics in India*, edited by C. Jaffrelot and T. Blom Hansen. Delhi: Oxford University Press, pp. 243–66.

Janson, M. 2021. *Crossing Religious Boundaries: Islam, Christianity, and 'Yoruba Religion' in Lagos, Nigeria*. Cambridge: Cambridge University Press.

Jayawardena, S. 2011. *Right of Way: A Journey of Resettlement*. Colombo: CEPA.

Jenkins, T. 1994. 'Fieldwork and the Perception of Everyday Life'. *Man* (N.S.) 29: 433–56.

Jevons, W.S. 1866. *The Coal Question: An Inquiry Concerning the Progress of the Nation, and the Probable Exhaustion of Our Coalmines*. 2nd edn, revised. London: Macmillan and Co.

Jodhka, S. 2002. 'Nation and Village: Images of Rural India in Gandhi, Nehru and Ambedkar'. *Economic and Political Weekly*, 37 (32): 3343–53.

Jodhka, S. and E. Simpson (eds). 2020. *India's Villages in the 21st Century: Revisits and Revisions*. New Delhi: Oxford University Press.

315

Joniak-Lüthi, A. 2015. 'Roads in China's Borderlands: Interfaces of Spatial Representations, Perceptions, Practices, and Knowledges'. *Modern Asian Studies*, 50 (1): 118–40.

Kakar, S. 1996. *The Colors of Violence: Cultural Identities, Religion, and Conflict*. Chicago, IL: University of Chicago Press.

Kay, J.H. 1997. *Asphalt Nation: How the Automobile Took Over America and How We Can Take It Back*. New York: Random House.

Kelman, I. 2010. 'Hearing Local Voices from Small Island Developing States for Climate Change'. *Local Environment*, 15 (7): 605–19.

Kerr, I.J. 2007. *Engines of Change: The Railroads That Made India*. Westport, CT: Praeger.

Khan, M. 2020. 'Making Them Look the Other Way! The (Ir)rationality of Road Building in the Sindh Borderlands of Pakistan'. PhD Thesis, SOAS University of London.

Khan, N. 2006. 'Flaws in the Flow: Roads and their Modernity in Pakistan'. *Social Text*, 24: 87–113.

Khanna, V.C. 2017. 'Review: *Look East to Act East Policy: Implications for India's Northeast* edited by Gurudas Das and C. Joshua Thomas *BCIM Economic Corridor: The Road Ahead* edited by Rajiv Bhatia and Rahul Mishra and *The Agartala Doctrine: A Proactive Northeast in Indian Foreign Policy* edited by Subir Bhaumik'. *China Report*, 53 (1): 59–64

Klaeger, G. 2009. 'Religion on the Road: The Spiritual Experience of Road Travel in Ghana'. In *The Speed of Change: Motor Vehicles and People in Africa, 1890–2000*, edited by J.-B. Gewald, S. Luning and K. van Walraven. Leiden: Brill. pp. 212–31.

Klaeger, G. 2013. 'Dwelling on the Road: Routines, Rituals and Roadblocks in Southern Ghana'. *Africa*, 83 (3): 446–69.

Klein, N. 2015. *This Changes Everything: Capitalism vs the Climate*. London: Penguin.

Knox, H. and P. Harvey. 2008. 'Otherwise Engaged: Culture, Deviance and the Quest for Connectivity through Road Construction'. *Journal of Cultural Economy*, 1 (1): 79–92.

Knox, H. and P. Harvey. 2011. 'Anticipating Harm: Regulation and Irregularity on a Road Construction Project in the Peruvian Andes'. *Theory, Culture & Society*, 28 (6): 142–63.

Krishna, S. 1994. 'Cartographic Anxiety: Mapping the Body Politic in India'. *Alternatives: Global, Local, Political*, 19 (4): 507–21.

Kulkarni, S. 2004. *Lal Krishna Advani's Patriotic Pilgrimage*. New Delhi: Ocean Books.

Kumar, A. and P. Kumar. 1999. 'User-friendly Model for Planning Rural Roads'. *Transportation Research Record*, 1652 (1): 31–9.

Kumar, A. and H.T. Tillotson. 1991. 'Planning Model for Rural Roads'. *Transportation Research Record*, 1291: 171–81.

Kuusisto, R. 2009. 'Roads and Riddles? Western Major Power Metaphors of Nonviolent Conflict Resolution'. *Alternatives*, 34: 275–97.

Kynnersley, T.R. 1945. *Roads for India*. Bombay: Tata Sons Limited.

Lampland, M. and S.L. Star. 2009. *Standards and their Stories: How Quantifying, Classifying and Formalizing Practices Shape Everyday Life*. Ithaca, NY: Cornell University Press.

Larkin, B. 2013. 'The Politics and Poetics of Infrastructure'. *Annual Review of Anthropology*, 42 (1): 327–43.

Latour, B. 2017. 'Why Gaia Is Not a God of Totality'. *Theory, Culture & Society*, 34 (2–3): 61–81.

Latour, B. 2018. *Down to Earth: Politics in the New Climatic Regime*. Cambridge: Polity.

Latour, B. 2019. *Facing Gaia: Eight Lectures on the New Climatic Regime*. Cambridge: Polity.

Latour, B. and T.M. Lenton. 2019. 'Extending the Domain of Freedom, or Why Gaia Is So Hard to Understand'. *Critical Inquiry*, 45 (3): 1–21.

Leach, E. 1968. *A Runaway World? The Reith Lectures*. Oxford: Oxford University Press.

Leavitt, H. 1970. *Superhighway–Superhoax*. Garden City, NY: Doubleday & Company.

Lewis, D. 1977. 'Estimating the Influence of Public Policy on Road Traffic Levels in Greater London'. *Journal of Transport Economics and Policy*, 11 (2): 155–68.

Li, T.M. 2007. *The Will to Improve: Governmentality, Development, and the Practice of Politics*. Durham, NC: Duke University Press.

Lipton, M. 1968. 'Strategy for Agriculture: Urban Bias and Rural Planning'. In *The Crisis of Indian Planning*, edited by P. Streeten and M. Lipton. London: Oxford University Press, pp. 83–147.

Ludden, D. 1996. *Contesting the Nation: Religion, Community, and the Politics of Democracy in India*. Philadelphia, PA: University of Pennsylvania Press.

Maçães, B. 2018. *Belt and Road: A Chinese World Order*. London: Hurst.

Maine, H. 1881 [1871]. *Village-Communities in the East and West*. London: John Murray.

Malm, A. 2016. *Fossil Capital: The Rise of Steam Power and the Roots of Global Warming*. London: Verso.

Marcus, G.E. 1995. 'Ethnography in/of the World System: The Emergence of Multi-sited Ethnography'. *Annual Review of Anthropology*, 24: 95–117.

Markovits, C. 2009. 'The Political Economy of Opium Smuggling in Early Nineteenth-century India: Leakage or Resistance?' *Modern Asian Studies*, 43 (1): 89–111.

Masquelier, A. 1992. 'Encounter With a Road Siren: Machines, Bodies and Commodities in the Imagination of a Mawri Healer'. *Visual Anthropology Review*, 8: 56–69.

Masquelier, A. 2002. 'Road Mythographies: Space, Mobility, and the Historical Imagination in Postcolonial Niger'. *American Ethnologist*, 29 (4): 829–55.

McNeill, J.R. and P. Engelke. 2014. *The Great Acceleration: An Environmental History of the Anthropocene Since 1945*. Cambridge, MA: Belknap Press of Harvard University Press.

Melly, C. 2013. 'Ethnography on the Road: Infrastructural Vision and the Unruly Present in Contemporary Dakar'. *Africa*, 83 (3): 385–402.

Merriman, P. 2007. *Driving Spaces: A Cultural-historical Geography of England's M1 Motorway*. Oxford: Wiley-Blackwell.

Miller, T. 2017. *China's Asian Dream*. London: Zed Books.

Misra, O.P. 1995. *Economic Thought of Gandhi and Nehru: A Comparative Analysis*. New Delhi: M.D. Publications Pvt Ltd.

Mitchell, T. 2013. *Carbon Democracy: Political Power in the Age of Oil*. London: Verso.

Mogridge, M.J.H. 1990. *Travel in Towns: Jam Yesterday, Jam Today and Jam Tomorrow?* London: Macmillan Press.

Mogridge, M.J.H., D.J. Holden, J. Bird and G.C. Terzis. 1987. 'The Downs–Thomson Paradox and the Transportation Planning Process'. *International Journal of Transportation Economics*, 14 (3): 283–311.

Mohapatra, J.K. and B.P. Chandrasekhar. 2007. 'Rural Roads'. In *India Infrastructure Report 2007: Rural Infrastructure*, edited by P. Kalra and A. Rastogi. New Delhi: Oxford University Press, pp. 109–37.

Moran, J. 2009. *On Roads: A Hidden History*. London: Profile Books.

Morley, F. 1961. *The Great North Road*. London: Hutchinson.

Mosse, D. 2004. *Cultivating Development: An Ethnography of Aid Policy and Practice*. London: Pluto.

Mostowlansky, T. 2011. 'Paving the Way: Isma'ili Genealogy and Mobility along Tajikistan's Pamir Highway'. *Journal of Persianate Studies*, 4: 171–88.

Mrázek, R. 2002. *Engineers of Happy Land: Technology and Nationalism in a Colony*. Princeton, NJ: Princeton University Press.

Mukherji, R. 2014. *Globalization and Deregulation: Ideas, Interests, and Institutional Change in India*. Oxford: Oxford University Press.

Mukhopadhyay, A. 2018. *Imperial Technology and 'Native' Agency: A Social History of Railways in Colonial India, 1850–1920*. London: Routledge.

Mumford, L. 1956. *From the Ground Up: Observations on Contemporary Architecture, Housing, Highway Building, and Civic Design*. New York: Harcourt, Brace & Company.

Murton, G. 2017. 'Making Mountain Places into State Spaces: Infrastructure, Consumption, and Territorial Practice in a Himalayan Borderland'. *Annals of the American Association of Geographers*, 107 (2): 526–45.

Murton, G. 2019. 'Facing the Fence: The Production and Performance of a Himalayan Border in Global Contexts'. *Political Geography*, 72: 31–42.

Nanda, B.R. 1981. *Mahatma Gandhi: A Biography*. Delhi: Oxford University Press.

Nehru, J. 1960–2017. *Selected Works of Jawaharlal Nehru*. New Delhi: Orient Longman Ltd.

Norgaard, K.M. 2011. *Living in Denial: Climate Change, Emotions, and Everyday Life*. Cambridge, MA: MIT Press.

Packard, V. 1992. *A Nation of Strangers*. Philadelphia, PA: David McKay Company.

Panda, P. 2015. 'Essays on Trade, Infrastructure, and Human Capital Outcomes in Developing Countries'. PhD Thesis, University of California, Riverside.

Parida, J.K. 2016. 'MGNREGS, Distress Migration and Livelihood Conditions: A Study in Odisha'. *Journal of Social and Economic Development*, 18: 17–39.

Parr, A. 2013. *The Wrath of Capital: Neoliberalism and Climate Change Politics*. New York: Columbia University Press.

Parry, J.P. 2003. 'Nehru's Dream and the Village Waiting Room: Long Distance Labour Migrants to a Central Indian Steel Town'. *Contributions to Indian Sociology*, 37 (1–2): 217–49.

Paterson, M. 2007. *Automobile Politics: Ecology and Cultural Political Economy*. Cambridge: Cambridge University Press.

Pawley, M. 1973. *The Private Future*. London: Thames and Hudson.

Pedersen, M.A. and M. Bunkenborg. 2012. 'Roads that Separate: Sino-Mongolian Relations in the Inner Asian Desert'. *Mobilities*, 7 (4): 555–69.

Phelan, J. 1950. *We Follow the Roads*. Bishopstone: Country Book Club.

Prabhu, N. 2017. *Reflective Shadows: Political Economy of the World Bank Lending to India*. New Delhi: Oxford University Press.

Prasad, R. 2015. *Tracks of Change: Railways and Everyday Life in Colonial India*. Daryaganj, Delhi: Cambridge University Press.

Pratap, K.V.C. and C. Rajesh. 2019. *Public–Private Partnerships in Infrastructure*. Singapore: Springer Verlag.

Raghavan, M.R. and D.L. Prasanna Rao. 1979a. 'Experimental Study of Forces in a *Bullock Cart*'. In *Proceedings of the Indian Academy of Science*, 1(C2, Part 4): 435–49.

Raghavan, M.R. and D.L. Prasanna Rao. 1979b. 'A Study on Bullock Carts: Part 2; Experimental Study of Forces in a Bullock Cart'. *Proceedings of the Indian Academy of Sciences: Section C; Engineering Sciences*, 2: 451–71.

Rahman, T. 2007. *Language and Politics in Pakistan*. New Delhi: Orient Longman.

Raikes, S. 1977 [1856]. *Memoir on the Thurr and Parkur District*. Karachi: Indus Publications.

Rajasekhar, D.S. Lakha and R. Manjula. 2013. 'How Effective Are Social Audits under MGNREGS? Lessons from Karnataka'. *Sociological Bulletin*, 62 (3): 431–55.

Ramanadham, V.V. 1948. *Road Transport in India*. Lucknow: Universal Publishers.

Ramnath, A. 2017. *The Birth of an Indian Profession: Engineers, Industry, and the State, 1900–47*. New Delhi: Oxford University Press.

Rankin, K., T.S. Sigdel, L. Rai, S. Kunwar and P. Hamal. 2017. 'Political Economies and Political Rationalities of Road Building in Nepal'. *Studies in Nepali History and Society*, 22 (1): 43–84.

Ravallion, M. 2012. 'Corruption in the MGNREGS: Assessing an Index'. *Economic and Political Weekly*, 47 (8): 13–15.

Rippa, A. 2018. 'Old Routes, New Roads: Proximity across the China–Pakistan Border'. In *Routledge Handbook of Asian Borderlands*, edited by A. Horstmann, M. Saxer and A. Rippa. London: Routledge, pp. 114–26.

Riverson, J., J. Gaviria and S. Thriscutt. 1994. 'Rural Roads in Sub-Saharan Africa: Lessons from World Bank Experience'. Technical Paper 141. Washington, DC: World Bank.

Rosa, H. 2013. *Social Acceleration: A New Theory of Modernity*. New York: Columbia University Press.

Roseman, S. 1996. '"How we built the road": The Politics of Memory in Rural Galicia'. *American Ethnologist*, 23 (4): 836–60.

Ross, K. 1996. *Fast Cars, Clean Bodies: Decolonization and the Reordering of French Culture*. Cambridge, MA: MIT Press.

Rudiak-Gould, P. 2013. *Climate Change and Tradition in a Small Island State: The Rising Tide*. New York: Routledge.

Rushdie, S. 1988. *The Satanic Verses*. London: Viking.

Sachs, W. 1992. *For the Love of the Automobile: Looking Back into the History of Our Desires*. Berkeley, CA: University of California Press.

Saha, J. 2016. 'Is It in India? Colonial Burma as a "Problem" in South Asian History'. *South Asian History and Culture*, 7 (1): 23–9.

Saunders, T. 2008. 'Buses in Bongoland: Seductive Analytics and the Occult'. *Anthropological Theory*, 8: 107–32.

Schendel, W. van. 2005. *The Bengal Borderland: Beyond State and Nation in South Asia*. London: Anthem Press.

Schipper, F. 2008. *Driving Europe: Building Europe on Roads in the Twentieth Century*. Eindhoven: Technische Universiteit Eindhoven.

Schipper, F. and J. Schot. 2011. 'Infrastructural Europeanism, or the Project of Building Europe on Infrastructures: An Introduction'. *History and Technology*, 27 (3): 245–64.

Schneider, K. 1971. *Autokind vs. Mankind*. New York: Norton.

Scott, J. 1999. *Seeing Like a State: How Certain Schemes to Improve the Human Condition Have Failed*. New Haven, CT: Yale University Press.

Sen, A. 1996. 'Economic Reforms, Employment and Poverty: Trends and Options'. *Economic and Political Weekly*, 31 (35/7): 2459–77.

Sen, G. 2011. *The Maharajas and their Magnificent Motor Cars*. Sparkford, Somerset: Haynes Publishing.

Shah, A. 2010. 'MGNREGS in Gujarat: Initial Experience and Early Signals'. *LBS Journal of Management & Research*, 8 (1): 35–56.

Shah, D. 1991. 'Gandhian Approach to Rural Development'. In *Gandhi and Economic Development*, edited by B.P. Pandey. London: Sangam Books Limited, pp. 3–6.

Shamdasani, Y. 2016. 'Rural Road Infrastructure & Agricultural Production: Evidence from India'. Job Market paper. Department of Economics, Columbia University.

Sheller, M. 2004. 'Automotive Emotions: Feeling the Car'. *Theory, Culture & Society*, 21 (4–5): 221–42.

Sieverts, T. 2003. *Cities Without Cities: An Interpretation of the Zwischenstadt*. London: Spon Press.

Simpson, E. 2006. 'The State of Gujarat and the Men without Souls'. *Critique of Anthropology*, 26 (3): 331–48.

Simpson, E. 2007. 'The History of Bhuj as Told by Its Own Historians'. In *Struggling with History: Islam and Cosmopolitanism in the Western Indian Ocean*, edited by E. Simpson and K. Kresse. London: Hurst, pp. 93–124.

Simpson, E. 2010. 'Introduction: The Parable of the Jakhs'. In *The Idea of Gujarat: History, Ethnography and Text*, edited by E. Simpson and A. Kapadia. Hyderabad: Orient Blackswan, pp. 1–19.

Simpson, E. 2013. *The Political Biography of an Earthquake: Aftermath and Amnesia in Gujarat, India*. London: Hurst.

Singh, J. 2019. *Global Players and the Indian Car Industry: Trade, Technology and Structural Change*. New Delhi: Routledge.

Sinha, N. 2012. *Communication and Colonialism in Eastern India, Bihar: 1760s–1880s*. London: Anthem Press.

Sinha, S. 2000. 'New Traditionalist Discourse of Indian Environmentalism'. *Journal of Peasant Studies*, 24 (3): 169–204.

Sinha, S., A. Baviskar and K. Philip, 2006. 'Rethinking Indian Environmentalism: Industrial Pollution in Delhi and Fisheries in Kerala'. In *Forging Environmentalism: Justice, Livelihood and Contested Environments*, edited by J. Bauer. New York: M.E. Sharpe, pp. 189–256.

Sinha, T.A. 2013. *India Aspires: Redefining Politics of Development*. New Delhi: Wisdom Press.

Small, A. 2020. *China–Pakistan Axis: Asia's New Politics*. New York: Oxford University Press.

Spodek, H. 1971. 'On the Origins of Gandhi's Political Methodology: The Heritage of Kathiawad and Gujarat'. *Journal of Asian Studies*, 30 (2): 361–72.

Star, S.L. 1999. 'The Ethnography of Infrastructure'. *American Behavioral Scientist*, 43 (3): 377–91.

Steinberg, R. and W.I. Zangwill. 1983. 'The Prevalence of Braess' Paradox'. *Transportation Science*, 17 (3): 301–18.

Stern, N. 2007. *The Economics of Climate Change: The Stern Review*. Cambridge: Cambridge University Press.

Stern, N. and J. Rydge. 2012. 'The New Energy-Industrial Revolution and International Agreement on Climate Change'. *Economics of Energy & Environmental Policy*, 1 (1): 101–20.

Stewart, K. 1996. *A Space on the Side of the Road: Cultural Poetics in an 'Other' America*. Princeton, NJ: Princeton University Press.

Swaminathan, C.G., N.B. Lal and A. Kumar. 1981. 'A Systems Approach to Rural Road Development'. *Journal of Indian Roads Congress*, 42-IV: 885–904.

Thrift, N. 2004. 'Driving the City'. *Theory, Culture & Society*, 21 (4/5): 41–59.

Tidrick, K. 2006. *Gandhi: A Political and Spiritual Life*. London: I.B. Tauris.

Trankell, I.-B. 1993. 'On the Road in Laos: An Anthropological Study of Road Construction and Rural Communities'. Uppsala Research Reports in Cultural Anthropology 12.

Uberoi, P. 2014. 'The BCIM Economic Corridor: A Leap into the Unknown?' Working Paper, Delhi: Institute of Chinese Studies.

Upadhyaya, D. 1965. *Integral Humanism*. New Delhi: Bharatiya Jan Sangh.

Urry, J. 2004. 'The "System" of Automobility'. *Theory, Culture & Society*, 21 (4–5): 25–39.

Urry, J. 2007. *Mobilities*. Cambridge: Polity.

Urry, J. 2011. *Climate Change and Society*. Cambridge: Polity.

Urry, J. 2013. *Societies beyond Oil: Oil Dregs and Social Futures*. London: Zed Books.

Vannini, P. 2010. 'Mobile Cultures: From the Sociology of Transportation to the Study of Mobilities'. *Sociology Compass*, 4: 111–21.

Veer, P. van der. 1988. *Gods on Earth: The Management of Religious Experience and Identity in a North Indian Pilgrimage Centre*. London: Athlone.

Veer, P. van der. 1994. *Religious Nationalism: Hindus and Muslims in India*. Berkeley, CA: University of California Press.

Virilio, P. 1986. *Speed and Politics*. New York: Semiotexte.

Waeyenberge, E. van and K. Bayliss. 2017. 'Unpacking the Public–Private Partnership Revival'. *Journal of Development Studies*, 54 (4): 577–93.

Wall, D. 1999. *Earth First! and Anti-roads Movement: Radical Environmentalism and Comparative Social Movements*. New York: Routledge.

Weber, B., M. Staub-Bisand and H.W. Alfen. 2016. *Infrastructure as an Asset Class: Investment Strategy, Sustainability, Project Finance and PPP*. 2nd edn. Chichester: Wiley.

Wengraf, L. 2018. *Extracting Profit: Imperialism, Neoliberalism and the New Scramble for Africa*. Chicago, IL: Haymarket Books.

Weston, K. 2012. 'Political Ecologies of the Precarious'. *Anthropological Quarterly*, 85 (2): 429–55.

Whitelegg, J. 1997. *Critical Mass: Transport, Environment and Society in the Twenty-first Century*. London: Pluto Press.

Whitelegg, J. 2016. *Mobility: A New Urban Design and Transport Planning Philosophy for a Sustainable Future*. CreateSpace Independent Publishing Platform.

Wilson, F. 2004. 'Towards a Political Economy of Roads: Experiences from Peru'. *Development and Change*, 35 (3): 525–46.

Wolf, S.O. 2020. *The China–Pakistan Economic Corridor of the Belt and Road Initiative: Concept, Context and Assessment*. Singapore: Springer.

Wolmar, C. 2016. *Are Trams Socialist? Why Britain Has No Transport Policy*. London: London Publishing Partnership.

Wynne, A.B. and F. Fedden. 1872. *The Geology of Kutch*. Calcutta: Geological Survey of India Memoir, V (IX), 1–294.

Yang, Y. and F. Li. 2019. *The Belt and Road Initiative: ASEAN Countries' Perspectives*. Singapore: World Scientific.

Yusoff, K. 2018. *A Billion Black Anthropocenes or None*. Minneapolis, MI: University of Minnesota Press.

Zeller, T. 2007. *Driving Germany: The Landscape of the German Autobahn, 1930–1970*. London: Berghahn.

INDEX

Note: Page numbers followed by '*n*' refer to notes.

Congress party, 119, 137, 147,
154, 189, 202, 233
'Bharat Nirman' (2005–9), 88,
143–4
vs. BJP supporters, 180
Gandhi's association with,
203–4
road networks impact on
election outcomes, 130
Upadhyaya against, 201
volunteers in Dandi Salt March
(12 Mar 1930), 114–15
consumerism, 69, 144
contemporary anthropology, 235
Contessa car, 138
core road network model, 92, 94
'corridor management', 144
corruption, 16, 32–3, 93, 163,
175
charges on Sharif family, 169,
170
high-profile leaks, 33
in Nigeria, 264
See also Panama Papers; Paradise
Papers (2017)
Council on Trade and Industry,
181
CPEC. *See* China–Pakistan
Economic Corridor (CPEC)
Criminal Tribes Act (1871), 21
CRISIL, 252
Critical Mass (Whitelegg), 41
CRRI. *See* Central Road Research
Institute (CRRI)
Cursetji Rustamji Thanewalla
(Diwan of Ratlam), 20

da Orta, Garcia, 276n5
daily wage migration, 103
Dalits, 119, 123
Daman, 18

Damania, Anjali, 248–9
Dandi Salt March (12 Mar 1930),
114–15, 146–7, 288n11
Danyor cemetery (Gilgit), 69–70
Darius the Great (Persian king),
118
Dawn (Pakistan newspaper), 38
deaths, 240, 241–2, 248, 263–4
De Dion-Bouton, 112
deforestation, 4, 182
Delhi
AHN meeting (1959), 72
IRF conference (Nov 2017),
224–5
Democracy, Carbon (Mitchell),
231
Democratic Front, 184, 185, 187
demolition, 13
Department for International
Development (DFID) (UK),
167
Depression (1930s), 113
Desai, Nitin, 88
Deshmukh, Vilasrao, 184, 185–6
development banks, 148–52,
158–9
dhabas (roadside eating houses),
17–18, 21–2
dharma, 190, 201
Dillen, Susanne van, 101
displacement, 56–7
Doxiadis, Constantinos, 107
Drive Electric Campaign, 226
drugs. *See* opium; heroin trade
drug mules, 26
Durgapur Expressway (West
Bengal), 132

earthquakes, 30, 131, 198, 203
East India Company, 19, 111–12
East Pakistan, 150

inequalities of, 117
of labour, 101, 103
levels of, 3
petro-mobility, 215
promotion of, 95
See also automobility; sustainable
    infrastructure / sustainable
    mobility
Model Concession Agreement, 144
modern economy, 130
Modi government, 73, 88
    Gadkari's role in, 188, 191
    See also 'Act East' policy;
        Bharatiya Janata Party (BJP);
        PMGSY (Pradhan Mantri
        Gram Sadak Yojana)
Modi, Narendra, 204, 88
    Planning Commission, closure
        of, 139–40
Mohapatra, Jugal, 85, 90, 91
money laundering, 251–2
Mookerjee, Syama Prasad, 190
morality, 19, 115, 117, 244
Moran Yacht & Ship, 258
Morley, Frank, 8, 49
morphine, 26
Morris, 138
Mossack Fonseca leak. *See* Panama
    Papers
'motor age', 109, 111, 124
motor roads (twentieth century),
    109–33, 135, 158
    demand for, 112
    See also bullock cart(s); cars;
        5-year plan; Gandhi,
        Mahatma; Nehru, Jawaharlal;
        20-year plan
motor vehicles, 110
    arrival of, 112
    Gandhi on growing number of,
        123

population, 115, 145, 217
    See also automobile
        manufacturing; cars
MP SH31. *See* SH31 (State
    Highway 31, Madhya Pradesh)
MSRDC. *See* Maharashtra State
    Road Development Corporation
    (MSRDC)
Mukhopadhyay, Partha, 84
Mumbai, 179, 215
    BOT project, first, 182
    flood and potholes, 248–9
    flyovers, 184–5
    'Infrastructure: Vision 2000'
        conference (1997), 177
    Mahim flyover, 183
    presidential rule, 185
    toll regime, public resistance to,
        183–4
    Vashi flyover, inauguration of,
        183
Mumbai–Ahmedabad Highway, 182
Mumbai–Pune Expressway, 176,
    177, 181, 182
Mumford, Lewis, 39
Mumtaz (firm), 54
Muniyappa, K.H., 146
Musharraf, Pervez, 165, 213
Muslims. *See* Hindus and Muslims
Myanmar, 73
    India-Myanmar border trade
        agreement (1994), 74
    India–Myanmar–Thailand
        'trilateral' highway, 74–6
    Indo-Myanmar friendship car
        rally, 76

Nagarjuna (firm), 54
Nagpur (Maharashtra), 174, 255
    bandh (strike) (20 Dec 1993),
        175